# ANNUAL REPORT

### OF THE

# AMERICAN HISTORICAL ASSOCIATION

#### FOR THE YEAR

## 1937

#### IN TWO VOLUMES

## VOLUME I

## PROCEEDINGS FOR 1937

UNITED STATES

GOVERNMENT PRINTING OFFICE

WASHINGTON : 1939

For sale by the Superintendent of Documents, Washington, D. C. - - - - - Price 75 cents (vellum)

VOLUME I OF THE ANNUAL REPORT OF THE
AMERICAN HISTORICAL ASSOCIATION
FOR THE YEAR 1937

# LETTER OF SUBMITTAL

---

THE SMITHSONIAN INSTITUTION,
*Washington, D. C., June 2, 1938.*

*To the Congress of the United States:*

In accordance with the act of incorporation of the American Historical Association, approved January 4, 1889, I have the honor of submitting to Congress the annual report of the Association for the year 1937.

I have the honor to be,

Very respectfully, your obedient servant,

C. G. ABBOT, *Secretary.*

# LETTER OF TRANSMITTAL

THE AMERICAN HISTORICAL ASSOCIATION,
740 FIFTEENTH STREET NW.,
*Washington, D. C., June 1, 1938.*

SIR: As provided by law, I submit herewith the annual report of the American Historical Association for the year 1937. This consists of two volumes, as follows:

Volume I contains the proceedings of the Association for 1937; the proceedings of the Pacific coast branch for 1937; the report of the Conference of Historical Societies for 1937; *Records of the United States District Courts, 1790–1870, deposited in the Copyright Office of the Library of Congress*, by Martin A. Roberts; *The record of American imprints*, by Douglas C. McMurtrie; and *List of manuscript collections received in the Library of Congress, July 1931 to July 1938*, compiled by C. Percy Powell.

Volume II contains a bibliography of writings on American History during the year 1937, compiled by Grace Gardner Griffin and associates.

LOWELL JOSEPH RAGATZ, *Editor.*

To the SECRETARY OF THE SMITHSONIAN INSTITUTION,
*Washington, D. C.*

# CONTENTS

# A LIST OF ILLUSTRATIONS

[All follow Page 106]

x

# ORGANIZATION AND ACTIVITIES OF THE AMERICAN HISTORICAL ASSOCIATION

## THE ASSOCIATION

The American Historical Association, incorporated by Act of Congress in 1889, is defined by its charter to be: *A body corporate and politic . . . for the promotion of historical studies, the collection and preservation of historical manuscripts, and for kindred purposes in the interest of American history, and of history in America.*

It is a society not only for scholars, though it has for the last half century included in its membership all the outstanding historical scholars in America, nor only for educators, though it has included all the great American teachers of history, but also for every man and woman who is interested in the study of history in America. Its most generous benefactors have been non-professionals who love history for its own sake and who wish to spread that love of history to a wider and wider circle.

## MEETINGS

It meets in the Christmas week in a different city each year to accommodate in turn members living in different parts of the country. The attendance at these meetings has been increasing steadily. In 1937 it exceeded 1,100. The formal programs of these meetings include important contributions to every field of historical scholarship, many of which are subsequently printed. The meetings also afford an excellent opportunity for maintaining contacts with professional friends and for exchanging ideas with others working in the same field.

## PUBLICATIONS

The publications of the Association are many and their scope is wide. The *Annual Report*, usually in two volumes, is printed for the Association by the United States Government and is distributed free to all members who ask for it. It contains *Proceedings*, valuable collections of documents, and *Writings on American History*, the standard annual guide to publications on the history of the United States. *The American Historical Review*, published quarterly and distributed free to all members of the Association, is the recognized organ of the historical profession in America. It prints authoritative articles and critical reviews of new books in all fields of history. The Association also cooperates with the National Council for the Social Studies in the publication of *Social Education*, one of the most important journals in America dealing with the problems of history teaching in the schools.

Besides these periodical publications, the Association controls a revolving fund donated by the Carnegie Corporation out of which it publishes from time to time historical monographs selected from the whole field of history. It has as well two separate endowment funds, the income from which is devoted to the publication of historical source material. The Albert J. Beveridge Fund was established as a memorial to the late Senator Beveridge by his wife, Catherine Beveridge, and a large group of his friends in Indiana. The income from this fund, the principal of which amounts to about $100,000, is applied to the publication of material relative to the history of the United States, with preference to the period from 1800 to 1865. The Littleton-Griswold Fund was established by Alice Griswold in memory of her father, William E. Littleton, and of her husband, Frank T. Griswold. The income from this fund, the principal of which amounts to $25,000, is applied to the publication of material relative to the legal history of the United States.

### OTHER ACTIVITIES

The Association from time to time, through special committees, interests itself actively in promoting the sound teaching of sound history in the schools. It has a continuing grant for helping small colleges remote from the great cultural centers to build up collections of rare books about America. It has done much and is doing more to collect and preserve historical manuscripts in public and private repositories. It has interested itself in developing the potentialities of the radio as an instrument of education, and it plans and directs historical radio broadcasts in which it seeks to combine the skill and popular appeal of the professional broadcaster with the learning of the professional scholar.

The Association maintains close relations with state and local historical societies through an annual conference which it has organized and the proceedings of which it prints in its *Annual Report*. It has also organized a Pacific coast branch for members living in the Far West.

## PRIZES

The Association offers the following prizes:

*The George Louis Beer Prize* of about $200 (being the annual income from an endowment of $5,000) is awarded annually for the best work on any phase of European international history since 1895. Competition is limited to citizens of the United States and to works in the English language actually submitted. A work may be submitted either in manuscript or in print.

*The John H. Dunning Prize* of $150 is awarded biennially in the even-numbered years for a monograph, either in print or in manuscript, on any subject relating to American history. In accordance with the terms of the bequest, competition is limited to members of the Association.

*The Justin Winsor Prize* of $200 is awarded biennially in the odd-numbered years for a monograph, in manuscript or in print, in the field of American history, including that of South America.

*The Herbert Baxter Adams Prize* of $200 is awarded biennially in the even-numbered years for a monograph, in manuscript or in print, in the field of European history.

In awarding these prizes the committees in charge will consider not only research accuracy and originality but also clearness of expression, logical arrangement, and general excellence of style. These prizes are designed particularly to encourage those who have not published any considerable work previously or obtained an established reputation.

All works submitted in competition for these prizes must be in the hands of the proper prize committees on or before June 1st of the year in which the award is made. The date of publication of printed monographs submitted in competition must fall within a period of two and one-half years prior to June 1st of the year in which the prize is awarded.

*The Jusserand Medal,* established by the American Historical Association in honor of Jean Jules Jusserand, one-time Ambassador from France to the United States and a former president of the Association, is awarded as occasion may arise for a published work of distinction on any phase of the history of the intellectual relations between the United States and any other country, written either by an American citizen or by a citizen of any other country. It is not limited to works in the English language.

The American Historical Association is in a position to do significant and useful work not only in the advancement of learning but also in the dissemination of sound knowledge. It commands the resources of the learned world, but it also recognizes the necessity of bringing the fruits of learning to the average American. It needs to be supported. Its endowment funds, amounting to about $240,000, are carefully managed by a board of trustees composed of men prominent in the world of finance. But most of the income from this endowment is earmarked for special publications. For its broader educational purposes it has to depend chiefly upon its membership dues. It has over 3,200 members, but needs many more. It welcomes to its ranks any individual subscribing to its purposes. Membership application blanks may be secured by addressing the Assistant Secretary at 740 Fifteenth Street NW., Washington, D. C.

# ACT OF INCORPORATION

*Be it enacted by the Senate and House of Representatives of the United States of America in Congress assembled,* That Andrew D. White, of Ithaca, in the State of New York; George Bancroft, of Washington, in the District of Columbia; Justin Winsor, of Cambridge, in the State of Massachusetts; William F. Poole, of Chicago, in the State of Illinois; Herbert B. Adams, of Baltimore, in the State of Maryland; Clarence W. Bowen, of Brooklyn, in the State of New York, their associates and successors, are hereby created, in the District of Columbia, a body corporate and politic by the name of the American Historical Association, for the promotion of historical studies, the collection and preservation of historical manuscripts, and for kindred purposes in the interest of American history, and of history in America. Said Association is authorized to hold real and personal estate in the District of Columbia so far as may be necessary to its lawful ends to an amount not exceeding $500,000, to adopt a constitution, and make bylaws not inconsistent with law. Said Association shall have its principal office at Washington, in the District of Columbia, and may hold its annual meetings in such places as the said incorporators shall determine. Said Association shall report annually to the Secretary of the Smithsonian Institution concerning its proceedings and the condition of historical study in America. Said Secretary shall communicate to Congress the whole of such report, or such portions thereof as he shall see fit. The Regents of the Smithsonian Institution are authorized to permit said Association to deposit its collections, manuscripts, books, pamphlets, and other material for history in the Smithsonian Institution or in the National Museum, at their discretion, upon such conditions and under such rules as they shall prescribe.

[Approved, Jan. 4, 1889.]

# CONSTITUTION [1]

## I

The name of this society shall be the American Historical Association.

## II

Its object shall be the promotion of historical studies.

## III

Any person approved by the council may become a member by paying $5 and after the first year may continue a member by paying an annual fee of $5. On payment of $100 any person may become a life member exempt from fees. Persons not resident in the United States may be elected as honorary or corresponding members and be exempt from the payment of fees.

## IV

The officers shall be a president, a first vice president, a second vice president, a secretary, a treasurer, an assistant secretary-treasurer, and an editor.

The president, vice presidents, secretary, and treasurer shall be elected by ballot at each regular annual meeting in the manner provided in the bylaws.

The assistant secretary-treasurer and the editor shall be elected by the council. They shall perform such duties and receive such compensation as the council may determine.

If the office of president shall, through any cause, become vacant, the first vice president shall thereupon become president, and the second vice president shall become first vice president whenever the office of first vice president shall have been vacated.

## V

There shall be a council, constituted as follows:

1. The president, the vice presidents, the secretary, and the treasurer.

2. Elected members, eight in number, chosen by ballot at the annual meeting of the Association. At the election of 1931 the persons so elected shall be assigned to four equal classes, the members of which shall be elected to serve respectively for 1, 2, 3, and 4 years. Subsequent elections in each class shall be for 4 years, except in the case of elections to complete unexpired terms.

3. The former presidents, but a former president shall be entitled to vote for the 3 years succeeding the expiration of his term as president, and no longer.

## VI

The council shall conduct the business, manage the property, and care for the general interests of the Association. In the exercise of its proper functions, the council may appoint such committees, commissions, and boards as it may

---

[1] As amended December 29, 1933.

deem necessary. The council shall make a full report of its activities to the annual meeting of the Association. The Association may by vote at any annual meeting instruct the council to discontinue or enter upon any activity, and may take such other action directing the affairs of the Association as it may deem necessary and proper.

For the transaction of necessary business when the council is not in session, the council shall elect annually an executive committee of not more than six members which shall include the secretary and the treasurer, and may include not more than two persons not members of the council. Subject to the general direction of the council, the executive committee shall be responsible for the management of Association interests and the carrying out of Association policies.

The council, or, when the council is not in session, the executive committee, shall have authority to appoint an executive secretary, delegating to him such functions as may from time to time seem desirable, and determining his compensation.

There shall be a board of trustees, five in number, consisting of a chairman and four other members, nominated by the council and elected at the annual meeting of the Association. The trustees elected in 1931 shall serve, respectively, as determined by lot, for 1, 2, 3, 4, and 5 years. Subsequent elections shall be in all cases for 5 years, except in the case of elections to complete unexpired terms. The board of trustees, acting by a majority thereof, shall have the power to invest and reinvest the permanent funds of the Association, with authority to employ such agents, investment counsel, and banks or trust companies as it may deem wise in carrying out its duties, and with further authority to delegate and transfer to any bank or trust company all its power to invest or reinvest; neither the board of trustees nor any bank or trust company to whom it may so transfer its power shall be controlled in its discretion by any statute or other law applicable to fiduciaries, and the liability of the individual members of the board and of any such bank or trust company shall be limited to good faith and lack of actual fraud or wilful misconduct in the discharge of the duties resting upon them.

## VIII

This constitution may be amended at any annual meeting, notice of such amendment having been given at the previous annual meeting or the proposed amendment having received the approval of the council.

# BYLAWS

## I

The officers provided for by the constitution shall have the duties and perform the functions customarily attached to their respective offices with such others as may from time to time be prescribed.

## II

A nomination committee of five members shall be chosen at each annual business meeting in the manner hereafter provided for the election of officers of the Association. At such convenient time prior to the 15th of September as it may determine, it shall invite every member to express to it his preference regarding every office to be filled by election at the ensuing annual business meeting and regarding the composition of the new nominating committee then to be chosen. It shall publish and mail to each member at least 1 month prior to the annual business meeting such nominations as it may determine upon for each elective office and for the next nominating committee. It shall prepare for use at the annual business meeting an official ballot containing, as candidates for each office or committee membership to be filled thereat, the names of its nominees and also the names of any other nominees which may be proposed to the chairman of the committee in writing by 20 or more members of the Association at least 1 day before the annual business meeting, but such nominations by petition shall not be presented until after the committee shall have reported its nominations to the Association as provided for in the present bylaw. The official ballot shall also provide, under each office, a blank space for voting for such further nominees as any member may present from the floor at the time of the election.

## III

The annual election of officers and the choice of a nominating committee for the ensuing year shall be conducted by the use of an official ballot prepared as described in bylaw II.

## IV

The Association authorizes the payment of traveling expenses incurred by the voting members of the council attending one meeting of that body a year, this meeting to be other than that held in connection with the annual meeting of the Association.

The council may provide for the payment of expenses incurred by the secretary, the assistant secretary-treasurer, and the editor in such travel as may be necessary to the transaction of the Association's business.

# PROCEEDINGS OF THE
# AMERICAN HISTORICAL ASSOCIATION
## FOR 1937

# ABSTRACT OF MINUTES OF EXECUTIVE COMMITTEE MEETINGS HELD DURING 1937

## Meeting of April 4, 1937

Present: Messrs. Guy Stanton Ford, chairman; James P. Baxter, III; Solon J. Buck; Wallace Notestein; Conyers Read.

The principal business before the meeting was the consideration of the following resolution from the minutes of the council meeting of December 28-29, 1936:

"Upon motion it was resolved that the whole question of the central administration of the American Historical Association be placed upon the agenda for the next meeting of the council, and that the council be invited at that time to consider the wisdom either of consolidating the two offices or else of modifying the salary scale."

At the request of President Ford, the executive secretary had already distributed to the members of the executive committee a memorandum on the existing organization of the American Historical Association. A copy of this memorandum is on file in the office of the executive secretary. Mr. Buck had also distributed to the members of the committee (1) a statement of receipts and expenditures of the American Historical Association for the period September 1, 1936, to February 28, 1937, and (2) a memorandum of the ordinary duties of the office of the American Historical Association in Washington.

Mr. Buck distributed at the meeting the following memoranda: (1) American Historical Association interest from investments applicable to unrestricted funds; (2) a comparative summary statement of receipts and expenditures of unrestricted funds for the years 1933-34 to 1935-36 (actual), and for the years 1936-37 and 1937-38 (estimated); (3) a statement of estimated receipts and expenditures for the year 1936-37 as compared with actual receipts and expenditures for the first 6 months of that year; (4) a conspectus of the changes in the set-up of the American Historical Association from 1927 to date.

All of these statements and memoranda are on file in the office of the executive secretary.

The discussion at the meeting turned during the morning session on the treasurer's memoranda and reports.

The following formal action was taken:

(1) Upon motion the treasurer was authorized to charge bills for current work on the *Bibliography of British History* and for other expenses authorized by the council or the executive committee and not otherwise provided for in the budget against the appropriation for council and council committees.

(2) Upon motion the sum of $189.81 returned by the executive secretary's office to the treasury of the Association and heretofore earmarked for "the necessary expenses of the executive committee" was allocated in the budget to the appropriation for council and council committees.

(3) Upon motion the appropriation in the budget for 1936-37 of $80 for auditing the treasurer's accounts was increased to $125, being the amount actually expended.

(4) Upon motion the treasurer was directed to transfer $25 in the budget of 1936-37 from the contingent fund to the equipment fund.

During the afternoon session the discussion turned upon the organization of the American Historical Association and various suggestions were offered,

3

but no formal action was taken. The president announced his intention of preparing a memorandum on the subject based upon the facts brought out in the discussion and of distributing this memorandum to a selected mailing list at his own expense.

The following resolutions were also passed:

(1) Upon motion the executive secretary was directed to advise the editor of the *Annual Report* that the correct title of Mr. Perkins was secretary of the Association and not secretary of the council, and was instructed to see to it that Mr. Perkins was so designated in the official records of the Association hereafter.

(2) Upon motion the treasurer was authorized to prepare an inventory of the records of the Association.

(3) Upon motion the treasurer was authorized to approach the officials of the Smithsonian Institution with a view to learning whether there was any possibility of securing permanent quarters for the Association in the projected new building of the Smithsonian Institution.

### Meeting of November 28, 1937

Present: Messrs. James P. Baxter, III, Solon J. Buck, Carlton J. H. Hayes, Wallace Notestein, Dexter Perkins, and Conyers Read. The finance committee (Buck, Perkins and Read) met concurrently.

The treasurer's report[1] was read and informally approved. There was some discussion of the form of the report. The treasurer proposes to present some part of the auditor's report, to summarize other pertinent financial material, and to multigraph the whole for distribution at the annual meeting. This plan of action was informally approved and in general left to his discretion.

The treasurer was authorized to change the form of the operating accounts of *Social Education*, the radio committee, the office of the executive secretary, and *The American Historical Review* to the form now used for the operating accounts of the Americana committee.

Mr. Schuyler's request that he be permitted to apply revenue received from the sale of periodicals out of his office and of books presented for review out of his office, to augment his budget, was approved. The executive secretary was directed to request Mr. Schuyler, editor of the *Review*, to send to the treasurer estimates of probable receipts from these sources.

The request from the committee on historical source materials for an appropriation of $50 was approved and the budget adjusted accordingly.

Mr. Leland's proposal that he manage the contribution of the American Historical Association to *The International Bibliography of Historical Sciences* from his office, and that the customary appropriation of $200 for that purpose be reduced to $100, was approved and the budget adjusted accordingly.

An appropriation of $300 for the membership committee, suggested by the outgoing chairman of that committee, was approved, the unexpended balance of $289.67 from the last appropriation to be used for that purpose and augmented so as to bring it to $300.

The budget for the years 1937–38 and 1938–39 as submitted by the treasurer, with a few minor changes, was adopted by the finance committee, approved by the executive committee, and recommended for approval by the council.

The treasurer asked for instructions regarding the keeping of expenditures strictly within the budget. No formal action was taken, but the sense of the meeting seemed to be that a certain amount of discretion should be exercised by the treasurer in such matters. The executive secretary was directed to refer the question to the decision of the council.

---

[1] See pp. 25 ff.

The executive committee saw no reason to change its attitude on the subject of the reorganization of the administration of the American Historical Association as revealed in the discussions at its last meeting, to wit: that the administrative organization, though it looked cumbersome, was operating efficiently, and that no economies could be effected by a concentration of offices great enough to justify a change. The executive secretary was directed to convey the sense of the meeting on this matter to the chairman of the executive committee, and to request him, since he already had contemplated such action, to prepare a written statement on the subject for distribution to the members of the executive committee, and with its approval for submission to the council.

A petition for a change in the method of election of officers of the American Historical Association, addressed to the council, was distributed by the president of the American Historical Association to the members of the executive committee for consideration. After an informal discussion of it, though it was voted to make no recommendations about the matter to the council, the sense of the meeting seemed to be—

(1) That the treasurer and the secretary of the American Historical Association, being administrative officers, should be appointed by the council, and the constitution of the American Historical Association amended accordingly.

(2) That members of the council and members of the nominating committee should be elected. No objection was raised to the election of these officers in the manner outlined in the petition, though some fear was expressed that it might lead to undesirable electioneering methods.

(3) Upon the question of electing the second vice president, presuming that his election was merely preliminary to his succession to the presidency, according to the current tradition, the sentiment of the executive committee was divided.

Page proof of the program for the Philadelphia meeting was presented for the inspection of the executive committee and was informally approved.

The question of publishing papers read at the Philadelphia meeting was considered. The executive secretary reported that he had been approached on the subject by Charles Scribner's Sons, Henry Holt & Co., and D. Appleton-Century Co. Upon motion, the question was referred to a committee of five as follows: Messrs. Conyers Read, chairman, Walton H. Hamilton, John A. Krout, Roy F. Nichols, and John H. Wuorinen, with power to act, subject to the following conditions:

(1) That no project of publication should involve a charge on the budget of the American Historical Association.

(2) That any book or books published should bear the name of the American Historical Association and should pay a royalty on sales to the American Historical Association.

The executive secretary reported that the cost of printing the program for the annual meeting in Philadelphia was being assumed by the local arrangements committee. This action was approved and the hope was expressed that it might serve as a precedent for subsequent meetings.

The place for the annual meeting in 1939 was informally discussed, and the suggestion from the secretary of the Modern Language Association for a joint meeting at New Orleans was referred to the council.

Mr. Read was invited to prepare an obituary notice for Mr. Charles H. Haskins.[2] The executive secretary was directed to invite Mr. Leland to prepare an obituary notice for Mr. J. Franklin Jameson.[3]

The ad interim appointment of Messrs. William E. Lingelbach, Roy F. Nichols, and Conyers Read to represent the American Historical Association at the

[2] See pp. 51 ff.
[3] See pp. 47 ff.

meeting of the American Academy of Political and Social Sciences in April, 1937, was approved.

The ad interim appointment of Mr. Tracy E. Strevey as secretary of the local arrangements committee for the annual meeting in Chicago in 1938 was approved.

Mr. T. R. Schellenberg was appointed delegate of the American Historical Association to the American Documentation Institute, but since some doubts were raised about his willingness to accept appointment, Mr. Douglas S. Freeman, Richmond, Va., was named as an alternate.

A vacancy in the representation of the American Historical Association on the Social Science Research Council will occur at the end of the current calendar year by reason of the expiration of the term of office of Mr. Guy S. Ford. It was the unanimous opinion of the executive committee that Mr. Ford's reappointment should be strongly urged upon the council.

The executive committee considered the resolutions submitted by Mr. H. K. Beale, concerning the publication of documents on the foreign relations of the United States, which were drafted for presentation to the appropriate committees of the Senate and House of Representatives. Upon motion they were referred to Mr. Sioussat and Mr. Malone, the representatives of the American Historical Association on the National Historical Publications Commission, without recommendation, with the request that they report back their recommendations to the council.

The executive secretary pointed out that the volumes of the Littleton-Griswold Committee were being published from his office at a very considerable saving to the American Historical Association and with a very considerable increase upon the burden of administrative work in his office. He reported that he had conferred with the chairman of the Littleton-Griswold Committee about the necessity of imposing some charge upon the committee for these services and that the chairman had approved. The executive secretary suggested that, with the approval of the executive committee, he would like to fix a charge of $100 a year for these services, the same to be added to the salary of Miss A. I. Gamber, his secretary, who had taken entire charge of this publication work. In the opinion of the executive committee this charge was not enough. They did not feel that the matter called for definite action, but were unanimously of the opinion that the executive secretary was justified in making a charge of $200 per annum for these services, the same to be added to the compensation of Miss A. I. Gamber.

Gifts of books from the University of Michigan Press to the Americana plan aggregating $3,100 were reported by the executive secretary. He was directed to convey the thanks of the Association to the director of the University of Michigan Press.

Reports of prize committees[4] were submitted to the executive committee. Some concern was expressed at the languid interest taken in the prizes, and it was suggested that the executive secretary urge upon the chairmen of prize committees the desirability of greater publicity. No formal action was taken.

The question of the exact amount to be paid in prizes was considered. In view of the fact that the George Louis Beer prize to be awarded this year had been announced as $250, the executive secretary was directed to ask the council to reverse its action fixing the amount of the prize and to authorize the payment of $250 for the prize this year. In general it was felt that the amount of this prize and of other prizes, the funds for which were derived from special endow-

---

[4] See pp. 60 ff.

ment, should hereafter be stated in terms of the actual yield from the principal of the endowment.

The treasurer was directed to transfer unexpended balances from income in the George Louis Beer prize fund to the principal account of the fund.

The treasurer asked for instructions regarding the accumulation of income in prize funds arising out of the fact that the prizes were not always awarded. The opinion was expressed that this accumulation of income should be added to the principal of the endowment for the prize, but the executive secretary was directed to present this question to the council for decision.

A petition from the history department of the University of Pennsylvania, directed to the council of the American Historical Association and urging that, in view of the death of Mr. Jameson, the American Historical Association should assume responsibility for the continuation of *Writings*, was laid before the executive committee. The sentiments expressed in the petition were unanimously endorsed. A letter from Miss Grace G. Griffin addressed to the executive committee was read, in which the whole question of the continuation of *Writings* was raised and an estimate of $2,000 submitted as the annual cost of editing the same. The treasurer was authorized to make payments to Miss Griffin for editorial expenses incurred in compiling *Writings*.

Upon motion the whole question of the continuation of *Writings* was referred to a special committee, with Mr. Stock as chairman, and Messrs. Buck and Leland as members, to consider and make recommendations to the council.

In this connection the question was raised as to the problem of handling the work heretofore done by Mr. Jameson for the American Historical Association. Upon motion it was voted to recommend to the council that Mr. Stock be appointed to replace Mr. Jameson as chairman of the publications committee, and that the two representatives of the American Historical Association on the National Historical Publications Commission, Mr. Sioussat and Mr. Malone, be appointed the other two members.

It was voted to request Mr. Stock to represent the interests of the American Historical Association at the forthcoming meeting of the appropriations committee of the House of Representatives. The question of a permanent arrangement for representing the American Historical Association in matters involving its contact with the United States Government was discussed, but no formal action was taken.

Mr. Hicks' report on the Carnegie revolving fund[5] was presented and attention called to his observations regarding the indifferent character of manuscripts submitted. The executive secretary was directed to place his suggestions on the agenda for consideration by the council.

The progress of the new magazine *Social Education* was described, and the request of the editor for a change in the method of making payments to him called to the attention of the treasurer. Satisfaction was expressed at the gratifying progress of the magazine. The question of payments from the treasurer was held to be covered by the general resolution referred to earlier which was passed in connection with the treasurer's report. The executive secretary was directed to advise the editor of *Social Education* accordingly.

Attention was drawn to the report transmitted by the treasurer on the archives of the American Historical Association in Washington, and general approval expressed of the plan to turn over papers not currently required to the Library of Congress for custody. But no formal action was taken since all the data were

---

[5] See pp. 58 ff.

not yet at hand upon which a definite policy could be based. The matter was referred for consideration to the council.

The executive secretary reported on informal conferences held by a self-constituted group in New York on the subject of a journal of popular history, which group included Mr. Langer, Mr. Commager, Mr. Nevins, Mr. DeVoto, Mrs. Braun, Mr. Lippmann, Mr. Cass Canfield, Mr. Read. A prospectus for such a journal prepared by Mr. Langer was laid before the executive committee. General approval of the project was expressed, and the desirability of identifying it closely with the American Historical Association emphasized. No formal action was taken.

Upon motion Miss Washington was directed to drop from the list of life members the following names since all communications addressed to them during the past 5 years have been returned: H. Otley Beyer, Maurice Arnold Deforest, George Fox Tucker. The executive secretary was directed to secure from the council some definition of policy in cases of this sort.

The executive secretary was directed to bring up for reconsideration by the council the question of supplying current mailing lists of members to other agencies, notably to Government agencies.

The executive secretary was directed to arrange for a short statement regarding the American Historical Association for distribution at the annual meeting, and to make plans for a reprinting of the usual folder of information about the American Historical Association for general distribution as required.[6]

## POLL VOTE OF EXECUTIVE COMMITTEE OF NOVEMBER 2, 1937

*Voted,* That the program committee for the meeting of the American Historical Association in Philadelphia in 1937, in view of the special commemorative significance of the occasion, be permitted to have the program printed in Philadelphia rather than in Washington as is customary.

## MINUTES OF THE MEETINGS OF THE COUNCIL OF THE AMERICAN HISTORICAL ASSOCIATION HELD IN PHILADELPHIA AT THE BELLEVUE–STRATFORD HOTEL, DECEMBER 28 AND 29, 1937

Present: Guy Stanton Ford, president; Frederic L. Paxson, second vice president; R. D. W. Connor; William L. Westermann; Bessie L. Pierce; Frederick Merk; Carl Wittke; Isaac J. Cox; Charles H. McIlwain; the treasurer; the secretary of the Association; and the executive secretary.

Upon motion the reading of the minutes of the last meeting was dispensed with. The minutes of the meeting of the executive committee on April 4, 1937,[7] and November 28, 1937,[8] were read and approved.

The report of the treasurer was presented by Mr. Buck,[9] together with the budget for the fiscal year 1937–38. It was voted to appropriate an additional $50 for *The American Historical Review,* for office assistance, and other expenses, this sum being likely to accrue from sales of periodicals and other sources. It was voted that the treasurer should pay no bills in excess of the estimates in the budget without the approval of the finance committee. The budget was approved.

It was voted to recommend to the business meeting that the annual meeting of the Association for 1939 be held in the city of Washington.

---

[6] See p. 10.
[7] See pp. 3 ff.
[8] See pp. 4 ff.
[9] See p. 25 ff.

The president presented a personal letter addressed to the members of the Association with regard to the administrative organization of the American Historical Association. Some discussion followed. No formal motion was passed, but the sense of the meeting was that the secretary of the Association should, in connection with his annual report to the members of the Association at the business meeting, present the point of view expressed in the minutes of the meeting of the executive committee of November 28.[10]

It being 1:30 p. m. the council adjourned for luncheon. The council reconvened at 2:30 p. m.

The executive secretary presented to the council a memorandum from 153 members of the Association making certain proposals with regard to the election of officers of the Association and members of the council and the nominating committee.

After some discussion on motion of Mr. Buck the following resolution was adopted:

*Resolved,* That the Association approves in principle the development of a procedure whereby the elective members of the council and the members of the nominating committee be chosen in an election conducted by mail from a list of nominees containing at least two names for each position to be filled, the nominees for these positions to be selected by the nominating committee after as complete a canvass as may be feasible of the members of the Association for suggestions, with the proviso that anyone nominated by petition with 20 signatures be included in the list. The executive committee is instructed to work out the details of such a procedure and embody them in a proposed amendment to the bylaws to be submitted to the next annual meeting of the Association.

The executive secretary raised the question of the continuation by the Association of the work known as *Writings on American History* which had previously been financed largely through the personal efforts of the late Dr. J. F. Jameson. He presented also a petition from the members of the University of Pennsylvania urging the council to take action. After some discussion it was voted to authorize the appointment of a special committee of the council to supervise *Writings on American History,* and assume responsibility for its publication, the personnel of this committee to be considered by the committee on appointments. The opinion was expressed that such a committee might undertake the raising of a special fund for the financing of *Writings* and that the bequest of Dr. Jameson to the Association might be regarded as the initial contribution to such a fund. It was also suggested that contributions to the endowment fund of the Association, some of which were given for the J. F. Jameson Fund, might be utilized in connection with *Writings.*

The executive secretary reported to the council with regard to the status of various projects: the magazine *Social Education,* the Americana plan, the work of the radio committee, the *Bibliography of American Travel,* the *Bibliography of British History,* and the Committee on Historical Source Material's activities. His comments on these matters will be found in his annual report, to be printed in the *Review,* April 1938.[11]

The council adjourned at 5:15 p. m. The council reconvened at 9:35 a. m. December 29.

Present: Guy Stanton Ford, president; Frederic L. Paxson, second vice-president; R. D. W. Connor; William L. Westermann; Bessie L. Pierce; Fred-

---

[10] See pp. 5 and 44 ff.
[11] On pp. 727 ff. of that issue.

erick Merk; Carl Wittke; Isaac J. Cox; the treasurer; the secretary of the Association; and the executive secretary.

The council proceeded to discuss certain questions arising in connection with the awarding of prizes. With regard to the George Louis Beer prize it was voted for the year 1937 to pay to the winner of said prize the sum of $250, but thereafter simply the annual income from invested funds. With regard to the Justin Winsor prize it was voted to pay the sum of $200 for the year 1937 with the understanding that this amount would be made available from contributions made or to be made, and the treasurer was requested to reach an arrangement with Professor Lybyer regarding the collection and allocation of funds contributed for this and the Herber Baxter Adams prize.

With regard to the Dunning prize it was voted that that prize, if and when awarded, would be paid on the basis of earlier council action. It was voted to authorize for this and other prizes the transfer of accumulated income to capital in units of $100 as occasion might arise. It was voted to refer to the executive committee with power to act the question of stimulating greater interest in the prizes of the Association, and the possibility of arranging the alternation of the Dunning and Justin Winsor prizes, and such other questions regarding the award of prizes as might arise in connection therewith.

The council discussed the status of the Carnegie revolving fund. It was voted that the names of the authors and titles of the works published under this fund should be announced at the same time that the prizes of the Association are announced.

The executive secretary presented certain resolutions from Prof. H. K. Beale with regard to the volumes known as *Foreign Relations of the United States*. It was voted to refer these resolutions, and the letter from Mr. Sioussat on the subject, to the National Historical Publications Commission.

The council discussed the question of the preparation of a new circular to be distributed to those interested in membership in the Association. It was voted to authorize the executive secretary to revise the existing circular, and after approval by the executive committee of his revision, to secure a supply of said circular sufficient for a period of two years.[12]

The executive secretary raised the question as to the terms on which the mailing list of the Association might be furnished to outsiders. The general opinion was expressed in conformity with the previous vote of the council that the list should, in most instances, be withheld. It was voted, however, that the executive secretary would be authorized to make the list available to organizations connected with the Federal Government, if in his opinion such action would be useful to the members of the Association, but not for purposes of solicitation.

The committee on appointments reported. Its recommendations were approved as indicated below. The chairman of each committee is the one named first.

*Executive committee.*—James P. Baxter, III, Williams College; Carlton J. H. Hayes, Columbia University; Frederick Merk, Harvard University; Laurence B. Packard, Amherst College; Solon J. Buck, Washington, D. C., *ex officio;* Dexter Perkins, University of Rochester, *ex officio.*

*Board of trustees.*—Shepard Morgan, Chase National Bank, New York City, 1939; Leon Fraser, First National Bank, New York City, 1938; Thomas I. Parkinson, Equitable Life Assurance Society, 1942.

*Committee on appointments.*—Miss Bessie L. Pierce, University of Chicago; Eugene C. Barker, University of Texas; Dexter Perkins, *ex officio;* Conyers Read, *ex officio.*

---

[12] Published in May 1938.

*Committee on program for 1938 meeting.*—Bernadotte E. Schmitt, *chairman*, with power to appoint his associates.

*Committee on local arrangements for 1938 meeting.*—Tracy E. Strevey, Northwestern University, *secretary*, with power to appoint his associates, recommending that representatives be appointed from the various institutions of higher learning in Chicago and thereabouts.

*Committee on Americana for college libraries.*—Randolph G. Adams, William L. Clements Library, University of Michigan; Kathryn L. Slagle, William L. Clements Library, University of Michigan; Thomas W. Streeter, Morristown, New York, *vice* Dr. J. F. Jameson, deceased, for a term expiring January 1, 1939; Julian P. Boyd, Historical Society of Pennsylvania, *vice* Leonard L. Mackall, deceased, for a term expiring January 1, 1940; Conyers Read, for a term expiring January 1, 1940.

*Board of editors of "Social Education."*—Erling M. Hunt, 204 Fayerweather Hall, Columbia University, *chairman;* Conyers Read, 226 South 16th Street, Philadelphia, *secretary;* Charles A. Beard, New Milford, Connecticut; Phillips Bradley, Amherst College; Margaret A. Koch, Fieldston School, New York City; Donnal V. Smith, State Teachers College, Albany, New York; Ruth Wanger, South Philadelphia High School for Girls; Louis Wirth, University of Chicago.

*Advisory board of "Social Education."*—For a 3-year term beginning January 1, 1938: Marjorie Dowling Brown, Manual Arts High School, Los Angeles, Calif.; Merle Curti, Teachers College, Columbia University; Elmer Ellis, University of Missouri; E. F. Hartford, duPont Manual Training High School, Louisville, Ky.; Howard C. Hill, University of Chicago; Ernest Horn, State University of Iowa; Tyler Kepner, public schools, Brookline, Mass.; Allen Y. King, public schools, Cleveland, Ohio; D. C. Knowlton, New York University; Martha Layman, State Teachers College, Valley City, N. Dak.; Miles Malone, Phillips Academy, Andover, Mass.; L. C. Marshall, Johns Hopkins University; Myrtle Roberts, High School, Dallas, Tex.; Arthur M. Schlesinger, Harvard University; Mabel Snedaker, University Elementary School, University of Iowa. Continuing from 1937: Robert I. Adriance, High School, East Orange, N. J.; Julian C. Aldrich, High School, Webster Groves, Mo.; Howard R. Anderson, Cornell University; Nelle E. Bowman, public schools, Tulsa, Okla.; Mary E. Christy, North High School, Denver, Colo.; Harley S. Graston, Woodlawn High School, Birmingham, Ala.; Eugene Hilton, Allendale Schools, Oakland, Calif.; George J. Jones, public schools, Washington, D. C.; A. K. King, University of North Carolina; Harrison C. Thomas, Richmond Hill High School, New York City; Ruth West, Lewis and Clark High School, Spokane, Wash.

*Committee on the Carnegie revolving fund for publications.*—John D. Hicks, University of Wisconsin; Kent R. Greenfield, Johns Hopkins University; Jakob A. O. Larsen, University of Chicago; William E. Lunt, Haverford College; Edward Whitney, Harvard University.

*Committee on the Albert J. Beveridge memorial fund.*—Roy F. Nichols, University of Pennsylvania; Arthur C. Cole, Western Reserve University; James G. Randall, University of Illinois.

*Committee on the Littleton-Griswold fund.*—Francis S. Philbrick, University of Pennsylvania Law School; Charles M. Andrews, Yale University; Carroll T. Bond, Baltimore, Md.; John Dickinson, University of Pennsylvania Law School; Walton H. Hamilton, Yale Law School; Richard B. Morris, College of the City of New York; Thomas I. Parkinson, New York City; Charles Warren, Washington, D. C.

*Jusserand medal committee.*—Louis R. Gottschalk, University of Chicago; Howard Mumford Jones, Harvard University; Frank Monaghan, Yale University.

*John H. Dunning prize committee.*—Kathleen Bruce, Chesterfield Apartments, Richmond, Va.; Marcus L. Hansen, University of Illinois; Viola F. Barnes, Mount Holyoke College.

*George Louis Beer prize committee.*—Raymond J. Sontag, Princeton University; David Harris, Stanford University; Alfred Vagts, Gaylordsville Post Office, Sherman, Conn.

*Justin Winsor prize committee.*—Caroline F. Ware, American University; W. P. Webb, University of Texas; Colin B. Goodykoontz, University of Colorado.

*Committee on historical source materials.*—T. R. Schellenberg, The National Archives, *chairman. Subcommittee on public archives:* A. R. Newsome, University of North Carolina; Robert C. Binkley, Western Reserve University; Francis S. Philbrick, University of Pennsylvania Law School. *Subcommittee on historical manuscripts:* Julian P. Boyd, Historical Society of Pennsylvania, Philadelphia; Theodore C. Blegen, University of Minnesota; Lester J. Cappon, University of Virginia.

*Board of editors, "American Historical Review."*—Referred to the committee on appointments with power.

*Committee on membership.*—Elmer Ellis, University of Missouri, *chairman*, with power to appoint his associates.

*Committee on the "Bibliography of American Travel."*—Frank Monaghan, Yale University; Julian P. Boyd, Historical Society of Pennsylvania; Harry M. Lydenberg, New York City Public Library.

*Committee on publication of the "Annual Report."*—Leo F. Stock, 231 First Street NE., Washington, D. C.; St. George L. Sioussat, University of Pennsylvania; Solon J. Buck, The National Archives, Washington, D. C.; Lowell J. Ragatz, The George Washington University.

*Committee on "Writings on American History."*—Referred to the committee on appointments with power.

*Committee on radio.*—Conyers Read, 226 South Sixteenth Street, Philadelphia; Evelyn Plummer Braun, Ardmore, Pa.; Felix Greene, American representative of the British Broadcasting System, New York City; John A. Krout, Columbia University; Walter C. Langsam, Columbia University; Ralph C. Rounds, 165 Broadway, New York City; Elizabeth Y. Webb, 1028 Connecticut Avenue, Washington, D. C.; Raymond Gram Swing, New York City.

*Representatives of the American Historical Association in allied bodies:*

*Social Science Research Council.*—Guy Stanton Ford, University of Minnesota, reappointed for a term of three years. *International Committee of Historical Sciences.*—Waldo G. Leland, American Council of Learned Societies; J. T. Shotwell, Columbia University. *Subcommittee of the same on archives.*—Robert D. W. Connor, The National Archives, Washington, D. C. *Subcommittee of the same on diplomatic history.*—Samuel F. Bemis, Yale University. *Subcommittee of the same on chronology.*—John La Monte, University of Cincinnati. *Subcommittee of the same on historical iconography.*—Leicester Holland, Library of Congress, Washington. D. C. *Subcommittee of the same on historical geography.*—Charles O. Paullin, 1718 N Street NW., Washington, D. C. *Subcommittee of the same on the International Bibliography of Historical Sciences.*—Waldo G. Leland, American Council of Learned Societies.

The meeting of the council was adjourned.

DEXTER PERKINS,
*Secretary of the Association.*

# THE CONSTITUTION OF THE UNITED STATES

*Its Background, its Content, its Repercussions in Europe and Elsewhere*

## WEDNESDAY, DECEMBER 29

### MORNING SESSIONS

### I

*The Background of the Idea of Representative Government*

NORTH GARDEN, 10:00 A. M.

Chairman, Nellie Neilson, Mount Holyoke College

Max Radin, University of California, "Delegation and Representation in Ancient Communities."

Carl Stephenson, Cornell University, "The Original Nature of the English Representative System." [1]

Louise Fargo Brown, Vassar College, "Ideas of Representation from Elizabeth to Charles II." [2]

### II

*The Southern Confederacy and the Constitution*

JOINT SESSION OF THE AMERICAN HISTORICAL ASSOCIATION AND THE
SOUTHERN HISTORICAL ASSOCIATION

PLANET ROOM, 10:00 A. M.

Chairman, Thomas P. Abernethy, University of Virginia

J. G. de Roulhac Hamilton, University of North Carolina, "State Courts and the Confederate Constitution." [3]

---

[1] Published in Conyers Read, ed., *The Constitution Reconsidered* (Columbia University Press, 1938). The titles of most of these collected papers were somewhat altered upon their publication in that volume.

[2] To be published in *The Journal of Modern History*.

[3] To be published in *The Journal of Southern History*.

William M. Robinson, Jr., Department of Natural Resources, Georgia, "A New Deal in Constitutions."

## III

*Agriculture and the Government*

JOINT SESSION OF THE AMERICAN HISTORICAL ASSOCIATION AND THE AGRICULTURAL HISTORY SOCIETY

ROSE GARDEN, 10 : 00 A. M.

Chairman, Robert E. Riegel, Dartmouth College

Albert V. House, Jr., Wilson Teachers College, "Proposals of Government Aid to Agricultural Settlement During the Depression of 1873–1879." [4]

Everett E. Edwards, United States Bureau of Agricultural Economics, "The Father of Co-operative Creameries in the Northwest." [5]

Paul H. Johnstone, Agricultural Adjustment Administration, "Turnips and Romanticism."

## LUNCHEON CONFERENCES

## I

*Luncheon Conference of the Society of American Archivists*

RED ROOM, 12 : 30 P. M.

Chairman, A. R. Newsome, University of North Carolina

Herbert W. K. Fitzroy, Princeton University, "The Importance of Legal Records." [6]

## II

*Luncheon Conference on Hispanic America*

JUNIOR ROOM, 12 : 30 P. M.

Chairman, Mary W. Williams, Goucher College

---

[4] Published in *Agricultural History,* January 1938.

[5] Published in *Minnesota History,* June 1938.

[6] Published in *The American Archivist,* July 1938, as "The Part of the Archivist in the Writing of American Legal History."

# III

*Luncheon Conference on Modern European History*

ROSE GARDEN, 12 : 30 P. M.

Chairman, George M. Dutcher, Wesleyan University

Carl L. Becker, Cornell University, "Some Rambling Remarks about Constitutions." [7]

## AFTERNOON SESSIONS

# I

*The Historical Aspects of the Constitution*

JOINT SESSION OF THE AMERICAN HISTORICAL ASSOCIATION AND THE AMERICAN PHILOSOPHICAL SOCIETY

INDEPENDENCE HALL, FIFTH AND CHESTNUT STREETS, 2 : 30 P. M.

Chairman, Frederic L. Paxson, University of California

Roland S. Morris, President, American Philosophical Society, "Welcome."

Charles A. Beard, "Historiography and the Constitution." [8]

Max Farrand, The Henry E. Huntington Library, "If James Madison Had Had a Sense of Humor." [9]

William W. Crosskey, University of Chicago, in collaboration with Leonard Bloomfield, University of Chicago, "The Language of the Fathers."

# II

*The Church and Constitutionalism*

JOINT SESSION OF THE AMERICAN HISTORICAL ASSOCIATION AND THE AMERICAN SOCIETY OF CHURCH HISTORY

ROOMS OF THE PRESBYTERIAN HISTORICAL SOCIETY
520 WITHERSPOON BUILDING, WALNUT AND JUNIPER STREETS, 2 : 30 P. M.

Chairman, H. W. Schneider, Columbia University

Irwin R. Goodenough, Yale University, "Philo's Political Theory and Practice." [10]

---

[7] Published in *The Constitution Reconsidered* (see note 1) and in *The Yale Review,* March 1938.

[8] Published in *The Constitution Reconsidered* (see note 1).

[9] Published in *The Pennsylvania Magazine of History and Biography,* April 1938.

[10] A condensation of one chapter of his *The Politics of Philo Judaeus* (Yale University Press, 1938).

Francis W. Buckler, Oberlin School of Theology, "The Establishment of the Church of England: Its Constitutional and Legal Significance."

Ray H. Abrams, University of Pennsylvania, "Suppression of Minority Opinion in Times of Crisis in America." [11]

Arthur C. Bining, University of Pennsylvania, "History and the Changing World." [12]

## III

*Reception Tendered by The American Philosophical Society to Members of The American Historical Association and Societies Meeting Concurrently*

AMERICAN PHILOSOPHICAL SOCIETY, FIFTH BELOW CHESTNUT, 4:30 P. M.

## IV

*Historical Vesper Service at Christ Church*

SECOND ABOVE MARKET, 5:30 P. M.

EXHIBIT OF HISTORICAL BOOKS AND MANUSCRIPTS IN THE MUNIMENT ROOM

### EVENING SESSIONS

## I

*Dinner of The Mississippi Valley Historical Association*

PLANET ROOM, 6:15 P. M.

Chairman, Clarence E. Carter, Department of State, Washington, D. C.

Guy Stanton Ford, President, American Historical Association, "Greetings."

Theodore C. Pease, University of Illinois, "The Ordinance of 1787."

## II

*Dinner of The Mediaeval Academy of America*

BALL ROOM, 6:15 P. M.

Chairman, William E. Lunt, Haverford College

Howard L. Gray, Bryn Mawr College, "The Commons and the Council in Fifteenth-Century England."

---

[11] Published in *The Crozer Quarterly*, April 1938.
[12] To be published in *The Crozer Quarterly*.

## III

### Reason and Tradition in the Political Thought of the Founding Fathers

BALL ROOM, 8:30 P. M.

Chairman, Louis R. Gottschalk, University of Chicago

Charles H. McIlwain, Harvard University, "The Fundamental Law Behind the Constitution of the United States." [13]

Roland H. Bainton, Yale University, "The Appeal to Reason." [14]

Robert H. MacIver, Columbia University, "European Doctrines of Sovereignty Bearing on the Constitution." [15]

Morris R. Cohen, College of the City of New York, "Constitutional and Natural Rights in 1787 and Since." [16]

## THURSDAY, DECEMBER 30

### MORNING SESSIONS

## I

### Varying American Attitudes Regarding Constitutionalism

PLANET ROOM, 10:00 A. M.

Chairman, Homer C. Hockett, Ohio State University

Curtis P. Nettels, University of Wisconsin, "The American Merchants and the Constitution."

Max Lerner, Editor, *The Nation*, "Minority Rule and the Constitutional Tradition." [17]

William Y. Elliott, Harvard University, "The Constitution as America's Social Myth." [18]

## II

### The Background of Political and Social Thinking Behind the Constitution

NORTH GARDEN, 10:00 A. M.

Chairman, Frederick L. Nussbaum, University of Wyoming

S. E. Thorne, Northwestern University, "English Private Law Background of Constitutional Ideas." [19]

---

[13] Published in *The Constitution Reconsidered* (see note 1).

[14] Published in *The Constitution Reconsidered* (see note 1).

[15] Published in *The Constitution Reconsidered* (see note 1) and in *The Journal of Social Philosophy,* April 1938, under the title "The Philosophical Background of the Constitution."

[16] Published in *The National Lawyers' Guild Quarterly,* February–March 1938.

[17] Published in *The Constitution Reconsidered* (see note 1) and in *The University of Pennsylvania Law Review,* March 1938.

[18] Published in *The Constitution Reconsidered* (see note 1).

[19] Published in *The Constitution Reconsidered* (see note 1).

Stanley Pargellis, Yale University, "The Theory of Balanced Government." [20]

Conyers Read, University of Pennsylvania, "Mercantilism: The Old English Pattern of a Controlled Economy." [21]

## III

### *The Background of the Bill of Rights*

JUNIOR ROOM, 10:00 A. M.

Chairman, C. Mildred Thompson, Vassar College

Gaetano Salvemini, Harvard University, "The Concepts of Democracy and Liberty in Eighteenth-century Europe." [22]

William Haller, Columbia University, "Liberty, Religion, and Union." [23]

Herbert W. Schneider, Columbia University, "Philosophical Differences Between the Constitution and the Bill of Rights." [24]

## IV

### *Appalachia, 1750–1800*

JOINT SESSION OF THE AMERICAN HISTORICAL ASSOCIATION AND THE MISSISSIPPI VALLEY HISTORICAL ASSOCIATION

ROSE GARDEN, 10:00 A. M.

Chairman, Charles H. Ambler, West Virginia University

E. Douglas Branch, University of Pittsburgh, "Henry Louis Bouquet, Professional Soldier." [25]

Randolph C. Downes, Hartwick College, "Appalachia in Transition: Indian *versus* White Man."

Richard H. Shryock, Duke University, "English Farmer *versus* German: the Hypothesis of Cultural Origins in the Old South." [26]

---

[20] Published in *The Constitution Reconsidered* (see note 1).
[21] Published in *The Constitution Reconsidered* (see note 1).
[22] Published in *The Constitution Reconsidered* (see note 1).
[23] Published in *The Constitution Reconsidered* (see note 1),
[24] Published in *The Constitution Reconsidered* (see note 1).
[25] Published in *The Pennsylvania Magazine of History and Biography,* January 1938.
[26] To be published in *The Mississippi Valley Historical Review.*

# V

*Joint Session of The American Historical Association and The Bibliographical Society of America*

THE HISTORICAL SOCIETY OF PENNSYLVANIA, 1300 LOCUST STREET, 10:00 A. M.

## Chairman, Earl G. Swem, College of William and Mary

Oliver Strunk, Princeton University, "Early Music Publishing in the United States."

E. H. O'Neill, University of Pennsylvania, "The Development of Biographical Writing in the United States."

Austin K. Gray, The Library Company of Philadelphia, "Peter Collinson: Agent of The Library Company of Philadelphia in London."

Samuel M. Wilson, Lexington, Ky., *"The Kentucky Gazette."* [27]

Martin A. Roberts, Library of Congress, "Records of the United States District Courts, 1790–1870, Deposited in the Copyright Office of the Library of Congress." [28]

### LUNCHEON CONFERENCE

*Complimentary Luncheon Tendered by the University of Pennsylvania to Members of The American Historical Association and Societies Meeting Concurrently*

BALL ROOM, 12:30 P. M.

## Chairman, Dixon Ryan Fox, Union College

Thomas S. Gates, President of the University of Pennsylvania, "The Possibilities of Philadelphia as a Center for Historical Research." [29]

### AFTERNOON SESSIONS

# I

*Judicial Interpretation of the Constitution*

BALL ROOM, 2:30 P. M.

## Chairman, Laurence M. Larson, University of Illinois

Edward S. Corwin, Princeton University, "What Kind of Judicial Review Did the Framers Have in Mind?" [30]

---

[27] To be published by the Bibliographical Society of America.
[28] Published in this volume, pp. 93 ff.
[29] Published in *The Pennsylvania Magazine of History and Biography*, April 1938.
[30] Excerpted from his *Court, Congress, Constitution* (Princeton University Press, 1938).

Walton H. Hamilton, Yale University, "The Path of Due Process of Law." [31]

## II

*Joint session of The American Historical Association and The Bibliographical Society of America*

LIBRARY COMPANY OF PHILADELPHIA, JUNIPER AND LOCUST STREETS

Chairman, Robert W. G. Vail, American Antiquarian Society

Mrs. George Butler, Edgefield, S. C., "Early Books Relating to Trees of America." [32]

James Mulhern, University of Pennsylvania, "Manuscript School Books." [33]

Chester T. Hallenbeck, Brooklyn College, "Book-trade Publicity Before 1800."

Mrs. Roswell Skeel, Jr., Northport, N. Y., "Noah Webster."

## III

*Business Session of The American Historical Association*

BALL ROOM, 4:00 P. M.

EVENING SESSIONS

## I

*Dinner of The American Historical Association*

BALL ROOM, 7:00 P. M.

Toastmaster, Roland S. Morris, American Philosophical Society

Announcement of prizes. Award of the Jusserand Medal.

Guy Stanton Ford, University of Minnesota, "Presidential Address." [34]

---

[31] Published in *The Constitution Reconsidered* (see note 1) and in *The International Journal of Ethics,* April 1938.

[32] Excerpted from her *Floralia: Garden Paths and By-paths of the Eighteenth Century* (University of North Carolina Press, 1938).

[33] To be published in *The Journal of Educational Research.*

[34] "Some Suggestions to American Historians," in *The American Historical Review,* January 1938.

## II

*Reception Tendered by The Historical Society of Pennsylvania to the Members of The American Historical Association and Societies Meeting Concurrently*

1300 LOCUST STREET, 9:30 P. M.

## FRIDAY, DECEMBER 31

### MORNING SESSIONS

## I

*Intellectual Aspects of the Constitution*

PLANET ROOM, 10:00 A. M.

### Chairman, W. T. Root, University of Iowa

Merle E. Curti, Columbia University, "Reformers Consider the Constitution."

Ralph H. Gabriel, Yale University, "Constitutional Democracy: A Nineteenth-century Faith." [35]

Henry S. Commager, New York University, "Constitutional History and the Higher Law." [36]

## II

*The Background of the Concept of Property in the Constitution*

NORTH GARDEN, 10:00 A. M.

### Chairman, Caroline F. Ware, American University

Francis S. Philbrick, University of Pennsylvania, "Changing Conceptions of Property in Law." [37]

Richard P. McKeon, University of Chicago, "The Development of the Concept of Property in Political Philosophy." [38]

John U. Nef, University of Chicago, "English and French Industrial History After the Reformation in its Relation to the Constitution." [39]

---

[35] Published in *The Constitution Reconsidered* (see note 1).
[36] Published in *The Constitution Reconsidered* (see note 1) and in *The Pennsylvania Magazine of History and Biography,* January 1938.
[37] Published in *The University of Pennsylvania Law Review,* May 1938.
[38] Published in *The International Journal of Ethics,* April 1938.
[39] Published in *The Constitution Reconsidered* (see note 1).

## III

*Repercussions of the Constitution on Modern Europe*

ROSE GARDEN, 10:00 A. M.

Chairman, Eber Malcolm Carroll, Duke University

A. Geoffrey Bruun, New York University, "The Constitutional Cult in the Early Nineteenth Century." [40]

Robert C. Binkley, Western Reserve University, "The Holy Roman Empire *versus* the United States: Patterns for Constitution-making in Central Europe." [41]

Hajo Holborn, Yale University, "The Influence of the American Constitution on the German Constitution of 1919." [42]

## IV

*Repercussions of the Constitution in the British Empire*

PINK ROOM, 10:00 A. M.

Chairman, Reginald G. Trotter, Queen's University, Canada

W. Menzies Whitelaw, The Public Archives of Canada, Ottawa, "American Influence on British Federal Systems." [43]

C. P. Wright, Wolfville, Nova Scotia, "Judicial Interpretation of the Canadian Constitution." [44]

Cornelis W. de Kiewiet, University of Iowa, "Frontier and Constitution in South Africa." [45]

## V

*The Development of Federalism in Hispanic America*

JUNIOR ROOM, 10:00 A. M.

Chairman, Arthur P. Whitaker, University of Pennsylvania

J. Lloyd Mecham, University of Texas, "Federalism in Mexico." [46]

Percy Alvin Martin, Stanford University, "Federalism in Brazil." [47]

Charles Lyon Chandler, Philadelphia, "Federalism in Argentina." Discussion led by C. H. Haring, Harvard University. [48]

---

[40] Published in *The Constitution Reconsidered* (see note 1).
[41] Published in *The Constitution Reconsidered* (see note 1).
[42] Published in *The Constitution Reconsidered* (see note 1).
[43] Published in *The Constitution Reconsidered* (see note 1).
[44] Published in *The Constitution Reconsidered* (see note 1).
[45] Published in *The Constitution Reconsidered* (see note 1).
[46] Published in *The Constitution Reconsidered* (see note 1) and to be published in *The Hispanic American Historical Review*.
[47] Published in *The Constitution Reconsidered* (see note 1) and in *The Hispanic American Historical Review*, May 1938.
[48] Published in *The Constitution Reconsidered* (see note 1) under the title "Federalism in Latin America."

LUNCHEON CONFERENCES

## I

*Luncheon Conference of the Agricultural History Society*

CLOVER ROOM, 12:30 P. M.

Chairman, Herbert A. Kellar, McCormick Historical Association

## II

*Luncheon Conference of Editors of Historical Publications*

JUNIOR ROOM, 12:30 P. M.

Chairman, Robert L. Schuyler, Columbia University

## III

*Luncheon Conference of the National Council for the Social Studies*

PLANET ROOM, 12:30 P. M.

Chairman, Elmer Ellis, University of Missouri

Carl Wittke, Oberlin College, "Freedom of Teaching in a Democracy." [49]

Ruth Wanger, South Philadelphia High School for Girls, "How Can the Academic Freedom of High School Teachers be Defended?"

AFTERNOON SESSION

*Joint Session of The American Historical Association and The Conference of State and Local Historical Societies*

THE HISTORICAL SOCIETY OF PENNSYLVANIA, 1300 LOCUST STREET, 2:30 P. M.

Chairman, Edward P. Alexander, New York State Historical Association

Mrs. Elinor Schafer Barnes, Philadelphia. "Philadelphia, Convention City of 1787." [50]

Douglas C. McMurtrie, Chicago, "The Record of American Imprints." [51]

Alexander J. Wall, New York Historical Society, "The Place of the Historical Society and Museum in the United States and Elsewhere." [52]

---

[49] Published in *Social Education*, February 1938.
[50] A condensation of her "A 'Faire Greene Country Towne' Plays Host: Philadelphia, 1787," in *The Social Studies*, November 1937.
[51] Published in this volume, pp. 107 ff.
[52] Published in *The Quarterly Bulletin of the New York Historical Society*, April 1938.

## MINUTES OF THE ANNUAL BUSINESS MEETING OF THE AMERICAN HISTORICAL ASSOCIATION FOR 1937

The meeting was called to order by President Ford at 4:20 p. m. on December 30, 1937. The treasurer presented his report,[1] which was approved and placed on file. The secretary of the Association presented his report,[2] which was approved and placed on file.

Mr. Waldo G. Leland read an obituary notice of the late J. Franklin Jameson[3] and Mr. Conyers Read read an obituary notice of the late Charles H. Haskins.[4]

The secretary of the Association read the list of the deceased members for the year 1937.[5]

The secretary of the Association presented a resolution from the council recommending to the business meeting that the annual meeting of the Association for the year 1939 be held in the city of Washington. The resolution was approved.

A resolution was presented by the secretary of the Association from the council in the following terms:

*Resolved*, That the Association approves in principle the development of a procedure whereby the elective members of the council an dthe members of the nominating committee be chosen in an election conducted by mail from a list of nominees containing at least two names for each position to be filled, the nominees for these positions to be selected by the nominating committee after as complete a canvass as may be feasible of the members of the Association for suggestions, with the proviso that anyone nominated by petition with 20 signatures be included in the list. The executive committee is instructed to work out the details of such a procedure and embody them in a proposed amendment to the bylaws to be submitted to the next annual meeting of the Association.

Mr. Howard K. Beale offered an amendment to the resolution providing that the second vice president of the Association should be elected by the method stipulated above. After some discussion the amendment to the resolution was rejected.

A resolution was presented to the meeting by Prof. Asa P. Martin, of Pennsylvania State College:

*Resolved*, That the outgoing president and the incoming president of the Association be authorized to appoint a committee on procedure and policy composed of 10 members to study the present organization and functions of the Association and to report its findings together with such recommendations as it may see fit to the next annual meeting of the Association.

The resolution was adopted.

The meeting then proceeded to the election of officers. It was moved to instruct the secretary of the Association to cast one ballot for the persons named on the official ballot prepared for the meeting and for the following three persons for the board of trustees: Leon Fraser, for the term expiring in 1938; Shepard Morgan, for the term expiring in 1939; and Thomas I. Parkinson, for the term expiring in 1942. The motion was adopted, and the following persons declared elected: Laurence M. Larson, president; Frederic L. Paxson, first vice president; William S. Ferguson, second vice president; Dexter Perkins, secretary; Solon J. Buck, treasurer; and Leon Fraser, Shepard Morgan, and Thomas I. Parkinson, trustees.

The meeting was adjourned.

DEXTER PERKINS,
*Secretary of the Association.*

---

[1] See p. 25 ff.
[2] See p. 44 ff.
[3] See p. 47 ff.
[4] See p. 51 ff.
[5] See p. 54 ff.

## ANNUAL REPORT OF THE TREASURER FOR THE FISCAL YEAR 1936–37

The financial assets of the American Historical Association on August 31, 1937, amounted to $289,562.17. Of that sum, $239,530.36 constitute the capital funds of the Association, which are in the custody of the Fiduciary Trust Co. of New York and are managed by it under the direction of the board of trustees. Of that amount $128,295 are credited to various special funds, leaving only $111,235.36, the income from which is unrestricted. The cash on hand in checking and savings accounts amounts to $50,031.81, of which sum $44,984.43 is restricted, leaving only $5,047.38 available for general purposes. The unrestricted balances in the custody of the treasurer amounted to $4,953.26, and the balance in the operating account of the executive secretary amounted to $94.12. The total of unrestricted funds, including both capital and expendable sums, amounted to $116,282.74, and that of restricted funds amounted to $173,279.43.

The expendable funds of the Association are administered through a general account, six special accounts, and four operating accounts. The general account includes, however, a number of special funds and grants, which are segregated from the unrestricted funds only by bookkeeping. The balances in this account are kept partly in a savings account and partly in a checking account, and transfers are made from one to the other as occasion arises. The balances in the special accounts are separately deposited, some in savings and some in checking accounts. The operating accounts are not administered by the treasurer, but the funds for them are supplied from the general or special accounts and their receipts are transmitted to the treasurer for deposit in the appropriate accounts.

The following tables present a condensed exhibit of the financial transactions of the Association during the year. The statement for the general fund is broken down into unrestricted funds and the various special funds and grants, and for the unrestricted funds the items for 1935–36 are included for purposes of comparison. Statements for the special accounts and the operating accounts follow, and there are a number of summaries.

The treasurer's accounts have been audited by F. W. Lafrentz & Co., certified public accountants; and their report, with the exhibits omitted, is reproduced herewith. The complete report is on file in the Washington office of the Association, where it may be examined by any interested member. The operating account of the committee on Americana for colleges has been audited by Price, Waterhouse & Co., certified public accountants; and the other operating accounts have been audited and certified to be correct by members of the Association appointed by the president for that purpose, as follows: The accounts of the executive secretary and the radio committee, by Leonidas Dodson and Roy F. Nichols; and the accounts of The Social Studies and Social Education, by Austin P. Evans and John A. Krout. Reports of these audits are also on file and available for inspection in the Washington office.

The last item presented herewith is the report of the board of trustees for the fiscal year ending August 31, 1937, which was submitted by Thomas I. Parkinson, chairman of the board.

SOLON J. BUCK, *Treasurer.*

## GENERAL ACCOUNT

*Comparative statement for 1935–36 and 1936–37 of receipts and disbursements of unrestricted funds*

|  | 1935–36 | 1936–37 |
|---|---|---|
| Cash on hand | $9, 535. 88 | $5, 685. 41 |
| Annual dues | 12, 764. 97 | 13, 417. 76 |
| Registration fees | 474. 00 | 885. 00 |
| Interest | 4, 053. 83 | 5, 170. 47 |
| *American Historical Review* | 5, 036. 19 | 5, 326. 30 |
| Miscellaneous | 218. 31 | 456. 14 |
| Total | 32, 083. 18 | 30, 941. 08 |

Disbursements:

|  | 1935–36 | 1936–37 |
|---|---|---|
| Office of the secretary and treasurer | 5, 020. 36 | 4, 771. 16 |
| Office of the executive secretary | 3, 856. 82 | 4, 400. 00 |
| Council and council committees | 862. 95 | 311. 20 |
| Committee on historical source material | 150. 00 | 3. 00 |
| Annual meetings | 742. 19 | 647. 89 |
| *Review*—editorial | 6, 815. 39 | 6, 533. 07 |
| *Review*—copies for members | 7, 391. 90 | 7, 871. 50 |
| *Writings on American History* | 500. 00 | 600. 00 |
| *International Bibliography of Historical Sciences* | 200. 00 | 200. 00 |
| International Committee—dues | 163. 40 | ———— |
| American Council of Learned Societies—dues | 75. 00 | 75. 00 |
| *Annual Report*—editorial | 419. 76 | 375. 00 |
| Pacific coast branch | 200. 00 | 200. 00 |
| Total | 26, 397. 77 | 25, 987. 82 |
| Balance | 5, 685. 41 | 4, 953. 26 |
|  | 32, 082. 18 | 30, 941. 08 |

*Statement of receipts and disbursements for 1936–37 of special funds and grants included in the general account*

|  | Receipts | Disbursements |
|---|---|---|
| **Endowment Fund:** |  |  |
| Life membership dues | $300. 00 | ———— |
| Transferred for investment | ———— | $300. 00 |
|  | 300. 00 | 300. 00 |
| **Andrew D. White Fund:** |  |  |
| Cash on hand Sept. 1, 1936 | 158. 78 | ———— |
| Interest | 48. 00 | ———— |
| Dues for 1937 to International Committee | ———— | 76. 35 |
| Balance, Aug. 31, 1937 | ———— | 130. 43 |
|  | 206. 78 | 206. 78 |
| **George Louis Beer Prize Fund:** |  |  |
| Cash on hand Sept. 1, 1936 | 466. 50 | ———— |
| Interest | 240. 00 | ———— |
| Balance Aug. 31, 1937 | ———— | $706. 50 |
|  | 706. 50 | 706. 50 |
| **John H. Dunning Prize Fund:** |  |  |
| Cash on hand Sept. 1, 1936 | 75. 09 | ———— |
| Interest | 80. 00 | ———— |
| Balance Aug. 31, 1937 | ———— | 155. 09 |
|  | 155. 09 | 155. 09 |

*Statement of receipts and disbursements for 1936–37 of special funds and grants, included in the general account*—Continued

| | Receipts | Disbursements |
|---|---|---|
| **Justin Winsor Prize Fund:** | | |
| Cash on hand Sept. 1, 1936 | $75.00 | |
| Contributions | 91.50 | |
| Balance Aug. 31, 1937 | | $166.50 |
| | 166.50 | 166.50 |
| **Herbert Baxter Adams Prize Fund:** | | |
| Contributions | 89.50 | |
| Balance Aug. 31, 1937 | | 89.50 |
| | 89.50 | 89.50 |
| **Subscriptions to *American Historical Review* Index:** | | |
| Cash on hand Sept. 1, 1936 | 126.00 | |
| Subscriptions | 3.00 | |
| Balance Aug. 31, 1937 | | 129.00 |
| | 129.00 | 129.00 |
| ***Writings on American History* Index:** | | |
| Cash on hand Sept. 1, 1936 | 500.00 | |
| Expenses | | 3.60 |
| Balance Aug. 31, 1937 | | 496.40 |
| | 500.00 | 500.00 |
| **Commission on the Social Studies:** | | |
| Cash on hand Sept. 1, 1936 | 10,048.35 | |
| Expenses | | 354.70 |
| Transferred to special account for *Social Education* | | 7,600.00 |
| Balance Aug. 31, 1937 | | 2,093.65 |
| | 10,048.35 | 10,048.35 |
| **Radio Committee Fund:** | | |
| Grant from McGregor Fund | 1,000.00 | |
| Grant from Keith Fund, Inc | 1,000.00 | |
| Transferred to Radio Committee | | 2,000.00 |
| | 2,000.00 | 2,000.00 |
| **Special accounts:** | | |
| Interest | 4,763.80 | |
| Transfers | | 4,763.80 |
| | 4,763.80 | 4,763.80 |

*Summary statement for 1936–37 of receipts and disbursements of funds in the general account*

| | Receipts | Disbursements |
|---|---|---|
| **Cash on hand Sept. 1, 1936:** | | |
| Unrestricted funds | $5,685.41 | |
| Special funds and grants | 11,449.72 | |
| | $17,135.13 | |
| **Income:** | | |
| Unrestricted funds | 25,255.67 | |
| Special funds and grants | 2,852.00 | |
| | 28,107.67 | |
| **Expenditures and transfers:** | | |
| Unrestricted funds | 25,987.82 | |
| Special funds and grants | 10,334.65 | |
| | | $36,322.47 |

*Summary statement for 1936–37 of receipts and disbursements of funds in the
general account*—Continued

| | | Receipts | Disbursements |
|---|---|---|---|
| Balance Aug. 31, 1937: | | | |
| Unrestricted funds | $4,953.26 | | |
| Special funds and grants | 3,967.07 | | |
| | | | $8,920.33 |
| Totals | | $45,242.80 | 45,242.80 |
| Interest received and transferred to special accounts | | 4,763.80 | 4,763.80 |
| Grand totals, general account | | 50,006.60 | 50,006.60 |

## SPECIAL ACCOUNTS

*Statement for 1936–37 of receipts and disbursements*

| | Receipts | Disbursements |
|---|---|---|
| Americana for College Libraries: | | |
| Transferred from operating account | $3,503.89 | |
| From the McGregor Fund | 10,928.41 | |
| From participating colleges | 3,750.00 | |
| Transferred to operating account | | $17,381.70 |
| Balance Aug. 31, 1937 | | 800.60 |
| | 18,182.30 | 18,182.30 |
| Carnegie Revolving Fund for Publications: | | |
| Cash on hand Sept. 1, 1936 | 8,377.89 | |
| Contribution | 243.87 | |
| Royalties | 1,322.32 | |
| Printing and storage | | 59.40 |
| Committee expenses | | 115.73 |
| Balance Aug. 31, 1937 | | 9,768.95 |
| | 9,944.08 | 9,944.08 |
| Albert J. Beveridge Memorial Fund: | | |
| Cash on hand Sept. 1, 1936 | 15,012.98 | |
| Interest | 3,930.27 | |
| Royalties | 1,345.60 | |
| Editorial and publication expenses | | 5,959.92 |
| Committee expenses | | 104.14 |
| Membership dues for contributors | | 415.00 |
| Balance Aug. 31, 1937 | | 13,809.79 |
| | 20,288.85 | 20,288.85 |
| Littleton-Griswold Fund: | | |
| Cash on hand Sept. 1, 1936 | 2,549.08 | |
| Interest | 1,042.75 | |
| Contribution from Mrs. Griswold | 500.00 | |
| Sales of publications | 811.50 | |
| Editorial and publication expenses | | 2,703.09 |
| Committee expenses | | 61.29 |
| Membership dues for contributor | | 5.00 |
| Balance Aug. 31, 1937 | | 2,133.95 |
| | 4,903.33 | 4,903.33 |
| Commission on the Social Studies, royalty account: | | |
| Cash on hand Sept. 1, 1936 | 7,190.55 | |
| Interest | 120.50 | |
| Royalties | 2,057.19 | |
| Royalty payments to authors | | 53.75 |
| Balance Aug. 31, 1937 | | 9,314.49 |
| | 9,368.24 | 9,368.24 |

*Statement for 1936–37 of receipts and disbursements*—Continued

| *The Social Studies* and *Social Education:* | Receipts | Disbursements |
|---|---|---|
| Cash on hand Sept. 1, 1936 | $73.33 | |
| Interest | 10.70 | |
| Transferred from special fund for Commission on the Social Studies | 7,600.00 | |
| Refund from *The Social Studies* | 3,301.30 | |
| Transferred from *Social Education* (advertising) | 331.50 | |
| Transferred to managing editor | | $9,900.00 |
| Legal services | | 100.00 |
| Balance Aug. 31, 1937 | | 1,316.83 |
| | 11,316.83 | 11,316.83 |

| Summary of special accounts: | | |
|---|---|---|
| Cash on hand Sept. 1, 1936 | 33,203.83 | |
| Income, including transfers | 40,799.80 | |
| Expenditures and transfers | | 36,859.02 |
| Balance Aug. 31, 1937 | | 37,144.61 |
| Total | 74,003.63 | 74.003.63 |

## GENERAL SUMMARY

*Summary statement for 1936–37 of funds in the general account and the special accounts*

| | | Receipts | Disbursements |
|---|---|---|---|
| Cash on hand Sept. 1, 1936: | | | |
| General account | $17,135.13 | | |
| Special accounts | 33,203.83 | | |
| | | $50,338.96 | |
| Income: | | | |
| General account | 28,107.67 | | |
| Special accounts | 40,799.80 | | |
| | 68,907.47 | | |
| Less duplication | 8,020.00 | | |
| | | 60,887.47 | |
| Expenditures and transfers: | | | |
| General account | 36,322.47 | | |
| Special accounts | 36,859.02 | | |
| | 73,181.49 | | |
| Less duplication | 8,020.00 | | |
| | | | $65,161.49 |
| Balance Aug. 31, 1937: | | | |
| General account | 8,920.33 | | |
| Special accounts | 37,144.61 | | |
| | | | 46,064.94 |
| Total | | 111,226.43 | 111.226.43 |

## OPERATING ACCOUNTS

*Statement for 1936–37 of receipts and disbursements of accounts not handled by the treasurer*

| Office of the executive secretary: | Receipts | Disbursements |
|---|---|---|
| Cash on hand, Sept. 1, 1936 | $289.81 | |
| Transferred from general account | 4,400.00 | |
| Refunded to general account | | $189.81 |
| Salaries | | 3,000.00 |
| Travel | | 321.36 |
| Rent | | 480.00 |
| Office expenses | | 604.52 |
| Balance Aug. 31, 1937 | | 94.12 |
| | 4,689.81 | 4,689.81 |

*Statement for 1936–37 of receipts and disbursements of accounts not handled by the treasurer*—Continued

### The Social Studies:

|  | Receipts | Disbursements |
|---|---|---|
| Cash on hand Sept. 1, 1936 | $3, 154. 91 | |
| Transferred from special account | 3, 200. 00 | |
| College Entrance Board reprints | 66. 00 | |
| Salaries, four months | | $2, 066. 66 |
| Review assistants and honoraria | | 257. 00 |
| Travel | | 130. 39 |
| Promotion and special expenses | | 131. 30 |
| Share of printing cost | | 298. 53 |
| Office expenses | | 235. 73 |
| Transferred to special account | | 3, 301. 30 |
| | 6, 420. 91 | 6, 420. 91 |

### Social Education:

|  | Receipts | Disbursements |
|---|---|---|
| Transferred from special account | 6, 700. 00 | |
| Subscriptions and advertising | 2, 105. 71 | |
| Salaries, 8 months | | 4, 083. 32 |
| Office assistant (advertising) | | 288. 00 |
| Review assistants | | 200. 00 |
| Travel | | 144. 55 |
| Office expenses | | 479. 33 |
| Transferred to special account (advertising) | | 331. 50 |
| Balance Aug. 31, 1937 | | 3, 279. 01 |
| | 8, 805. 71 | 8, 805. 71 |

### Radio Committee:

|  | Receipts | Disbursements |
|---|---|---|
| Transferred from general account | 2, 000. 00 | |
| Honoraria for broadcasts | | 600. 00 |
| Historical director, 4⅙ months | | 625. 00 |
| Rent of office space, 5 months | | 25. 00 |
| Stenographic and typing services | | 211. 25 |
| Travel and meetings | | 270. 24 |
| Office expenses | | 235. 22 |
| Balance Aug. 31, 1937 | | 33. 29 |
| | 2, 000. 00 | 2, 000. 00 |

### Committee on Americana for College Libraries, Aug. 1–Dec. 31, 1936 [1]

|  | Receipts | Disbursements |
|---|---|---|
| Cash on hand Aug. 1, 1936 | 3, 310. 99 | |
| From McGregor Fund | 6, 100. 00 | |
| From participating colleges | 4, 000. 00 | |
| Books and repairs | | 7, 404. 86 |
| Gift to Wake Forest College | | 100. 00 |
| Salaries | | 1, 450. 00 |
| Other expenses | | 952. 24 |
| Transferred to special account | | 3, 507. 89 |
| | 13, 410. 99 | 13, 410. 99 |

### Committee on Americana for College Libraries, Jan. 1–Aug. 31, 1937 [1]:

|  | Receipts | Disbursements |
|---|---|---|
| Transferred from special account | 17, 381. 70 | |
| Books | | 12, 128. 09 |
| Salaries | | 3, 309. 90 |
| Other expenses | | 1, 383. 26 |
| Balance Aug. 31, 1937 | | 560. 45 |
| | 17, 381. 70 | 17, 381. 70 |

---

[1] Prior to Jan. 1, 1937, the committee received its funds directly from the McGregor Fund and the participating colleges; since that date the funds have been received by the Association and deposited in a special account, from which transfers are made to the committee as needed in its operations.

## FINANCIAL ASSETS

| | | |
|---|---:|---:|
| Securities as appraised Aug. 31, 1937 | | $239,530.36 |
| Credited to— | | |
|   Albert J. Beveridge Memorial Fund | $94,095 | |
|   Littleton-Griswold Fund | 25,000 | |
|   Andrew D. White Fund | 1,200 | |
|   George Louis Beer Prize Fund | 6,000 | |
|   John H. Dunning Prize Fund | 2,000 | |
| | | 128,295.00 |
| Unrestricted | | 111,235.36 |
| Cash in checking and savings accounts | | 50,031.81 |
|   Special accounts | 37,144.61 | |
|   Credited to special funds | 3,967.07 | |
|   Operating accounts, restricted | 3,872.75 | |
| | | 44,984.43 |
| Unrestricted | | 5,047.38 |

### SUMMARY

| | | |
|---|---:|---:|
| Unrestricted funds: | | |
|   Securities | $111,235.36 | |
|   Cash in custody of the treasurer | 4,953.26 | |
|   Cash in custody of the executive secretary | 94.12 | |
| | | $116,282.74 |
| Restricted funds: | | |
|   Securities | 128,295.00 | |
|   Cash in custody of the treasurer | 41,111.68 | |
|   Cash in the operating accounts | 3,872.75 | |
| | | 173,279.43 |
| Total | | 289,562.17 |

## REPORT ON EXAMINATION

OCTOBER 9, 1937.

AMERICAN HISTORICAL ASSOCIATION,
*Washington, D. C.*

DEAR SIRS: We have examined your accounts from September 1, 1936, to August 31, 1937, and submit herewith our report including seven exhibits and three schedules.

### CASH RECEIPTS AND DISBURSEMENTS

A summary of the cash receipts and disbursements of the various funds, as detailed in exhibits A to G, inclusive, is as follows:

| Exhibit | Account | Balance Sept. 1, 1936 | Cash receipts | Subtotal | Cash disbursements | Balance Aug. 31, 1937 |
|---|---|---:|---:|---:|---:|---:|
| A | General account | $17,135.13 | $32,871.47 | $50,006.60 | $41,086.27 | $8,920.33 |
| B | Carnegie Revolving Fund for Publications | 8,377.89 | 1,566.19 | 9,944.08 | 175.13 | 9,768.95 |
| C | Albert J. Beveridge Memorial Fund | 15,012.98 | 5,275.87 | 20,288.85 | 6,479.06 | 13,809.79 |
| D | Littleton-Griswold Fund | 2,549.08 | 2,354.25 | 4,903.33 | 2,769.38 | 2,133.95 |
| E | Commission on the Social Studies, royalty account | 7,190.55 | 2,177.69 | 9,368.24 | 53.75 | 9,314.49 |
| F | Commission on the Social Studies in Schools | 73.33 | 11,243.50 | 11,316.83 | 10,000.00 | 1,316.83 |
| G | Committee on Americana for college libraries | | 18,182.30 | 18,182.30 | 17,381.70 | 800.60 |
| | Total | 50,338.96 | 73,671.27 | 124,010.23 | 77,945.29 | 46,064.94 |

Recorded cash receipts were checked against the bank deposits and the cash disbursements were supported by cancelled checks and approved vouchers.

The cash in banks at August 31, 1937, amounting to $46,064.94, was reconciled with bank statements and pass books and confirmed by correspondence with the depositories. A summary of the cash balances in the various funds at August 31, 1937, is as follows:

| | | | |
|---|---|---:|---:|
| Riggs National Bank: Checking account No. 1 | | | $9,768.95 |
| Union Trust Co.: | | | |
|    Checking account No. 2 | $4,332.42 | | |
|    Savings account No. 3 | 4,587.91 | | |
| | | $8,920.33 | |
|    Savings account No. 4 | | 9,314.49 | |
|    Savings account No. 5 | | 13,809.79 | |
|    Savings account No. 6 | | 2,133.95 | |
|    Savings account No. 7 | | 1,316.83 | |
|    Special checking account | | 800.60 | |
| | | | 36,295.99 |
|     Total | | | 46,064.94 |

### INVESTMENTS

A summary of the transactions made by the Fiduciary Trust Co. of New York, for your account from August 12, 1936, to August 11, 1937, inclusive, as detailed on schedule No. 1, is as follows:

| | | |
|---|---:|---:|
| Cash balance at Aug. 12, 1936 | $252.19 | |
| Add receipts | 83,659.23 | |
| | | $83,911.42 |
| Deduct disbursements | | 77,166.57 |
|    Cash balance at Aug. 11, 1937 | | 6,744.85 |

On August 31, 1937, the amount of $300 was transferred from the general account to the Fiduciary for investment and was entered accordingly on your records, but same was not included in their report as their fiscal year ended August 11, 1937.

A summary of the purchase and sale of securities made by the Fiduciary Trust Co. of New York for your account from August 12, 1936, to August 11, 1937, inclusive, as detailed on schedule No. 2, is as follows:

| | | |
|---|---:|---:|
| Securities on hand at Aug. 12, 1936 | $225,971.04 | |
|   Add— | | |
|     Purchases | 67,558.41 | |
|     Adjustment to restore book value of American Car & Foundry Co. stock | 1,018.75 | |
| | | $294,548.20 |
| Deduct sales and payment on bonds of International Match Corporation | | 73,894.14 |
|    Total securities, schedule No. 3 | | 220,654.06 |

A summary of all securities, or certificates of deposit covering same, in the hands of the Fiduciary Trust Co. of New York at August 11, 1937, in accordance with statements submitted to us by your Association, computed at par and book value, as detailed on schedule No. 3, is as follows:

| | | |
|---|---:|---:|
| Bonds: | | |
|    Interest paying, par value | $148,000.00 | |
|    In default of interest, par value | 10,000.00 | |
|    In receivership—par value, less dividends | 2,539.52 | |
| | | $160,539.52 |

Stocks:
   Preferred:

| | | |
|---|---|---|
| Interest paying, book value | $13,049.75 | |
| Nonpaying, book value | 6,018.75 | |
| | | $19,068.50 |
| Common, book value | | 41,046.04 |
| **Total securities, schedule No. 3** | | 220,654.06 |

### INCOME FROM INVESTMENTS

The total net income received from securities by the Fiduciary Trust Co. of New York and transmitted to the Association during the year ended August 11, 1937, amounted to $10,176.66, as shown on schedule No. 1. The total interest and dividends on securities, as shown by the records, was accounted for with the following exceptions:

| Par value | Bond | Rate | Due at— | Interest in arrears |
|---|---|---|---|---|
| $5,000.00 | Chicago, Milwaukee & St. Paul Ry. Co., 1989 | 4½s | July 1, 1937 | $337.50 |
| 5,000.00 | Missouri Pacific R. R. Co., 1978 | 5s | May 1, 1937 | 1,125.00 |
| 2,539.52 | International Match Corporation, c/d, 1947 | do | do | 805.81 |
| | | | | 2,268.31 |

In addition to the above arrearages the dividend of 7 percent on the preferred stock of the American Car & Foundry Co. was not paid during the year under review.

Respectfully submitted.

F. W. LAFRENTZ & Co.,<br>
*Certified Public Accountants.*

EXHIBIT A.—*Statement of cash receipts and disbursements—General account, from Sept. 1, 1936, to Aug. 31, 1937*

#### RECEIPTS

| | | | |
|---|---|---|---|
| Annual dues | | | $13,417.76 |
| Life memberships | | | 300.00 |
| Registration fees | | | 885.00 |
| Royalties | | | 192.86 |
| Publications | | | 61.27 |
| Interest: | | | |
|   Savings account | | $125.61 | |
|   Investments—Fiduciary Trust Co. of New York: | | | |
|     Unrestricted funds | | $5,044.86 | |
|     Special funds: | | | |
|       Andrew D. White Fund | $48.00 | | |
|       George Louis Beer Prize Fund | 240.00 | | |
|       John H. Dunning Prize Fund | 80.00 | | |
| | | 368.00 | |
| | | 5,412.86 | |
| | | | 5,538.47 |
| Contributions: | | | |
|   Justin Winsor Prize Fund | | 91.50 | |
|   Herbert Baxter Adams Prize Fund | | 89.50 | |
|   Radio committee | | 2,000.00 | |
| | | | 2,181.00 |
| Refund, office of executive secretary | | | 189.81 |
| Fiduciary Trust Co. of New York for transfer to other funds | | | 4,763.80 |
| Miscellaneous | | | 12.20 |

EXHIBIT A.—*Statement of cash receipts and disbursements—General account, from Sept. 1, 1936, to Aug. 31, 1937*—Continued

RECEIPTS—continued

*American Historical Review:*
 The Macmillan Co.:
  Editorial expenses_____ $2,400.00
  Profit for the year ended July 15, 1937_____ 2,391.30
  Subscriptions to proposed index to vols. 21–40__ 3.00
  Periodicals purchased_____ 535.00
                   $5,329.30

   Total receipts_____ 32,871.47
Cash on hand, Sept. 1, 1936:
 Union Trust Co.:
  Checking account_____ $5,547.22
  Savings account_____ 11,587.91
                   17,135.13

                        50,006.60

DISBURSEMENTS

Administrative expenses:
 Salaries_____ $2,400.00
 Temporary clerical assistance_____ 456.88
 Rent_____ 578.84
 Janitor service and office expense_____ 15.72
 Stationery, printing, and office supplies_____ 442.05
 Equipment_____ 74.10
 Postage _____ 258.57
 Telephone and telegraph_____ 52.23
 Auditing_____ 125.00
 Bonding_____ 25.00
 Contingent fund_____ 263.22
Council and executive committee meetings_____ 311.20
 Annual meetings:
  Providence meeting:
   Program _____ $379.81
   Local arrangements_____ 99.20
   Nominating committee____ 31.00
            $510.01

   Philadelphia meeting:
   Program_____ 109.63
   Nominating committee____ 28.25
            137.88
                 647.89
  *Annual Report* of the Association_____ 375.00
  Pacific coast branch_____ 200.00
  Miscellaneous_____ 79.55
                   6,305.25
Historical activities:
 *Writings on American History*_____ 603.60
 Dues to American Council of Learned Societies_____ 75.00
 Committee on historical source material_____ 3.00
 *International Bibliography of Historical Sciences*____ 200.00
 Andrew D. White Fund_____ 76.35
 Committee on the Social Studies:
  Salaries_____ $325.00
  Committee expense_____ 29.70
  Transfer to special account_____ 7,600.00
             7,954.70
                   8,912.65
Radio committee_____ 2,000.00
Executive secretary:
 Salaries_____ $3,000.00
 Office expenses_____ 1,400.00
                   4,400.00

EXHIBIT A.—*Statement of cash receipts and disbursements—General account, from Sept. 1, 1936, to Aug. 31, 1937*—Continued

DISBURSEMENTS—continued

*American Historical Review:*

| | | |
|---|---:|---:|
| Salaries | | $5,722.72 |
| Stationery, printing, and supplies | | 134.81 |
| Postage and express | | 252.49 |
| Payment for notes contributed | | 180.75 |
| Copies to members | $7,871.50 | |
| Copies to European libraries | 40.00 | |
| | | 7,911.50 |
| Publications | | 15.52 |
| Binding | | 2.60 |
| Equipment | | 110.30 |
| Miscellaneous | | 73.88 |
| | | $14,404.57 |
| Fiduciary Trust Co. of New York, for investment | | 300.00 |
| Transfers to other funds | | 4,763.80 |
| | | |
| Total disbursements | | 41,086.27 |
| Cash on hand, Aug. 31, 1937, Union Trust Co.: | | |
| Checking account | $4,332.42 | |
| Savings account | 4,587.91 | |
| | | 8,920.33 |
| | | |
| | | 50,006.60 |

*Summary of balances, general account, Union Trust Co., at Aug. 31, 1937*

| | | | |
|---|---:|---:|---:|
| Savings account: | | | |
| Cash on hand, Sept. 1, 1936 | $11,587.91 | | |
| Interest | 125.61 | | |
| | 11,713.52 | | |
| Transfer to checking account | 7,125.61 | | |
| | | $4,587.91 | |
| Checking account | | 4,332.42 | |
| For credit of— | | | |
| Operating expense and historical activities | $4,953.26 | | |
| Subscriptions for *Review* index | 129.00 | | |
| Herbert Baxter Adams Prize Fund | 89.50 | | |
| George Louis Beer Prize Fund | 706.50 | | |
| John H. Dunning Prize Fund | 155.09 | | |
| Andrew D. White Fund | 130.43 | | |
| Justin Winsor Prize Fund | 166.50 | | |
| *Writings on American History:* American Council of Learned Societies, for cumulative index | 496.40 | | |
| Commission on Social Studies | 2,093.65 | | |
| | 8,920.33 | | |
| | | 8,920.33 | |

EXHIBIT B.—*Statement of cash receipts and disbursements—Carnegie Revolving Fund for Publications, from Sept. 1, 1936, to Aug. 31, 1937*

RECEIPTS

| | | |
|---|---:|---:|
| Contributions: The University of London, toward publication cost of Hoon's *English Customs System* | | $243.87 |
| Royalties on volumes by authors noted: | | |
| Allyn | $19.95 | |
| Barnes | 67.20 | |
| Bemis | 283.73 | |
| Brown | 29.86 | |
| Bruce | 28.80 | |

**EXHIBIT B.**—*Statement of cash receipts and disbursements—Carnegie Revolving Fund for Publications, from Sept. 1, 1936, to Aug. 31, 1937*—Continued

RECEIPTS—continued

Royalties on volumes by authors noted—Continued.

| | | |
|---|---|---|
| Carroll | $26. 13 | |
| Dietz | 29. 87 | |
| Garrett | 118. 40 | |
| Hubbart | 382. 66 | |
| Lonn | 11. 20 | |
| Ragatz | 29. 33 | |
| Sanborn | 10. 66 | |
| Shryock | 42. 67 | |
| Swann | 12. 80 | |
| Sydnor | 69. 06 | |
| Whitaker | 123. 20 | |
| White | 36. 80 | |
| | | $1, 322. 32 |
| Total receipts | | 1, 566. 19 |
| Cash on hand, Sept. 1, 1936, Riggs National Bank | | 8, 377. 89 |
| | | 9, 944. 08 |

DISBURSEMENTS

| | | |
|---|---|---|
| Storage, Bemis volume | | $59. 40 |
| Committee expenses: | | |
| Clerical services and reading of manuscripts | $96. 70 | |
| Postage and supplies | 19. 03 | |
| | | 115. 73 |
| Total disbursements | | 175. 13 |
| Cash on hand, Aug. 31, 1937, Riggs National Bank | | 9, 768. 95 |
| | | 9, 944. 08 |

**EXHIBIT C.**—*Statement of cash receipts and disbursements—Albert J. Beveridge Memorial Fund, from Sept. 1, 1936, to Aug. 31, 1937*

RECEIPTS

| | | |
|---|---|---|
| Interest: | | |
| Investments | $3, 763. 80 | |
| Savings account | 166. 47 | |
| | | $3, 930. 27 |
| Royalties: | | |
| Dumond—*Southern Editorials on Secession* | 64. 00 | |
| Barnes and Dumond—*Weld-Grimké Letters* | 224. 00 | |
| Labaree—*Royal Instructions to British Colonial Governors* | 624. 00 | |
| Case—*French Opinion on the United States and Mexico* | 182. 93 | |
| Binkley—*Official Correspondence of the Texan Revolution* | 250. 67 | |
| | | 1, 345. 60 |
| Total receipts | | 5, 275. 87 |
| Cash on hand, Sept. 1, 1936, Union Trust Co. savings account | | 15, 012. 98 |
| | | 20, 288. 85 |

**Exhibit C.**—*Statement of cash receipts and disbursements—Albert J. Beveridge Memorial Fund, from Sept. 1, 1936, to Aug. 31, 1937*—Continued

### DISBURSEMENTS

Expenses of volumes:

| | | |
|---|---|---|
| Dumond—*Southern Editorials on Secession*_____ | $74.49 | |
| Binkley—*Official Correspondence of the Texan Revolution* _____ | 3,528.08 | |
| Pargellis—*Military Affairs of North America, 1748–1765* _____ | 2,357.35 | |
| | | $5,959.92 |
| Postage, express, and other committee expenses_____ | | 104.14 |
| Dues to American Historical Association of Life Members_____ | | 415.00 |
| | | |
| Total disbursements_____ | | 6,479.06 |
| Cash on hand, Aug. 31, 1937, Union Trust Co. savings account_____ | | 13,809.79 |
| | | |
| | | 20,288.85 |

**Exhibit D.**—*Statement of cash receipts and disbursements—Littleton-Griswold Fund, from Sept. 1, 1936, to Aug. 31, 1937*

### RECEIPTS

Interest:

| | | |
|---|---|---|
| Investments _____ | $1,000.00 | |
| Savings account_____ | 42.75 | |
| | | $1,042.75 |
| Contributions from Mrs. Frank T. Griswold_____ | | 500.00 |
| Proceeds of sales of publications: | | |
| Volumes: | | |
| Bond—*Proceedings of Maryland Court of Appeals, 1695–1729*_____ | 62.98 | |
| Morris—*Select Cases of the Mayor's Court, New York City, 1674–1784*_____ | 122.57 | |
| Towle and Andrews — *Records of the Vice-Admiralty Court of Rhode Island, 1716–1752*____ | 625.95 | |
| | | 811.50 |
| | | |
| Total receipts_____ | | 2,354.25 |
| Cash on hand, Sept. 1, 1936, Union Trust Co. savings account_____ | | 2,549.08 |
| | | |
| | | 4,903.33 |

### DISBURSEMENTS

Expenses:

| | | |
|---|---|---|
| Volumes: | | |
| Bond—*Proceedings of Maryland Court of Appeals, 1695–1729* _____ | $3.13 | |
| Morris—*Select Cases of the Mayor's Court, New York City, 1674–1784*_____ | 4.79 | |
| Towle and Andrews—*Records of the Vice-Admiralty Court of Rhode Island, 1716–1752*_____ | 2,695.17 | |
| | | $2,703.09 |
| Committee expenses and miscellaneous_____ | | 66.29 |
| | | |
| Total disbursements_____ | | 2,769.38 |
| Cash on hand, Aug. 31, 1937, Union Trust Co. savings account_____ | | 2,133.95 |
| | | |
| | | 4,903.33 |

EXHIBIT E.—*Statement of cash receipts and disbursements, Commission on the Social Studies—Royalty account from Sept. 1, 1936, to Aug. 31, 1937*

### RECEIPTS

| | | |
|---|---:|---:|
| Interest on savings account | | $120. 50 |
| Royalties: | | |
| Volumes: | | |
| Beale—*Are American Teachers Free?* | $8. 43 | |
| Beard—*A Charter for the Social Sciences* | 122. 16 | |
| Beard—*The Nature of the Social Sciences* | 78. 48 | |
| Bowman—*Geography in Relation to the Social Sciences* | 90. 44 | |
| Clark—*Exercises in Historical Evidence* | 9. 79 | |
| Counts—*Social Foundations of Education* | 657. 23 | |
| Curti—*The Social Ideas of American Educators* | 226. 12 | |
| Johnson—*Introduction to the History of the Social Sciences in Schools* | 14. 99 | |
| Kelly and Krey—*Tests and Measurements* | 90. 23 | |
| Kelty-Moore—*Tests of Concepts* | 5. 36 | |
| Marshall - Goetz — *Curriculum - making in the Social Studies* | 177. 45 | |
| Merriam—*Civic Education in the United States* | 60. 77 | |
| Newlon—*Educational Administration as Social Policy* | 91. 35 | |
| Pierce—*Citizens Organizations and the Civic Training of Youth* | 36. 00 | |
| Tyron—*Social Sciences as School Subjects* | 233. 32 | |
| Wesley—*Tests* | 30. 09 | |
| *Conclusions and Recommendations* | 141. 84 | |
| | | 2, 057. 19 |
| | | |
| Total receipts | | 2, 177. 69 |
| Cash on hand Sept. 1, 1936, Union Trust Co., savings account | | 7, 190. 55 |
| | | 9, 368. 24 |

### DISBURSEMENTS

| | |
|---|---:|
| Royalty payments to authors: | |
| Johnson | $10. 50 |
| Pierce | 25. 20 |
| Wesley | 18. 05 |
| Total disbursements | 53. 75 |
| Cash on hand Aug. 31, 1937, Union Trust Co., savings account | 9, 314. 49 |
| | 9, 368. 24 |

EXHIBIT F.—*Statement of cash receipts and disbursements, Commission on the Social Studies in the Schools, from Sept. 1, 1936, to Aug. 31, 1937*

### RECEIPTS

| | |
|---|---:|
| Interest on savings account | $10. 70 |
| Advertising in *The Social Studies* | 331. 50 |
| Refund by *The Social Studies* of balance at Dec. 31, 1936 | 3, 301. 30 |
| Transfer from the general funds of the Commission | 7, 600. 00 |
| Total receipts | 11, 243. 50 |
| Cash on hand, Sept. 1, 1936, Union Trust Co., savings account | 73. 33 |
| | 11, 316. 83 |

### DISBURSEMENTS

| | |
|---|---:|
| To managing editor for editorial work and office expenses | $9, 900. 00 |
| Legal services | 100. 00 |
| Total disbursements | 10, 000. 00 |
| Cash on hand Aug. 31, 1937, Union Trust Co., savings account | 1, 316. 83 |
| | 11, 316. 83 |

Exhibit G.—*Statement of cash receipts and disbursements, Committee on Americana for College Libraries, from Jan. 19, 1937, to Aug. 31, 1937*

### RECEIPTS

| | |
|---|---:|
| The McGregor Fund | $11,081.25 |
| Participating colleges | 7,101.05 |
| | 18,182.30 |

### DISBURSEMENTS

Operating expenses:

| | | |
|---|---:|---:|
| To establish bank account | | $2,000.00 |
| Book inventory | | 10,697.73 |
| Book expense | | 125.68 |
| Bond (Kathryn L. Slagle) | | 25.00 |
| Engraving and framing portraits | | 83.75 |
| Office supplies and equipment | | 322.17 |
| Postage and express | | 68.05 |
| Printing pamphlets, etc | | 374.83 |
| Refunded to McGregor Fund | | 50.00 |
| Salaries: | | |
|     Director and office assistant | $2,992.00 | |
|     Clerical help | 317.90 | |
| | | 3,309.90 |
| Telephone and telegraph | | 85.52 |
| Travel | | 220.91 |
| Miscellaneous | | 34.63 |
| | | 17,398.17 |
| Less refunds of expenses | | 16.47 |
| | | 17,381.70 |
| Cash on hand Aug. 31, 1937, Union Trust Co., special account | | 800.60 |
| | | 18,182.30 |

Schedule No. 1.—*Statement of cash receipts and disbursements of The Fiduciary Trust Co. of New York from Aug. 12, 1936, to Aug. 11, 1937*

[In accordance with statement submitted by American Historical Association]

### RECEIPTS

| | | |
|---|---:|---:|
| Interest on securities | | $10,787.40 |
| Proceeds from sale of securities | | 72,495.49 |
| American Historical Association, for investment | | 376.34 |
| Total receipts | | 83,659.23 |
| Cash in hands of Fiduciary Aug. 12, 1936 | | 252.19 |
| | | 83,911.42 |

### DISBURSEMENTS

| | | |
|---|---:|---:|
| Securities purchased | $65,398.76 | |
| Accrued interest | 179.43 | |
| Commissions, taxes, etc | 279.22 | |
| Fee to Fiduciary Trust Co. of New York | 1,132.50 | |
| Total disbursements | 66,989.91 | |
| Cash in hands of Fiduciary Aug. 11, 1937 | 6,744.85 | |
| | | 73,734.76 |

Payments to American Historical Association:

| | | |
|---|---:|---:|
| Exhibit A—General account | 5,412.86 | |
| Exhibit B—Albert J. Beveridge Memorial Fund | 3,763.80 | |
| Exhibit D—Littleton-Griswold Fund | 1,000.00 | |
| | | 10,176.66 |

SCHEDULE No. 2.—*Purchase and sale of securities by The Fiduciary Trust Co. of New York from Aug. 12, 1936, to Aug. 11, 1937*

[In accordance with statement submitted by American Historical Association]

| | | | |
|---|---|---:|---:|
| Securities in hands of Fiduciary at Aug. 12, 1936 | | | $225,971.04 |
| Add: | | | |
|   Securities purchased: | | | |
|     Bonds, per list (par value) | | $36,000.00 | |
|     Stocks, preferred, per list (book value) | | 13,049.75 | |
|     Stocks, common, per list (book value) | | 18,508.66 | |
|   Adjustment to restore book value of American Car & Foundry Co. stock | | 1,018.75 | |
| | | | 68,577.16 |
| | | | 294,548.20 |
| Deduct: | | | |
|   Securities sold: | | | |
|     Bonds, per list (par value) | | 65,400.00 | |
|     Stocks, preferred, per list (book value) | | 3,500.00 | |
|     Stocks, common, per list (book value) | | 4,687.15 | |
|   Dividend on bonds of International Match Corp., in receivership | | 306.99 | |
| | | | 73,894.14 |
| Securities in hands of Fiduciary at Aug. 11, 1937: | | | |
|   Bonds, per list (par value) | | 148,000.00 | |
|   Bonds in default of interest, per list (par value): | | | |
|     Chicago, Milwaukee & St. Paul Ry. Co., 4½s, 1989 | $5,000.00 | | |
|     Missouri Pacific R. R. Co., 5s, 1978 | 5,000.00 | | |
| | | 10,000.00 | |
|   Bonds of International Match Corp., c/d, in receivership: | | | |
|     Par value | 3,000.00 | | |
|     Less dividends received to date | 460.48 | | |
| | | 2,539.52 | |
| | | 160,539.52 | |
|   Stocks, per list: | | | |
|     Preferred (book value) | 19,068.50 | | |
|     Common (book value) | 41,046.04 | | |
| | | 60,114.54 | |
| | | | 220,654.06 |

SCHEDULE No. 3.—*Securities, at Aug. 11, 1937, in hands of The Fiduciary Trust Co. of New York*

[In accordance with statement submitted by the American Historical Association]

Bonds:

| | |
|---|---:|
| American Gas & Electric Co. 5s, 2028 | $7,000.00 |
| Bell Telephone Co. of Canada 5s, 1957 | 5,000.00 |
| Brooklyn Edison Co., Inc., 3¼s, 1966 | 7,000.00 |
| Canadian National Railways 5s, 1969 | 5,000.00 |
| Consolidated Edison Co. of N. Y., Inc., 3¼s, 1946 | 10,000.00 |
| Detroit Edison Co., series F, 4s, 1965 | 6,000.00 |
| General Motors Acceptance Corporation 3s, 1946 | 10,000.00 |
| Louisville & Nashville Railroad Co. 4s, 1940 | 10,000.00 |
| Massachusetts Utilities Associates, series A, 5s, 1949 | 5,000.00 |
| Mobile and Birmingham Railroad Co. 4s, 1945 | 5,000.00 |
| National Steel Corporation 4s, 1965 | 10,000.00 |
| New York, Chicago & St. Louis R. R. Co. series A, 5½s, 1974 | 4,000.00 |
| North American Co. 5s, 1961 | 5,000.00 |

Schedule No. 3.—*Securities, at Aug. 11, 1937, in hands of The Fiduciary Trust Co. of New York*—Continued

**Bonds—Continued.**

| | | | |
|---|---|---|---|
| Ontario Power Co. of Niagara Falls 5s, 1943 | $5,000.00 | | |
| Oregon-Washington Railroad & Navigation Co. 4s, 1961 | 5,000.00 | | |
| Pacific Gas & Electric Co., series G, 4s, 1964 | 10,000.00 | | |
| Pennsylvania Railroad Co., series D, 4¼s, 1981 | 12,000.00 | | |
| Pittsburgh, Bessemer & Lake Erie R. R. Co. 5s, 1947 | 2,000.00 | | |
| Railway Express Co., Inc., series A, 5s, 1949 | 5,000.00 | | |
| Southern Pacific Co. 4½s, 1981 | 10,000.00 | | |
| Union Electric Co. of Missouri 3s, 1942 | 10,000.00 | | |
| | | $148,000.00 | |
| In default: | | | |
| Chicago, Milwaukee & St. Paul Ry. Co. 4½s, 1989 | 5,000.00 | | |
| Missouri Pacific R. R. Co. 5s, 1978 | 5,000.00 | | |
| | | 10,000.00 | |
| In receivership: | | | |
| International Match Corporation 5s, 1947 c/d (par value $3,000.00, dividends received $460.48) | 2,539.52 | | |
| | | | $160,539.52 |

**Stocks:**

Preferred:

| | | | |
|---|---|---|---|
| 50 American Car & Foundry Co. 7 percent, non-cumulative | $6,018.75 | | |
| 100 E. I. Dupont de Nemours & Co., $4.50 cumulative | 10,512.50 | | |
| 30 Electric Bond & Share Co., $6 cumulative | 2,537.25 | | |
| | | 19,068.50 | |

Common:

| | | | |
|---|---|---|---|
| 20 American Can Co | 1,817.55 | | |
| 30 Bethlehem Steel Corporation | 2,796.00 | | |
| 25 Chrysler Corporation | 886.08 | | |
| 30 Commercial Investment Trust Corporation | 2,000.00 | | |
| 60 Continental Oil Co | 1,051.92 | | |
| 30 General Motors Corporation | 834.60 | | |
| 10 Guaranty Trust Co. of N. Y | 3,090.00 | | |
| 20 Ingersoll-Rand Co | 2,729.30 | | |
| 30 International Harvester Co | 1,150.95 | | |
| 30 International Nickel Co. of Canada, Ltd | 700.20 | | |
| 50 Kennecott Copper Corporation | 1,060.75 | | |
| 40 Loew's, Inc | 2,965.60 | | |
| 25 New York Air Brake Co | 1,885.38 | | |
| 50 Pacific Gas & Electric Co | 1,966.40 | | |
| 40 J. C. Penney Co | 1,834.60 | | |
| 20 Pittsburgh Plate Glass Co | 2,565.10 | | |
| 50 Standard Oil Co. of N. J | 2,122.65 | | |
| 40 Union Carbide and Carbon Corporation | 1,649.60 | | |
| 15 United Fruit Co | 1,329.98 | | |
| 20 United States Gypsum Co | 916.50 | | |
| 25 Westinghouse Electric & Manufacturing Co | 3,567.28 | | |
| 40 Youngstown Sheet & Tube Co | 2,125.60 | 41,046.04 | 60,114.54 |
| Total | | | 220,654.06 |

## REPORT OF THE BOARD OF TRUSTEES

DECEMBER 6, 1937.

To THE TREASURER OF THE AMERICAN HISTORICAL ASSOCIATION.

SIR: I beg to submit herewith a report of the board of trustees of the American Historical Association for the fiscal year ending August 31, 1937.

The securities held in trust for the Association on the 31st day of August 1937 were as follows:

### *Bond account*

| | Approximate | | Estimated annual income |
| --- | --- | --- | --- |
| | Price | Value | |
| **Railroad bonds:** | | | |
| $5,000—Chicago, Milwaukee & St. Paul Ry. Co., genl. mtge. ser. E 4½ percent, due 5/1/89, 7/1/35 to 7/1/36, incl.; cpns. stpd. $15, J & J 1 pd. 7/1/35 and S C A; paid two-thirds of 1936 interest | 50 | $2,500.00 | $150.00 |
| $10,000—Louisville & Nashville R. R. Co., unified 4 percent, due 7/1/1940; J & J 1 int., $200 | 107 | 10,700.00 | 400.00 |
| $5,000—Oregon-Washington Railroad & Navigation Co., 1st & ref. mtge. ser. A gtd. 4 percent, due 1/1/1961; J & J 1 int., $100 | 106 | 5,300.00 | 200.00 |
| $12,000—Pennsylvania R. R. Co., genl. mtge. ser. D, 4¼ percent, due 4/1/1981; A & O 1 int., $255 | 106 | 12,720.00 | 510.00 |
| $2,000—Pittsburgh, Bessemer & Lake Erie R. R. Co. cons. 1st. mtge. 5 percent, due 1/1/1947; J & J 1 int., $50 | 117 | 2,340.00 | 100.00 |
| $5,000—Railway Express Agency, Inc., ser. A, 5 percent, due 3/1/1949; M & S 1 int., $125 | 109 | 5,450.00 | 250.00 |
| $10,000—Southern Pacific Co., 4½ percent, due 5/1/81; M & N 1 int., $225 | 82 | 8,200.00 | 450.00 |
| **Public-utility bonds:** | | | |
| $7,000—American Gas & Electric Co., deb. 5 percent, due 5/1/2028; M & N 1 int., $175 | 107 | 7,490.00 | 350.00 |
| $7,000—Brooklyn Edison Co. Inc., cons. mtge. 3¼ percent, due 5/15/66; M & N 15 int., $113.75 | 101 | 7,070.00 | 227.00 |
| $10,000—Consolidated Edison Co. of N. Y., Inc., deb. 3¼ percent, due 4/1/46; A & O 1 int., $162.50 | 105 | 10,500.00 | 325.00 |
| $6,000—Detroit Edison Co. genl. & ref. mtge. ser. F 4 percent due 10/1/65; A & O 1 int., $120 | 108 | 6,480.00 | 240.00 |
| $5,000—Massachusetts Utilities Associates deb. ser. A 5 percent due 4/1/49; A & O 1 int., $125 | 104 | 5,200.00 | 250.00 |
| $5,000—North American Co. deb. 5 percent due 2/1/61; F & A 1 int. $125 | 104 | 5,200.00 | 250.00 |
| $10,000—Pacific Gas & Electric Co. 1st & ref. mtge. ser. G 4 percent due 12/1/64; J & D 1 int., $200 | 107 | 10,700.00 | 400.00 |
| $10,000—Union Electric Co. of Missouri notes 3 percent due 7/1/42; J & J 1 int., $150 | 103 | 10,300.00 | 300.00 |
| **Industrial bonds:** | | | |
| $10,000—National Steel Corporation 1st coll. mtge. 4 percent due 6/1/65; J & D 1 int., $200 | 107 | 10,700.00 | 400.00 |
| $1,000—Socony Vacuum Oil Co., Inc., deb. 3½ percent due 10/15/50; A & O 15 int., $17.50 | 105 | 1,050.00 | 35.00 |
| $10,000—General Motors Acceptance Corporation deb. 3 percent due 8/1/46; F & A 1 int., $150 | 103 | 10,300.00 | 300.00 |
| **Canadian bonds:** | | | |
| $5,000—Bell Telephone Co. of Canada 1st mtge. ser. B 5 percent, due 6/1/1957; J & D 1 int., $125 | 120 | 6,000.00 | 250.00 |
| $5,000—Canadian National Rwys. Co. gtd. 5 percent due 10/1/1969; A & O 1 int., $125 | 118 | 5,900.00 | 250.00 |
| $5,000—Ontario Power Co. of Niagara Falls 1st mtge. 5 percent due 2/1/43; F & A 1 int., $125 | 114 | 5,700.00 | 250.00 |
| **Preferred stock:** | | | |
| 100 shares E. I. duPont de Nemours & Co. $4.50 cum. pfd. no par rate $4.50; JJ AO 25 div., $112.50 | 110 | 11,000.00 | 450.00 |
| **Miscellaneous stock:** | | | |
| 6 shares International Match Realization Co., Ltd., V. T. C. par L 1; first liquidating div. of $12.50 per share paid 8/31/37 | 61 | 366.00 | |
| Securities value | | 161,166.00 | |
| Principal cash balance | | 7,585.80 | |
| Total bond account | | 168,751.80 | 6,337.00 |

*Special account*

| | Approximate | | Esti-mated annual income |
| --- | --- | --- | --- |
| | Price | Value | |
| Railroad bonds: | | | |
| $5,000—Missouri Pacific R. R. Co. 1st & ref. mtge. ser. G 5 percent due 11/1/1978; 11/1/33 & S. C. A.; not paying | 36 | $1,800.00 | |
| $5,000—Mobile & Birmingham R. R. Co. 1st mtge. 4 percent due 7/1/1945, $200 denominations; J & J 1 int., $100 | 69 | 3,450.00 | $200.00 |
| $4,000—N. Y., Chicago & St. Louis R. R. Co. ref. mtge. ser. A 5½ percent due 4/1/1974; A & O 1 int., $110 | 97 | 3,880.00 | 220.00 |
| Preferred stocks: | | | |
| 30 shares Electric Bond & Share Co. $6 cum. pfd.; no par rate, $6; FA MN 1 div., $45 | 68 | 2,040.00 | 180.00 |
| 50 shares American Car & Foundry Co. 7 percent non cum. pfd., par. $100; $4 paid 4/20/37 JJ AO 1 | 72 | 3,600.00 | 200.00 |
| Industrial common stocks: | | | |
| 15 shares United Fruit Co. no par rate $3; $1.25 extra paid in 1936; JJ AO 15 div., $11.25 | 71 | 1,065.00 | 64.00 |
| 20 shares American Can Co. par $25, rate $4; $2 extra paid in 1936; FA MN 15 div., $20 | 103 | 2,060.00 | 120.00 |
| 40 shares J. C. Penney Co. no par rate $4; $7.25 paid in 1936; MS JD 30 div. $40 | 98 | 3,920.00 | 290.00 |
| 40 shares Loew's, Inc., no par rate irregular, $6 paid to 8/25/37, MS JD 30 | 81 | 3,240.00 | 240.00 |
| 40 shares Union Carbide & Carbon Corporation no par rate $3.20; JJ AO 1 div., $32 | 98 | 3,920.00 | 128.00 |
| 60 shares Continental Oil Co. par $5; rate, $1; 50 cents extra declared to 9/30/37; MS JD 30 div., $15 | 43 | 2,580.00 | 90.00 |
| 50 shares Standard Oil Co. of New Jersey par $25; rate $1; $1 extra paid in 1936, 75 cents extra paid 6/15/37; J & D 15 div., $25 | 65 | 3,250.00 | 100.00 |
| 25 shares Chrysler Corporation par $5; rate irregular; $12 paid in 1936; MS JD 15 $7 declared to 9/10/37 | 109 | 2,725.00 | 300.00 |
| 30 shares General Motors Corporation par $10; rate irregular; $4.50 paid in 1936; MS JD 12; $2.25 declared to 9/13/37 | 54 | 1,620.00 | 135.00 |
| 30 shares International Harvester Co. no par; rate, $2.50; JJ AO 15 div., $18.75 | 112 | 3,360.00 | 75.00 |
| 25 shares New York Air Brake Co. no par; rate, $2; $2.50 paid in 1936; MS JD 1 div., $12.50 | 65 | 1,625.00 | 62.00 |
| 25 shares Westinghouse Elec. & Mfg. Co. par $50, rate $4; $5.50 paid in 1936; FA MN 30 div., $25 | 145 | 3,625.00 | 138.00 |
| 20 shares Ingersoll-Rand Co. no par rate irregular; $6 paid in 1936 MS JD 1; $3 declared to 9/1/37 | 128 | 2,560.00 | 120.00 |
| 30 shares Bethlehem Steel Corporation no par; $2.50 declared to 9/15/37 | 93 | 2,790.00 | 75.00 |
| 40 shares Youngstown Sheet & Tube Co. no par rate $3; JJ AO 1 div., $30 | 87 | 3,480.00 | 120.00 |
| 20 shares Pittsburgh Plate Glass Co. par $25, rate irregular; $6 paid in 1936 JJ AO 1; $5.50 declared to 10/1/37 | 123 | 2,460.00 | 120.00 |
| 20 shares U. S. Gypsum Co. par $20, rate $2; $1.25 extra paid in 1936; JJ AO 1 div., $10 | 108 | 2,160.00 | 65.00 |
| 50 shares Kennecott Copper Corporation no par, rate irregular; $2 declared to 9/30/37; MS JD 30 (estimated rate $3) | 59 | 2,950.00 | 150.00 |
| 50 shares Pacific Gas & Electric Co. par $25, rate $2; JJ AO 15 Div., $25 | 31 | 1,550.00 | 100.00 |
| Financial common stocks: | | | |
| 10 shares Guaranty Trust Co. of New York par $100; rate $12; JJ AO 1 div., $30 | 322 | 3,220.00 | 120.00 |
| 30 shares Commercial Investment Trust Corporation no par, rate $4; JJ AO 1 div., $30; $4.90 paid in 1936 | 61 | 1,830.00 | 147.00 |
| Securities value | | 70,760.00 | |
| Principal cash balance | | 18.56 | |
| Total special account | | 70,778.56 | 3,559.00 |
| Total bond account | | 168,751.80 | 6,337.00 |
| Grand total | | 239,530.36 | 9,896.00 |

All the securities listed above are in the custody of the Fiduciary Trust Co. of New York. It will be borne in mind that the securities in the bond account are under the direct control of the board of trustees and are neither bought nor sold except with the written approval of a majority of the board. The securities in the special account are bought and sold at the discretion of the Fiduciary Trust Co. This account was created in June 1934. As originally constituted it was made up of securities which the trustees believed it desirable to sell, and as sales were made it was largely invested in common stocks in order to provide some measure of insurance against what was believed at the time to be an impending danger of inflation. The discretionary power conceded to the Fiduciary Trust Co. in the management of this special account can be terminated at any time by the board of trustees upon thirty days' notice to that effect in writing.

During the year securities at a cost price of $34,137.50 have been purchased for the bond account, and securities at a sales price of $41,536.70 have been sold from the bond account. Securities at a cost price of $19,045.91 have been purchased for the special account, and securities at a sales price of $19,441.85 have been sold from the special account. A list of these purchases and sales is on file at the office of the chairman of the board of trustees.

A comparison of the holdings of the American Historical Association as of August 31, 1937, with its holdings as of August 31, 1936, reveals the following:

|  | Value of principal | Income |
|---|---|---|
| Bond account: | | |
| 1936 | $171,806.60 | $6,631.00 |
| 1937 | 168,751.80 | 6,337.00 |
| Special account: | | |
| 1936 | 71,370.37 | 2,386.50 |
| 1937 | 70,778.56 | 3,559.00 |

The net result, therefore, of the year's operation has been that the total value of the securities now held for the Association has decreased from $243,176.97 to $239,530.36, a decrease of 1½ percent, while the income has increased from $9,017.50 to $9,896, an increase of nearly 10 percent. It will be observed that the income from the bond account has decreased by $294, a decrease which is explained in large part by the fact that there was in the bond account on the 31st of August 1937, a cash balance of $7,585.80 awaiting investment and, therefore, not at the time the account was taken showing any yield in income. A few days after the account was taken, $7,000 of this balance was invested in bonds which show a yield in income of $245, thus reducing the apparent decrease in revenue from the bond account to less than $50.

The striking increase in income from the special account is, of course, a reflection of the greatly increased dividend payments on common stocks during the fiscal year.

During the fiscal year the trustees received from the Association $374.34 for investment.

The charges made by the Fiduciary Trust Co. for the management of securities amounted during the current year to $1,132.50. The brokerage charges on purchases and sales amounted to $279.22. The board of trustees itself incurred no expenses in the performance of its services.

THOMAS I. PARKINSON, *Chairman.*

## ANNUAL REPORT OF THE SECRETARY FOR 1937

No doubt the most important single question with which my report should concern itself this year is that of the administrative set-up of our Association. President Ford, acting on his own initiative, has submitted to the members a statement which is in your hands. In conformity with the desire expressed in the council, I should like to supplement that statement by some further observations, chiefly of an historical character.

The present organization of the Association, as historians will not find it difficult to believe, is not the product of logic but of circumstances. Theoretically, the affairs of the Association might reasonably be centralized in a single place. Practically, matters have worked otherwise. Even so long as 17 years ago, when the affairs of the Association were infinitely simpler than they are now, there was no complete centralization in Washington, for on the resignation of Waldo G. Leland as secretary, Professor Bassett, of Smith College, was appointed to the post thus vacated. On Professor Bassett's tragic death in 1928, the office of Secretary devolved upon me and was discharged by me as one of the two principal administrative officers of the organization until 1933. There existed in the Association, however, a strong feeling that a full-time secretariat ought to be created, and in the year just mentioned the generosity of the Carnegie Corporation made possible such action.

In seeking to fill the office of executive secretary, the members of the council selected Dr. Conyers Read, of Philadelphia, and his selection determined the establishment of the executive offices of the Association in that city. The Carnegie Corporation not continuing its grant on a scale sufficient to maintain a full-time officer, Mr. Read continued to serve after 1933 on part time. The vigor and competence which he had brought to the management of the affairs of the Association determined his continuance in the work of executive secretary.

With regard to the *Review*, the transfer of Dr. Jameson from the Carnegie Institution to the Library of Congress in 1929 presented a new situation to the council. After a brief term we had the good fortune to find in Washington a highly competent editor in the person of Professor H. E. Bourne; but on Mr. Bourne's resignation at the end of 1935, in seeking to select the best possible editor available, it was necessary to transfer the *Review* to New York. Meanwhile, the activities of the Association had brought about the raising of the endowment fund, and made it desirable that the heavy responsibility for the investments of the Association should not be vested in one man alone, such as the treasurer. A board of trustees was accordingly created, and in the nature of the case the appointments to such a board centered in New York.

Out of the Commission on the Social Studies in the Schools grew a magazine now known as *Social Education*, and here again the choice of the best possible editor resulted in the selection of New York as the centre of administration for this new enterprise.

From this brief historical review it will be seen, then, that the diffusion of the activities of the Association is the result of the efforts of the council to secure the best possible administrative officers to carry on the various functions of the Association. It should also be said that this diffusion is less important than might appear for, with the exception of the *Review* and of the financial affairs of the Association, administrative responsibility is centered in the executive secretary. Nonetheless, as has already been made clear to you, the executive committee has been concerned with the problem of administrative reorganization, which was the subject of two resolutions, one of December 28, 1935, and one of December 28–29, 1936. The question of our administrative set-up was to be reconsidered, and at the outset it was thought that important economies might be effected by some simplification of the present structure. As a matter of fact, this appears less clear on examination. The only rents paid by the Association are those for the Philadelphia and Washington offices, and the total amount for the two together is only $1,059. For administrative services Miss Patty W. Washington is maintained in the Washington office and Miss Ann I. Gamber in the office of the Association here in Philadelphia, but it does not appear from an examination of the work of these offices that either one of these two highly competent persons is without sufficient work, nor is it clear in what way a saving could here be effected by any process of consolidation.

The administrative expenses of the *Review* are, as will be seen from the figures in Mr. Ford's letter, quoted from the treasurer's report, actually less today than they were when the *Review* was in Washington. There has also been effected since the separation of the *Review* and the Washington office a saving of $400 in the expenses of the latter. Taking all these facts into consideration, neither the executive committee nor the council has found it possible as yet to recommend a change in the existing set-up. The matter, however, is obviously one which is the concern of all the members of the Association and on which they may take such action as circumstances seem to warrant.

The council at its meeting on Tuesday received a memorandum signed by a considerable number of the more active members of the Association with regard to the method of election of officers. The views expressed in this memorandum met with much support, though not entire concurrence. At the same time practical problems in connection with the alteration of our electoral procedure made it impossible to draft in the limited time at our disposal an amendment to be submitted to this meeting. I shall, however, present to you a resolution which has the unanimous support of all the members of the council.[1]

The membership of the Association has increased during the last year and now stands, or stood on November 30, 1937, at 3,236. Three hundred and eight new members were added during the last year and 260 were lost, making a total gain of 48 members, and giving us the largest membership we have had in at least 5 years. The thanks of the Association are due to Professor Miller and his associates, who have given much time and energy to the membership problem. At the same time it ought to be emphasized that no membership committee can do for the Association what individual members can do if they will consider it a part of their function to secure new additions to our rolls. An increase of 500 members would immensely simplify the problems of the Association. The council has this problem very much in mind, but hopes also for the cooperation of all those interested in the affairs of our Association.

Some concern has been expressed during the past year at the slight interest taken in the prizes of the Association and in the relatively small number of desirable applications made to the committee on the Carnegie Revolving Fund. We shall hope, in the course of the next year, to ask the members of the larger graduate schools to give wider publicity to the existence of these prizes and of this Fund. Two years ago it seemed as if the generous gift of the Carnegie Corporation to permit the publication of manuscripts of importance might be approaching exhaustion. It has, however, been replenished by royalties, and there should be no hesitation in submitting any worthy project to the chairman of the committee which administers this fund, Prof. John D. Hicks. The widest publicity which can be given to the existence of this source of assistance to scholars should certainly be given.

In the same way the generous initiative of Professor Lybyer, of the University of Illinois, in securing funds for the reestablishment of the Justin Winsor and Herbert Baxter Adams prizes should not be unknown to the members of the Association in general.

In the course of the last year there have appeared the last of the studies prepared as a result of the work of the Commission on the Social Studies. As is, I hope, known to the members of the Association, the remainder of the

---

[1] See pp. 9 and 24.

funds have been used in the establishment of a new magazine, *Social Education*, the number of whose subscribers in the last year has increased from 1,855 to 3,436. In the liquidation of the affairs of the Commission, and in the establishment of the new magazine, the energy and interest of the executive secretary have been particularly valuable.

The publication program of the Association will be outlined in detail in the report of the executive secretary, which will be published in the April number of *The American Historical Review*.[2] The committees of the Association charged with publication are all active. The Beveridge Memorial Committee expects to publish in 1938 the papers of James G. Birney. The Littleton-Griswold Committee expects to publish the reports of the Superior Court of Connecticut, 1772–73, by William Samuel Johnson, and the minutes of the Supreme Court of West New Jersey, 1681–1709, these to be edited, respectively, by John T. Farrel and by Henry Clay Reed in collaboration with George J. Miller.

The *Bibliography of American Travel*, long a concern of the Association, is advancing towards publication, and the consummation of this work will depend upon further funds.

One of the most interesting activities of the Association during the past year has been its radio program. In the winter of 1937 twelve talks were given over the Columbia Broadcasting System network. These broadcasts were entitled *"The History Behind the Headlines,"* and each of them was prepared by a competent scholar. The actual broadcasting was done by a trained broadcaster of the Columbia System. It is much to be hoped that funds will be found for the carrying on of this work.

The Association has had a prosperous and an effective year. Its activities have undeniably widened in their scope as time has gone on. Such matters as the new magazine, *Social Education*, the conclusion of the program set in motion by the Commission on the Social Studies in the Schools, and the publication through the office of the executive secretary of the Littleton-Griswold volumes have increased the burden imposed upon Mr. Read, the administerial officer of the Association. They have also increased the usefulness of our body to the causes of historical scholarship. That its role may expand rather than contract with time is, I am sure, the earnest wish of every member of the Association.

DEXTER PERKINS,
*Secretary of the Association.*

## JOHN FRANKLIN JAMESON

The death on September 28, 1937, of John Franklin Jameson removed a notable figure from among the historians of the world and lost to the American Historical Association one who for 53 years had been to it a principal and unfailing source of strength and reputation.

Born on September 19, 1859, he had not reached his twenty-fifth birthday when he took part in the founding of the Association, as one of that small group, of which there is now but one survivor, who met for the purpose in Saratoga on September 9, 1884. Twenty-two years later he was elected president of the Association.

The Association has been fortunate above many organizations in the number and quality of those of its members who have devoted to it their interest, their affection, and their labors. Among these Jameson was preeminent, not only for the length and unselfishness of his service but also for its unfailing regularity, its quality of wisdom, and its creative resourcefulness. Without this service the history of the Association would have been different and less distinguished.

---

[2] See pp. 727 ff. of that issue.

The biography of Jameson, when it comes to be written, will reveal the notable influence that he exercised upon the progress of historical studies in the United States as an inspiring teacher, as a writer of uncommon charm and lucidity, as an editor of uncanny omniscience, as a far-seeing administrator, and as a leader in many undertakings of major importance.

Jameson was born in Somerville, a part of the Boston metropolitan district. He prepared for Harvard College at the Roxbury Latin School, but although admitted to Harvard, the appointment of his father to the postmastership of Amherst, Mass., made it expedient for him to take his undergraduate work at Amherst College, from which he graduated in 1879. He decided to prepare himself for a career of scholarship in the field of history, although the opportunities for gainful occupation in that field were at that time few and precarious, and so he entered the newly founded Johns Hopkins University as a graduate student, where, like so many others of the early pillars of the Association, he came under the influence of Herbert Adams. He received his doctorate from Johns Hopkins in 1882, and remained there as assistant and associate in history until 1888, when he became professor of history in Brown University, a position which he held until 1901, when he was called to the University of Chicago as successor to Von Holst, and head of the department of history. Four years later, in 1905, he was appointed director of the department of historical research in the Carnegie Institution of Washington, remaining there for 23 years until his retirement in 1928, when he was called to the Library of Congress as the first occupant of the chair of American history and chief of the Division of Manuscripts. Here his career found a fitting culmination amid congenial surroundings, in a high position which he distinguished by enlarging its opportunities for public service and leadership.

Jameson was a teacher for 26 years, and an administrator for 32 years; during the 58 years of his career he was constantly engaged in good works for the advancement of his profession, and these exercised a constant influence upon the course of historical studies in the United States. As a teacher of undergraduates, Jameson was admired and beloved by the small number of students who had the intellectual courage to elect a course that was reputed to be one of the most exacting and difficult of the curriculum. Those who had such courage look back upon "Jamie's History" as one of the most inspiring of their college experiences. Behind the cold, rather stern expression that he habitually wore they discovered a wealth of practical wisdom and far-seeing philosophy, as well as a most unexpected fund of humor. His personal interest in his students was very keen, and in countless ways he showed himself their friend and won their affection. His learning, the range of his knowledge, and his extraordinary memory, together with the perfection of his conversational lectures, made him almost the object of a cult among his students. As a teacher, or rather a leader of graduate students, Jameson, during the 4 short years at Chicago, bade fair to become the founder of a school, not because he specialized in an attractive hypothesis or opened up a new field of study but because of the high quality of his scholarship and because of the fresh points of view that he brought to bear upon the history of the United States.

The change from teaching to administration was made in full knowledge of all that it implied, because Jameson saw in the new Carnegie Institution an opportunity to realize a dream that he and others had long cherished of establishing in Washington a central institute for historical research. The Carnegie Institution, to be devoted entirely to research, seemed to offer an ideal setting for such an institute, in the form of one of its departments. As chairman of an advisory committee appointed by the trustees of the Institution, Jameson was able to lay before that body a plan which won their support, and so, in an organization given over very largely to research in the sciences, a place was made for history. When, 2 years later, Jameson came to the department as its director, succeeding the organizing director, Andrew C. McLaughlin, he had a definite program well in hand.

This included, first of all, a systematic exploration of the archives and other historical depositories of foreign countries for the discovery of materials on American history. These explorations, conducted under his active direction and in some of which he took part, resulted in a series of published guides relating to materials in Canada, Mexico, Cuba, and the West Indies, on this side of the Atlantic, and in Great Britain, France, Spain, Italy, Germany, Austria, Switzerland, and Russia on the other side; while information was gathered, although not yet published, in the Netherlands and the Scandinavian countries.

A direct result of this exploration was the commencement, generally under the direction of the authors of the various guides, of the work of transcribing selected documents for deposit in the Library of Congress. The great extension of this work, made possible by photography and the generosity of Mr. Rockefeller, has now brought to the Library an unparalleled collection of materials, increasing manyfold the opportunities for research in American history in this country.

The program also included important series of documentary publications bearing upon American history at points where much new work remains to be done, such as *Letters of Members of the Continental Congress, Proceedings and Debates of the British Parliament respecting North America, European Treaties Relating to the History of the United States and its Dependencies, Judicial Cases Relating to Slavery, Documents Illustrative of the History of the Slave Trade in the United States, Correspondence of Andrew Jackson*, and, in a different category of material, the *Atlas of the Historical Geography of the United States*.

Jameson's interests were not, however, confined to the program of his department, and some of his most notable achievements were personal. Among these stands, first and foremost, the successful conduct of a long, difficult, and nearly always discouraging campaign for a national archives building and establishment. The structure on Pennsylvania Avenue that he lived to see completed and in operation is as much a monument to him as though it bore his name. Another achievement was the creation, as a part of the Archives establishment, of the National Historical Publications Commission, a direct, though deferred, result of the report of a special committee, organized by Jameson and appointed by President Theodore Roosevelt, on governmental historical documentary publications. Still another achievement was the maintenance, year after year, by means of small personally-solicited contributions, of *Writings on American History*. Finally in this group of achievements must be mentioned the *Dictionary of American Biography*, for the inception, planning, and support of which Jameson was chiefly responsible, and to the progress of which, as chairman of the committee of management, he contributed constantly and helpfully. This great work, which he lived to see completed, is also in a very real sense a monument to him.

It was while at Brown that Jameson commenced some of his most valuable services to the American Historical Association. In 1890 he conducted for the Association an inquiry into the expenditures of foreign governments on behalf of history, the results of which were published in the *Annual Report* for 1891.

Shortly after this he became chairman of the Historical Manuscripts Commission, which he himself had fashioned upon the model of the Royal Historical Manuscripts Commission.

In 1895 he became managing editor of the newly founded *American Historical Review*, which, although not owned by the Association until 20 years later, became almost at once its official organ and a focal point of American historical interests. This editorship he held until 1928, except for the 4 years from 1901 to 1905 that he spent at Chicago. It was as editor that Jameson displayed some of his most characteristic qualities, and perhaps exercised his greatest influence upon historical studies. The editorial function, which includes so much of drudgery, seemed not to be irksome to him; it stimulated him, rather, and in its performance he was greatly aided by the superior powers that he possessed of orderliness, consistency, and memory. But above all it afforded him the opportunity of setting the highest standards for historical scholarship. So successful was his direction of the *Review* that Gabriel Monod, the editor of the *Revue Historique*, pronounced it to be the best historical journal.

In the midst of these occupations and achievements it was inevitable that Jameson should find little opportunity and less time for research and writing of his own, and yet his accomplishment was very considerable in amount and of the highest order. His doctoral dissertation on William Usselinx, founder of the Dutch and Swedish West India Companies, appeared in 1887, and was a model of scholarship dealing with European and American history. His little *History of Historical Writing in America* (1891) displayed a complete and critical knowledge of American historiography. A *Dictionary of American History* (1894) became a standard reference work for librarians and students; his consummate skill as an editor was demonstrated in an edition of the correspondence of John C. Calhoun (1900), in the series *Original Narratives of Early American History* (1906–1907), both of these for the American Historical Association, and in *Privateering and Piracy* (1923), while his power of philosophic interpretation was revealed in *The American Revolution Considered as a Social Movement* (1926).

It is impossible in a single concluding paragraph to characterize a man such at Jameson. His personality, not easily revealed except to those close to him, was simple and magnetic. A reserved exterior concealed a warm and sincere friendliness and a belief in the fundamental goodness of his fellow beings. His sense of humor was extraordinarily keen, and found constant expression. He was never unjust, and could not endure injustice on the part of others. He possessed and practiced the noblest part of the Puritan tradition. His mind was open to new ideas, and generated many, and his point of view was that of the intelligent liberal. He had a strong historical sense, and realized that the present and the future are anchored in the past, and that any attempt to cut them loose is futile. Change for its own sake he disliked; he preferred to hold fast to what had been proved, and to that extent he was a conservative.

He was essentially and completely unselfish. He was ambitious only for historical scholarship, never for himself. Honors came to him, but he was as incapable of seeking them as he was of an ungenerous action. This is the sort of man he was. The influence of his character and of his work continues and will be felt throughout the lifetime of the Association, becoming a part of its tradition and of the inheritance of future generations of scholars.

WALDO G. LELAND.

## CHARLES HOMER HASKINS

Charles Homer Haskins was born in Meadville, Pa., on December 21, 1870. He died after a long illness on May 14, 1937, at Cambridge, Mass.

He was a great scholar, a great educator, a great administrator, and on one notable occasion revealed the qualities of a great diplomatist. To those who worked with him and beside him he will be remembered best as a great teacher and a great friend. The learned world at large associates his name with those of Henry C. Lea and Charles Gross as one of the three great American medievalists. As a matter of fact, his doctoral dissertation at Johns Hopkins—and he took his B. A. degree there when he was 16 and his Ph. D. degree there before he was 20—was in American history and his first published contribution to historical scholarship belongs in the same field. But his major historical interest almost from the start lay overseas, and his first professorship, which came to him at the University of Wisconsin when he was 22, was in European history. The great creative period of his life began after he went to Harvard in 1902, and all of his published books fall within the last 20 years of his active life.

His outstanding contributions to scholarship have to do with Norman institutions and with medieval science, and most of them were printed first as short monographs on special subjects and gathered together later into book form. The greatest of them appeared in 1918 under the title of *Norman Institutions* and in 1924 under the title *Studies in the History of Mediaeval Science*. Both of these books were addressed to the world of scholars, but Charles Haskins did not disdain to distill the essence of his learning for a wider audience. His *Normans in European History* (1915), his *Rise of Universities* (1923), and his *Renaissance of the Twelfth Century* (1927) are as delightful as they are learned. And no one who heard them is likely to forget those brilliant masterpieces of vulgarization—his lectures on medieval history to Harvard freshmen.

Charles Haskins was much more than a great scholar. He was also a great educator. As a member of the famous committee of seven of the American Historical Association he played a very active part in planning a curriculum for the study of history in secondary schools which still remains a classic in the literature of American pedagogy. For 16 years (1908–24) he was dean of the Graduate School at Harvard, and he had a great deal to do with development of what is today certainly one of the greatest, if not the greatest, graduate schools of history in America. It was characteristic of his breadth of interest that he should have made such important contributions to the teaching of history both at the secondary school level and at the postgraduate level.

Those of us here present will not forget his great services to the cause of American historical scholarship at large and to the general advancement of humanistic learning in America. For 12 years he served this Association, first as corresponding secretary (1901–8) and then as secretary of the council (1909–13). He was our president in 1921. Dr. Jameson, not many weeks before he went to join his colleague, wrote of him in words which deserve to be remembered:

"His most conspicuous relation to the American Historical Association lay in the service he performed as secretary of the council. During most of the time that he so served, Leland was secretary of the Association, and it is hard to separate the services of two men composing such a team. Certainly it can be said, however, that Haskins was an invaluable secretary, and that, as the older of the two, he may rightly be given the larger share of the credit for most of the excellent things which the Association did in those years. . . .

"Haskins had all the society's business and operations at his fingers' ends (as, indeed, he seemed to have almost everything else that had ever come under his eye). He was full of ingenuity, of fairness toward all interests, and of insight into future needs. . . . Typical of his attitude was this: I remember his saying once, when there was some discussion of elections to the council, 'There is So-and-So, an angular person, difficult to get on with, and one who will be found far from agreeable in the council, but he has ideas of his own and will do us all good.' "

In the same letter Dr. Jameson also called attention to the very significant part which Charles Haskins played in the organization of the American Council of Learned Societies.

"Haskins," he wrote, "and Leland and I set it going, but Leland would not think it unjust, large as was his part in the matter, to say that Haskins, with his varied learning as well as his executive abilities, had very much the leading part—and, of course, I, though I tried to be useful in the organization, am well aware that my part was the least of the three representatives of history. Haskins was chairman of the Council until his physical condition made it impossible for him to continue, and his wide knowledge, his good judgment, and his wide acquaintance with similar scholars in Europe, did manage to give the A. C. L. S. (as Leland has since continued to give it) the large influence it has in the Union Académique Internationale."

Nor must we forget that he had much to do with the formation of the Mediaeval Academy.

The one interruption in his academic career came at the end of the Great War when Charles Haskins was selected by President Wilson as Chief of the Division of Western Europe in the American delegation to the Peace Conference at Versailles. His most distinguished service there was in connection with the difficult problem of redefining the eastern frontier of France. With Tardieu of France, and Headlam-Morley of England, he made one of a committee of three responsible for the settlement of the Saar Valley. There can be little doubt that the knowledge and wisdom and skill which he displayed in these high matters opened doors for him to a brilliant diplomatic career. But he was not tempted. I remember asking him just after he had returned from Europe, heavy with honors, whether he would ever be content to return again to medieval documents. His answer was characteristic: "I want nothing in the world," he said, "quite so much. The past at any rate is secure."

Those of us who studied under Charles Haskins or made one of that shining company of his assistants—and it is amazing how many of the outstanding historians in America today have touched at least the hem of his garments—will remember him best as a great teacher and a great friend. I dare not dwell upon this, but those among you who knew him well know how much the best of him was that part which he saved for the closer circle of his intimates.

The final period of his life, following that mysterious collapse which made him a helpless invalid for 6 weary years, has been appraised by one of his close colleagues and old friends:

". . . this lamentable breakdown of a great career was mastered by Haskins with the strength with which he mastered everything. Even in the latter years, in the latter months of his life, his friends who were permitted brief visits saw within the prison of the body the will of iron, the keen mind, the gay humor, the loyal friendship that they had known of yore. Those who were his constant attendants, his devoted wife and children, his faithful nurses, heard no syllable of discontent, no sound of pain escape his lips. It was the triumph, not the defeat of Charles Haskins, and the best of his legacies to our age. Far more notable even than his works in the world of scholars and of nations was the molding of a noble soul through joys and pain. *Requiescat in pace, anima candida.*"

Conyers Read.

*Statistics of membership, Nov. 30, 1937*

### I. GENERAL

Total membership:
  Individuals:
    Life_____ 519 [1]
    Annual_____ 2, 336
  Institutions:
    25-year membership_____ 6
    Annual_____ 375

                                          3, 236

Total paid membership, including life members_____ 2, 593
Delinquent_____ 643
Loss:
  Deaths _____ 38
  Resignations_____ 49
  Dropped_____ 150

                                          237

New members:
  Life_____ _____
  Annual:
    Individuals_____ 350
    Institutions_____ 39

                                          389

Net gain_____ 152
Membership, Dec. 9, 1936_____ 3, 084
New members, 1937_____ 389
Deaths, resignations, etc., 1937_____ 237

                                          152

Total membership, Nov. 30, 1937_____ 3, 236

### II. BY REGIONS

New England: Maine, New Hampshire, Vermont, Massachusetts, Rhode Island, Connecticut_____ 513
North Atlantic: New York, New Jersey, Pennsylvania, Delaware, Maryland, District of Columbia_____ 1, 018
South Atlantic: Virginia, North Carolina, South Carolina, Georgia, Florida_ 200
North Central: Ohio, Indiana, Illinois, Michigan, Wisconsin_____ 668
South Central: Alabama, Mississippi, Tennessee, Kentucky, West Virginia_ 119
West Central: Minnesota, Iowa, Missouri, Arkansas, Louisiana, North Dakota, South Dakota, Nebraska, Kansas, Oklahoma, Texas_____ 343
Pacific Coast Branch: Montana, Wyoming, Colorado, New Mexico, Idaho, Utah, Nevada, Arizona, Washington, Oregon, California, Hawaii_____ 274
Territories and dependencies: Puerto Rico, Alaska, Philippine Islands, Canal Zone_____ 3
Other countries_____ 98

                                          3, 236

[1] On Dec. 9, 1936, there were 524 life members. During the year 8 life members have died, and 3 members who had annual memberships have changed them to life memberships.

*Statistics of membership, Nov. 30, 1937*—Continued

III. BY STATES

| | New members, 1937 | | | New members, 1937 |
|---|---|---|---|---|
| Alabama | 22 | 2 | New Hampshire | 30 | 2 |
| Alaska | 1 | ------ | New Jersey | 81 | 10 |
| Arizona | 9 | ------ | New Mexico | 9 | 2 |
| Arkansas | 5 | 1 | New York | 466 | 52 |
| California | 174 | 17 | North Carolina | 63 | 8 |
| Canal Zone | ------ | ------ | North Dakota | 10 | 1 |
| Colorado | 21 | 2 | Ohio | 150 | 16 |
| Connecticut | 112 | 10 | Oklahoma | 21 | 7 |
| Delaware | 11 | ------ | Oregon | 11 | 1 |
| District of Columbia | 158 | 17 | Pennsylvania | 235 | 34 |
| Florida | 19 | 2 | Philippine Islands | 2 | ------ |
| Georgia | 23 | 1 | Puerto Rico | ------ | ------ |
| Hawaii | 6 | ------ | Rhode Island | 32 | 6 |
| Idaho | 5 | ------ | South Carolina | 19 | 4 |
| Illinois | 217 | 32 | South Dakota | 7 | 2 |
| Indiana | 147 | 17 | Tennessee | 41 | 5 |
| Iowa | 38 | 5 | Texas | 60 | 10 |
| Kansas | 37 | 4 | Utah | 4 | ------ |
| Kentucky | 26 | 3 | Vermont | 10 | 5 |
| Louisiana | 19 | 1 | Virginia | 76 | 10 |
| Maine | 17 | 4 | Washington | 23 | 1 |
| Maryland | 67 | 10 | West Virginia | 21 | 1 |
| Massachusetts | 312 | 38 | Wisconsin | 63 | 3 |
| Michigan | 91 | 11 | Wyoming | 2 | ------ |
| Minnesota | 65 | 13 | Canada | 34 | 2 |
| Mississippi | 9 | 2 | Cuba | 1 | ------ |
| Missouri | 53 | 6 | Latin-America | 3 | ------ |
| Montana | 7 | 1 | Foreign | 60 | 5 |
| Nebraska | 28 | 3 | | | |
| Nevada | 3 | ------ | | 3,236 [2] | 389 |

*Deaths Reported, December 9, 1936, to November 30, 1937*

Elizabeth Briggs, Cambridge, Mass. (life member); died May 14, 1937.

Frank Cundall, Institute of Jamaica, Kingston, Jamaica; died November 15, 1937.

Richard Edwin Day, Albany, N. Y.; died December 14, 1936.

George Francis Dow, Topsfield, Mass.; died June 5, 1936.

Bell Merrill Draper (Mrs. Amos G.), Washington, D. C. (life member); died October 12, 1937.

Barnett A. Elzas, New York, N. Y.; died October 1936.

William Crowninshield Endicott, Boston, Mass.; died November 28, 1936.

Henry C. Ford, Lexington, Va.; died September 1, 1936.

Samuel M. Foster, Fort Wayne, Ind. (life member); died April 4, 1935.

Rt. Rev. Michael Gallagher, Detroit, Mich. (life member); died January 20, 1937.

Reuben Post Halleck, Louisville, Ky.; died December 24, 1936.

Charles Homer Haskins, Cambridge, Mass.; died May 14, 1937.

Msgr. Patrick J. Healy, Washington, D. C.; died May 18, 1937.

John Franklin Jameson, Washington, D. C. (charter member); died September 28, 1937.

William Lee Jenks, Port Huron, Mich.; died December 4, 1936.

Charles Knapp, New York, N. Y.; died September 12, 1936.

George Herbert Locke, chief librarian, Public Library of Toronto, Toronto, Canada; died January 28, 1937.

---

[2] This includes the 389 new members.

Leonard Leopold Mackall, Savannah, Ga.; died May 19, 1937.
Charles Meyerholz, Chicago, Ill. (life member) ; died 1937 (?).
George H. Moore, Boston, Mass.; died July 11, 1936.
Henry R. Mueller, Allentown, Pa.; died May 3, 1937.
Grenville Howland Norcross, Boston, Mass.; died February 12, 1937.
Rev. Albert O'Brien, St. Bonaventure, N. Y.; died July 16, 1937.
Mary F. O'Brien (Mrs. M. W.), Detroit, Mich.; died October 23, 1936.
Thomas Walker Page, Washington, D. C.; died January 13, 1937.
George Arthur Plimpton, New York, N. Y. (life member) ; died July 1, 1936.
Rev. Ralph B. Pomeroy, West Orange, N. J.; died August 1935.
Harrington Putnam, Brooklyn, N. Y.; died April 7, 1937.
Warren Bartlett Ranney, Washington, D. C.; died April 20, 1937.
Oliver Huntington Richardson, Seattle, Wash.; died 1936 (?).
Hon. Simon W. Rosendale, Albany, N. Y. (life member) ; died April 22, 1937.
Arthur H. Seymour, Aberdeen, S. D.; died September 29, 1936.
Oliver Joseph Thatcher, San Bernardino, Calif.; died August 19, 1937.
Charles F. Thwing, D. D., Cleveland, Ohio; died August 29, 1937.
Ethelbert Dudley Warfield, D. D., Chambersburg, Pa.; died July 1936.
Mildred Salz Wertheimer, New York, N. Y.; died May 6, 1937.
Allen Brown West, Cincinnati, Ohio; died September 18, 1936.
Horace L. Wheeler, Boston, Mass.; died 1937 (?).

## COMMITTEE REPORTS FOR 1937

### Report of the Nominating Committee

NOVEMBER 6, 1937.

Your Committee on Nominations, in compliance with the requirements of the bylaws, reports the following nominations for elective offices and committee members of the Association for the ensuing year 1937–38.

President: Laurence M. Larson, University of Illinois, Urbana, Ill.

First vice president: Frederic L. Paxson, University of California, Berkeley, Calif.

Second vice president: William Scott Ferguson, Harvard University, Cambridge, Mass.

Secretary: Dexter Perkins, University of Rochester, Rochester, N. Y.

Treasurer: Solon J. Buck, Washington, D. C.

Council (for 4 years ending 1941) : Eugene C. Barker, University of Texas, Austin, Tex.; Laurence B. Packard, Amherst College, Amherst, Mass.

Nominating committee: Violet Barbour, Vassar College, Poughkeepsie, N. Y., *chairman;* Edgar E. Robinson, Stanford University, Calif.; A. C. Krey, University of Minnesota, Minneapolis, Minn.; Kent R. Greenfield, Johns Hopkins University, Baltimore, Md.; Frank Owsley, Vanderbilt University, Nashville, Tenn.

J. FRED RIPPY, *Chairman.*
VIOLET BARBOUR.
M. E. CURTI.
EDGAR ROBINSON.
A. C. KREY.

### THE COMMITTEE ON THE ALBERT J. BEVERIDGE MEMORIAL FUND

The Committee on the Albert J. Beveridge Memorial Fund reports the completion of one of its projects during the past year, the papers of James G. Birney, which have been edited by Dwight L. Dumond without expense to our committee. This work has been forwarded to us and we are about to publish it in two volumes, which will appear in the spring.

The projects of Messrs. Monaghan, Perkins, and Easterby, though delayed, are nearing completion.

The committee has agreed to print a series of documents illustrating the history of the first Bank of the United States, to be edited by James O. Wettereau, of New York Univerity. The committee has also agreed to print a collection of the writings of Christopher Gadsden, Revolutionary patriot, to be collected and edited by R. H. Woody, of Duke University.

The report of the sales of the various publications of the committee is encouraging and the fund is augmenting itself somewhat through royalty.

ROY F. NICHOLS, *Chairman.*

NOVEMBER 1, 1937.

## THE COMMITTEE ON THE LITTLETON-GRISWOLD FUND

I beg to submit my report on the activities of the Committee on the Littleton-Griswold Fund during the last year.

The committee has met only once—in New York City, on February 20 of this year. At that meeting various publications were agreed upon; some definitely, others tentatively. To the former class should be assigned *The Reports of the Superior Court of Connecticut, 1772-73,* by William Samuel Johnson, and *The Minutes of the Supreme Court of West New Jersey, 1681-1709.* The volumes tentatively agreed upon were a minute book of the county courts of Bucks County, Pa., 1684-1715; a volume of Vice Admiralty Records of New York, Philadelphia, and Charleston, 1700-1783; and a composite volume of records of New Jersey county courts. Still other materials are under contemplation.

Work on the Johnson volume is far advanced. The materials for this include a diary by Chief Justice Johnson in which he recorded the substance of the decisions rendered in some 125 cases, and file papers and minutes relating to the same cases. An editor of colonial records finds it necessary in most cases to make his own selections of those judged most worthy of reproduction; in this instance the chief justice has himself made the selection for us, thus immensely simplifying our task. At the same time, his diary is one of the rare surviving records of decisions in cases of the colonial period. Dr. Farrell was awarded the doctoral degree at Yale in June of this year, and his thesis, which was a discussion of the materials above mentioned, will be utilized in revised form as an introduction to the volume. Inasmuch as this publication must satisfy Yale's requirements for the printing of his thesis, the substance of the latter cannot be greatly changed. It is believed that the Johnson volume will be of very special interest to practicing lawyers, since it deals very largely with the use of the common-law actions and legal procedure of Connecticut at that time. In order to make the volume of still greater interest to lawyers of the present day, the committee has secured the cooperation of Dean Charles E. Clark, of the Yale School of Law, who will advise Dr. Farrell on technical matters as his work progresses and will contribute a discussion of the relation between the procedure of Chief Justice Johnson's time and that of today. Dean Clark is nationally known as an authority on civil procedure, and has only recently served as chairman of a committee appointed by the Supreme Court of the United States to draft new rules of procedure for that tribunal. It is a great satisfaction to the committee to have secured his aid.

The minutes of the Supreme Court of West New Jersey will be edited by Professor Reed, of the University of Delaware, and by George J. Miller, State superintendent in New Jersey of the Historical Records Survey. Professor

Reed is the author of a volume on the administration of criminal justice in New Jersey which will appear in the series edited for that state by Professor Wertenbaker. He is, therefore, very familiar with the New Jersey records and already has at his command the entire background required for his editorial work upon our volume. Mr. Miller has for years been active in legal practice, has published various booklets on the legal history of New Jersey, and has, of course, an unrivaled knowledge of the state's records. The entire volume has been transcribed, the editors have had meetings, and their work is progressing.

The Historical Records Survey of Pennsylvania has offered to prepare a transcript of the Bucks County volume above referred to—which will presumably be supplemented by materials properly belonging in it, but mistakenly bound in another volume. The exact contents of the volume, however, have not been as yet determined. Mr. Harry E. Sprogel, a recent graduate of the University of Pennsylvania Law School and former editor in chief of its *Law Review*, and Mr. Herbert K. Fitzroy, a graduate of both the college and the Law School of the same university and now an instructor in history at Princeton University, will serve as editors.

Plans for the last two of the six proposed publications above referred to still remain indefinite, and further comments upon them may be reserved for a later report. It may be said, merely, that the labors of the Federal Archives Survey have left the materials of the suggested admiralty volume accessible and arranged to a degree which might no longer characterize them if years should be allowed to pass without their utilization.

It may be mentioned that several meetings were held last year—in Philadelphia, Trenton, and in New York—to discuss a project for microfilming the more important court records of the five Middle Atlantic States. The number who attended at these meetings steadily increased, and great interest was manifested in the proposed undertaking. Manufacturers of cameras and projectors attended the meeting in Trenton and explained and illustrated the operation of their instruments. In the end the Historical Records Survey undertook the project with the idea of carrying it forward as far as circumstances might permit. Some 20 volumes of New Jersey records, including more than 5,000 pages, have already been microfilmed. It is understood that the work will now be carried on in other states. The microfilming of the New Jersey records will lay the basis for work upon the last of the five publications above referred to as those for which the committee has already rather definitely planned.

There was a balance of funds in hand, at the end of the Association's fiscal year, of $2,133.95. Most important and heartening to the committee has been the offer by Mrs. Griswold to continue her special contribution of $1,000 yearly toward its work.

Francis S. Philbrick, Chairman.

December 13, 1937.

### The Committee on Membership

Activity on the part of the committee seems almost useless except in the months of October to December, inclusive, when the beginning of our Association year and the opening of school year give point to our work. That activity for the current year is now being carried on with as yet undetermined results. This office has sent approximately 2,000 letters direct to prospective members and has sought in each of 300 institutions the help of a member in the effort to interest his colleagues.

One item the chairman would like to present—not as a criticism but as a problem: In November 1934, roughly, the date of the appointment of the present committee, there were 2,991 members; in 1935, 245 were added; and in 1936, 308. Up to the date of September 27 this year the central office has sent me the names of 322 new members, which, of course, is incomplete. This means a total of 875 new names, or an increase of 33 percent. Actually, the net increase for the first 2 years was only 45 and 50, respectively. The net gain for 1937 has not yet been determined. The task of the membership committee seems unhappily parallel to that of filling a basket at a well.

The chairman has no specific suggestion to make. It would seem to him, however, that the cost and effort of adding a member is sufficiently large to justify extraordinary efforts to hold those we have. I am convinced that lapses in membership are not due to failing interest or other dissatisfaction, but in a large measure are attributable to individual carelessness and negligence.

A program for a membership campaign ought to be planned for 2 or 3 years and the new committee should be given the presumption of appointment for such a time. I would suggest that once in that term a sizable appropriation—say $300 to $500—should be made to permit active and energetic work, and that in other years a nominal sum of say $50 should be made available. The fact that the present committee has spent only a little over $200 during its 3 years is due to the fact that its work has been subsidized by the universities in a most generous and unexpected manner; we can hardly hope for permanent aid of that sort.

Needless to say, your chairman, having served 3 years, expects to be replaced at this time. He cannot close, however, without expressing again his appreciation to the following men who have served as members of the committee: Mr. Gray C. Boyce, Princeton University; Mr. Culver H. Smith, University of Chattanooga; Mr. George B. Manheart, DePauw University; Mr. A. T. Volwiler, Ohio University; Mr. J. L. Sellers, University of Nebraska; Mr. Max Seville, Stanford University.

R. C. MILLER, *Chairman.*

NOVEMBER 3, 1937.

### THE COMMITTEE ON THE CARNEGIE REVOLVING FUND FOR PUBLICATIONS

This committee was somewhat retarded in its labors by the difficulty of educating a new chairman. This work, however, was undertaken cordially by the former chairman, Professor Cheyney, and by late spring the records were fully transferred.

Two books have been ordered published this year, both on recommendation of the old committee. They are:

Ranck: *Albert Gallatin Brown.*
Hoon: *Organization of the English Customs System.*

The former is already published; the latter is to be published soon. Payment for these publications will reduce the fund to five or six thousand dollars, so that the amount of money now on hand is comparatively small.

The new committee has done more by way of rejecting manuscripts than by way of accepting them. Only one, Priestley's *France Overseas,* to which the old committee was in some degree committed, has been accepted, and this only on condition that about half the cost of publication will be borne by the American Council of Learned Societies. Our application to the A. C. L. S. for this grant-in-aid has been made but has not yet been acted upon.

The chairman is much disappointed at the character of manuscripts presented to the committee. They represent, for the most part, two types: (1) Long treatises of so many volumes that publication is virtually impossible without a heavier subsidy than we can afford, and (2) treatises of indifferent merit that have been repeatedly turned down by publishers, both commercial and otherwise.

Suggestions as to how better manuscripts can be obtained are definitely in order. One that has come to the chairman, but has not yet been submitted to the committee, is this: Let publication by the Carnegie revolving fund be treated as a sort of prize, the same to be awarded each year to the best manuscript submitted (if worthy of publication). Have the specifications clear as to length of manuscript, time of submission, character of the study. The long manuscripts could thus be eliminated, the borderliners that are not really history could be shaved off, and the opportunity for making a comparative study could be given. Acceptance of a manuscript could be announced at the annual meeting at the same time and in the same way as other awards, such as the Pulitzer Prize. The opinion of the council on this plan of procedure would be most gratefully received.

JOHN D. HICKS, Chairman.

NOVEMBER 1, 1937.

### THE COMMITTEE ON THE "BIBLIOGRAPHY OF AMERICAN TRAVEL"

For the earlier work of your committee we refer you to our reports of December 24, 1935, and of December 1, 1936. The work accomplished by your committee since that second report may be briefly summarized under the following six entries:

(1) The committee has been in touch with Dr. James R. Masterson, of Hillsdale, Mich., who is a possible editor for the period from 1750 to 1830. Dr. Masterson has already done distinguished work in the bibliography of travel in America in the 1770's and it is very possible that he can be persuaded to undertake the editorial work, under the direction of the central board of editors, for the entire second period. Since the whole project is lacking funds, still tentative, we have made no definite arrangements.

(2) Mr. Henry Madden, recently returned from a period of study in Hungary, has generously offered to become a member of our board of advisory editors and will be responsible for all Hungarian travelers in the United States.

(3) A complete bibliography of Japanese travelers in the United States from the earliest times to 1900 has been received from the America-Japan Society. The Polish Government has supplied voluminous materials on Polish travelers in the United States and is prepared to go into any additional field of investigation that we set for them. These are the first fruits of that cooperation which your committee predicted we would receive from various diplomatic contacts.

(4) The C. R. B. Educational Foundation is prepared to put to work two very capable Belgian scholars as soon as we are definitely prepared to go on with the bibliography. Arrangements for this are completed.

(5) The chairman of your committee has continued his work of collecting the records of *French Travelers in the United States.* Since that bibliography was first published by the New York Public Library in 1933 more than 200 items have been found for the period from 1765 to 1860. These are all prepared for insertion in the bibliography of American travel—the concern of your committee.

(6) By a coincidence your chairman is also historical advisor to the New York World's Fair of 1939 and in that capacity comes into contact with the diplomatic representatives of all the important foreign nations. In the course

of the past 6 months the subject of the bibliography has been presented to a number of them, and the prospects for a hearty and serious cooperation are even better than your committee has formerly indicated.

This is progress which we wish to report. We are still without any source of funds; we still require $3,000 to prepare the manuscript. We have not been able, lacking these funds, to make any formal commitments to the various persons and institutions standing ready to assist the bibliography to the fullest degree. This is the problem which requires the earliest solution. With that, the work may be speedily begun; without it, not even posterity will see the consummation of our plans.

In the midst of this paucity of funds your committee has been most frugal. We have not yet called upon the Association to make any expenditure, although several small sums have been appropriated for our needs. Some expenses have been incurred during the course of our work which the members of the committee do not feel they can carry. A statement of these will shortly be submitted; they are all covered by the current appropriation.

FRANK MONAGHAN, *Chairman.*

NOVEMBER 24, 1937.

### THE COMMITTEE ON THE GEORGE LOUIS BEER PRIZE

The George Louis Beer Prize Committee has voted to award the prize for this year to Mr. Charles W. Porter for his study *The Career of Théophile Delcassé* (University of Pennsylvania Press, 1936). Mr. Porter's book was one of three submitted.

The expenses incurred by the committee have been nominal and have been taken care of by the members. The committee has no recommendations to make beyond those which it submitted last year.

E. N. ANDERSON, *Chairman.*

NOVEMBER 3, 1937.

### THE COMMITTEE ON THE JUSSERAND MEDAL

After considerable correspondence with the other two members of my committee, namely, Prof. Ralph H. Lutz, of Stanford, and Prof. Eloise Ellery, of Vassar, I am ready to report the unanimous decision of the committee to award the medal to Prof. Samuel E. Morison, of Harvard University. We are making this award primarily because of Professor Morison's outstanding volume on *The Founding of Harvard College* and because of his other studies in New England cultural and intellectual history. All of this work, we think, constitutes a genuine contribution to the history of the intellectual relations of the United States and Europe and, therefore, falls quite properly within the scope of the award as defined by the donor of the medal.

CARL WITTKE, *Chairman.*

OCTOBER 14, 1937.

### THE COMMITTEE ON THE JOHN H. DUNNING PRIZE

The John H. Dunning Prize Committee received two works submitted for this prize. After reading them the committee concluded that neither was of the standard expected to attain the award of that prize, and therefore made no award for the year 1937.

L. B. SHIPPEE, *Chairman.*

NOVEMBER 1, 1937.

## THE COMMITTEE ON THE JUSTIN WINSOR PRIZE

Early in the year announcement was made through various historical reviews and journals that the prize would be awarded this year. In the spring, in conjunction with the Committee on the Herbert Baxter Adams Prize, the committee prepared an extended statement with respect to the two prizes, which was mailed through the Washington office to the Departments of History in about 150 colleges and universities in the United States and Canada.

As a result of this publicity, two books and five manuscripts were submitted for consideration by the committee. The members of the committee are unanimous in their recommendation that the Justin Winsor Prize for 1937 be awarded to Carl Bridenbaugh for his manuscript study entitled *Cities in the Wilderness: The First Century of Urban Life in America, 1625–1742*.

The expenses incurred by the activities of the committee are a bill of $4.50 for duplicating the announcement of the prize and $4.52 for the postage necessary to mail the announcement to the various institutions throughout the country. These items, I believe, are charged against the Washington office of the Association. Since the Winsor Prize will not be awarded in 1938, it would seem that the committee would require no appropriation for the year.

The committee recommends that an earlier date than September 1 be set for the submission of essays for the prize competition.

JAMES B. HEDGES, *Chairman.*

NOVEMBER 5, 1937.

## THE COMMITTEE ON AMERICANA FOR COLLEGE LIBRARIES

We beg to present herewith a report of the work of the Committee on Americana for College Libraries of the American Historical Association for 1937; and herewith also to submit our estimated needs for the next year (i. e., calendar year of 1938).

The so-called "McGregor Plan" was operated after Mr. McGregor's death, in his offices in Washington, until the headquarters were moved to Ann Arbor, January 1937. At the time of Mr. McGregor's death 10 colleges were participating. At present we have the quota of 15, having added within the period the following: Pomona College, California; Albion College, Michigan; Baylor University, Texas; Western Kentucky State Teachers College; and Birmingham-Southern College, Alabama. As Birmingham-Southern was not admitted until late in the year 1937, it was decided that the participation of that institution should not begin until the fall of 1937. In view of this the College of William and Mary was asked to contribute an additional $500 this year, which was matched by the committee with the unused appropriation intended for Birmingham-Southern, thus setting up a credit of $2,000 instead of $1,000 for 1937 for William and Mary. This plan seemed advisable in order to extinguish the "overdrafts" of that college which had accumulated under Mr. McGregor's encouragement and approval.

During the year we published a pamphlet entitled *The McGregor Plan for the Encouragement of Book Collecting by American College Libraries*, a copy of which was sent to each of the trustees of the McGregor Fund and to each member of the committee of the American Historical Association. This is an explanation of what we are doing. In distributing the books we have published two catalogs wherein we have listed and given a critical note on each title offered for distribution. A third catalog has been printed and will be distributed this fall.

During the past year two members of the committee on Americana for college libraries have passed away, Mr. Leonard L. Mackall and Dr. J. Franklin

Jameson.  Their places will be filled at the December meeting of the American Historical Association.

A well-framed photograph of Mr. McGregor, bearing a small metal nameplate, has been sent to 11 of the colleges on the plan, to be hung in their rare book rooms.

As byproducts of the plan the friends of the participating colleges have already bestirred themselves to do something for their own institutions.  This is particularly notable at Albion, William and Mary, Western Kentucky, and Wesleyan College.

Another happy result of the plan was the gift by the University of Michigan of copies of every book published by the University of Michigan Press, which the press had in stock and which the colleges participating in the McGregor Plan lacked.  This gift amounted to $3,019.41, an amount which does not appear on our financial statement but which should be recognized by the trustees and committee members as being an additional benefaction conferred by the McGregor Plan.

The principal problem with which we have been faced this year was how to handle with limited help the enormous amount of detail involved in properly operating the plan.  It has proved to be physically impossible for Mr. Adams and Miss Slagle alone to do all the work, so a part-time assistant has been employed and paid for out of the unexpended balances in the travel and equipment funds. This assistant is employed on a monthly basis until some more satisfactory arrangement can be reached.  We are therefore asking the McGregor Fund for $225 more for next year in order to take care of this extra part-time assistant.

The need for this extra help is imperative.  Distributing rare books is not analogous to the acquisition and distribution of other property which may be the object of charitable enterprises.  Rare books must be carefully "collated" (i. e., tested, leaf by leaf, to assure their perfection and authenticity) and must be packed for shipment with more than usual care.  No one would care to participate, either as the distributor or the receiver, in such a plan as this unless these safeguards were observed.  There are cases when the collation of a single title involves more than one full day's work.  But all the property in question must be "expertized" in this fashion, or we would become involved in interminable difficulties.

A financial statement of the conduct of our affairs from August 1, 1936, through August 31, 1937 (13 months), is attached hereto.  (See Appendix A.)

A "property account," summarized as "book inventory," August 1, 1936, to August 31, 1937, is also attached.  (See Appendix B.)

The above give an accounting of the funds and property entrusted to us through August of 1937.  An audit by Price, Waterhouse & Co. was made in September, and a copy of the report has been sent to the executive secretary of the American Historical Association.

Since the above does not take into account the activities of the Plan from August 31, 1937, to date, we submit herewith a statement of the expenditures from January 1, 1937, through October, with the anticipated expenses to the end of the calendar year 1937, which is also the fiscal year of the McGregor Fund and the termination of our appropriation.  (See Appendix C.)

We beg to submit herewith a statement of our estimated needs for the coming year and respectfully request from the trustees of the McGregor Fund the sum of $15,000, of which $7,500 will be used for the purchase of books and $7,500 for operating expenses.  It must also be borne in mind that another $7,500 comes from the participating colleges.  (See Appendix D for an analysis of the needs for 1938 and a comparison with this year's budget and expenditures.)

Inasmuch as more than 65 colleges have now applied for participation in the McGregor Plan, 7 of which stand ready to put up their own $500 at once, we also respectfully request the trustees of the McGregor Fund to grant us an additional $2,500 for books, thus making it possible for us to increase our quota to twenty participating institutions. We are convinced that this unique project, which is serving such a definite need in the field of education, is truly worthy of serious consideration and expansion. And it is our opinion that the expense budget as submitted for 1938 would be sufficiently large to maintain twenty colleges, with the possible exception of transportation and book expenses.

In conclusion, the administrators of the McGregor Plan beg to express their appreciation of the generosity of the McGregor Fund, and of the helpful co-operation and advice given by the members of the committee of the American Historical Association.

RANDOLPH G. ADAMS, *Chairman.*

NOVEMBER 3, 1937.

APPENDIX A.—*Financial report, Aug. 1, 1936, to Aug. 31, 1937*

| | | |
|---|---:|---:|
| Cash on hand, Aug. 1, 1936 | | $3,310.99 |
| Received from the McGregor Fund Aug. 1, 1936, to Dec. 31, 1936 | 6,100.00 | |
| Received from colleges Aug. 1, 1936, to Dec. 31, 1936 | 4,000.00 | |
| Received from American Historical Association office, Jan. 1, 1937, to Aug. 31, 1937 | 17,381.70 | |
| | 27,481.70 | |
| | 30,792.69 | |
| Cash on hand at Jan. 1, 1937, turned over to American Historical Association | 3,503.89 | |
| To be accounted for | | $27,288.80 |
| Books purchased, bindings, etc., including accounts payable at Aug. 1, 1936 | | $19,532.95 |
| Special gift to Wake Forest, as appropriated and designated by the McGregor Fund | | 100.00 |
| Expenses: | | |

| | | | |
|---|---:|---:|---:|
| Office salaries | $4,759.90 | | |
| Rent, telephone, and telegraph | 290.21 | | |
| Traveling expense | 490.05 | | |
| Office equipment and supplies | 391.41 | | |
| Insurance on books and bond | 89.45 | | |
| Auditing service at July 31, 1936 | 250.00 | | |
| Cost of pictures, frames, plate | 80.25 | | |
| Printing and engraving catalogues and McGregor Plan pamphlets | 374.83 | | |
| Book expense: Bookplates, transportation, duties, etc | 369.30 | | |
| | | 7,095.40 | |
| | | 26,728.35 | |
| Cash on hand at Aug. 31, 1937 [1] | | 560.45 | |
| Accounted for | | | 27,288.80 |

[1] See the following:

CASH

| | |
|---|---:|
| Balance in Ann Arbor Savings & Commercial Bank | $535.45 |
| Petty cash on hand | 25.00 |
| Balance Aug. 31, 1937 | 560.45 |

NOTE.—At the end of the period, the American Historical Association held in its account for us $800.60.

APPENDIX B.—*Book inventory, Aug. 1, 1936, to Aug. 31, 1937*

| | |
|---|---:|
| Inventory of books on hand Aug. 1, 1936 (605 titles) | $12,622.99 |
| Books purchased during period (468 titles) | 18,054.19 |
| | 30,677.18 |
| Cost of books disbursed to colleges (471 titles) | 14,984.17 |
| Inventory of books on hand Aug. 31, 1937 (602 titles) | 15,693.01 |

### APPENDIX C

Appropriated for the calendar year 1937:

| | |
|---|---:|
| For books (plus $7,500 from colleges) | $15,000.00 |
| For operating expenses | 7,275.00 |
| | 22,275.00 |

Expended therefrom to and for Oct. 31, 1937:

| | |
|---|---:|
| For books | 13,428.72 |
| For operating expenses | 5,641.12 |
| | 19,069.84 |
| Balance unexpended at Nov. 1, 1937 | 3,205.16 |

Anticipated expenditures for the months of November and December 1937:[2]

| | |
|---|---:|
| For books | 1,571.28 |
| For operating expenses | 1,622.78 |
| | 3,194.06[3] |
| Possible balance unexpended at Dec. 31, 1937 | 11.10 |

### APPENDIX D—*Regarding the budget*

| | Appropriation for 1937 | Expended and anticipated for 1937 | Budget for 1938 |
|---|---:|---:|---:|
| For books: | | | |
| Contributed by the McGregor Fund | $7,500 | $15,000.00 | $7,500 |
| Contributed by colleges | 7,500 | | 7,500 |
| For operating expenses: | | | |
| Salaries | 4,500 | 5,112.90 | 5,500 |
| Communication | 150 | 117.62 | 125 |
| Transportation | 500 | 358.20 | 400 |
| Travelling | 1,250 | 404.74 | 500 |
| Office equipment | 500 | 158.21 | 0 |
| Office supplies and expense | | 226.00 | 250 |
| Bookplates and labels | | 74.50 | 70 |
| Insurance and bond | | 26.60 | 80 |
| Printing and engraving | | 480.38 | 300 |
| Framing pictures of Mr. McGregor | | 29.75 | 0 |
| Auditing of accounts | 250 | 275.00 | 275 |
| Miscellaneous | 125 | 0 | 0 |
| | 7,275 | 7,263.90 | 7,500 |
| Total | 22,275 | 22,263.90 | 22,500[4] |

[2] Report thereon of actual expenditures will be submitted in formal annual statement to the Trustees of the McGregor Fund.

[3] Present invoices for payment in November total $2,253.77.

| | |
|---|---:|
| [4] Requested from the McGregor Fund for calendar year 1938 | $15,000 |
| Contributions from colleges | 7,500 |
| | 22,500 |
| Additional request from the McGregor Fund in order to increase the number of colleges from 15 to 20, 5 at $500 each | 2,500 |
| Total requested from the McGregor Fund for 1938 | 17,500 |

### The Committee on Historical Source Materials

In accordance with plans outlined in its last annual report, the Committee on Historical Source Materials restricted its functions to planning and advisory work. Certain phases of the plans presented in the last annual report were accordingly refined and elaborated.

At a session of the committee in Providence during the meetings of the American Historical Association, the question of bringing the manuscript resources of this country under control was discussed. On the basis of this discussion, it was suggested to Dr. Luther H. Evans, national director of the Historical Records Survey, that a preliminary survey of institutions maintaining manuscript resources be undertaken. The purpose of such a preliminary survey, it was pointed out, should be two-fold: First, to assemble a body of data to be used in formulating a program of relief work in accumulating information on manuscript collections, and, second, to assemble a body of data to be used by scholars in determining whether manuscript materials are available for research purposes.

In making this survey, it was suggested that information should be secured on the following three points: First, the volume of manuscript materials existing in various institutions in this country; second, the proportion of this volume under control; and, third, the method by which it has been placed under control. Under the first point, estimates should be made on the basis of a rapid inspection of the surveyor or custodian of the linear footage of manuscript materials of varying sizes existing in any given institution. Under the second point, estimates should be secured from the custodian as to the proportion of the above volume under control. Under the third point information should be secured on the method of control. The following methods were suggested for consideration:

a. Inventories.

b. Finding lists.

c. Guides (either published or unpublished).

d. Indexes.

e. Catalogs.

f. Classification schemes.

It was suggested also that an attempt should be made to determine whether all or any part of the manuscript materials were ever before surveyed, either by officials of the institutions or by relief workers under local C. W. A. or E. R. A. projects and that, if such surveys were made, the resulting inventories, etc., should be accumulated at the Washington office of the Historical Records Survey.

On the basis of information accumulated by the above survey of institutions, which is now under way, plans might be formulated for a comprehensive listing of the manuscript collections of this country by relief labor. Since a similar project relating to Federal archives was sponsored cooperatively by the National Archives and the Works Progress Administration, is it not expedient that the project relating to manuscript collections receive direction and aid from the Manuscript Division of the Library of Congress?

In view of the fact that the functions of the committee are being restricted to planning, a budget not exceeding $50 is sufficient to cover secretarial expenses, stationery, and postage.

T. R. Schellenberg, *Chairman.*

November 1, 1937.

## COMMITTEE ON RADIO

The experimental series of radio talks outlined in the report of the executive secretary for last year, to finance which the sum of $2,000 was given by the Keith Fund and the McGregor Fund, was broadcast during the period from mid-January to mid-April 1937. Twelve talks were given over the Columbia Broadcasting System network. No real effort was made to get "fan mail" because the funds available were not sufficient to take care of such mail in any quantity or to distribute copies of talks or other material. In spite of that many letters did come in expressing interest in the talks, desire to read on the subjects and hope that the series would continue. Every letter was answered individually by the director, bibliographies were suggested and locations of libraries indicated. With sufficient money available a very significant educational work could be done in follow-up for the history program.

Plans are under way for a second series of history radio talks. Raymond Gram Swing, well-known radio commentator, has consented to do the broadcasting. The plan of operation with Mr. Swing as broadcaster will be the same as that followed in the experimental series. That series proved beyond a doubt that the technique of cooperation between learned men and a professional broadcaster is entirely practicable. We shall have to pay Mr. Swing an honorarium. But there is no doubt that he will be much better than the type of announcer which the commercial company would supply. The American commercial companies have not yet got to the point where they are ready to spend "good money" on educational talks. They control the nation-wide networks. Therefore it seems fairly obvious that those who believe in radio as an educational medium will have to find the funds to finance sound history on the radio. The commercial companies will give free time on the air. They expect sensational results from a large investment. They must be shown that such a series as the American Historical Association is prepared to sponsor will, if well done, have a real appeal to the radio audience. Members of the Radio committee and other members of the American Historical Association are working on the problem of raising the money. Until this is accomplished the work of the Radio committee is temporarily at a standstill.

CONYERS READ, *Chairman.*

NOVEMBER 1, 1937.

### THE COMMITTEE ON THE CONTENTS OF THE "ANNUAL REPORT"

At a meeting held on May 28, 1937 (present: Mr. Jameson, chairman; Mr. Connor and Mr. Stock), it was voted that the *Annual Report* for 1936 should consist of three volumes: I. Combining the usual proceedings and official papers for 1936 and including the matter of the Pacific coast branch, the report of the Conference of Historical Societies, and the Fauchet document edited by Mr. Lokke; II. Miss Griffin's annual bibliography, *Writings on American History* (1936); III. Instructions, 1791–1812, of the British foreign secretaries to their envoys in the United States, edited by Prof. Bernard Mayo.

LEO F. STOCK, *Chairman.*

NOVEMBER, 1937.

### THE COMMITTEE TO CONSIDER "WRITINGS ON AMERICAN HISTORY"

Your special committee of Leo F. Stock (chairman), Solon J. Buck and Waldo G. Leland, appointed to consider the future of *Writings on American History*, the management and financing of which has for many years been unselfishly undertaken by Dr. Jameson, met on December 13. After full discussion and consideration of all problems involved, it was agreed:

1. That this annual bibliography should under no circumstances be permitted to lapse. Apart from its own indispensable value and utility, it was felt that its discontinuance just when *Writings on British History* has been begun would for many reasons be most unfortunate.

2. That the Association should assume full responsibility for the undertaking.

3. That a permanent committee should be appointed to devise ways and means of establishing a Jameson Memorial Fund of sufficient principal and income accounts to bear the expense, estimated at $2,000 per annum (provided the printing subsidy be continued by Congress), of compilation, proofreading, and indexing.

4. That the legacy of $400 bequeathed by will of Dr. Jameson to the Association be made the first contribution to the proposed Memorial Fund.

5. That that portion of the proceeds of the endowment campaign of some years ago which was to be set aside for a Jameson Fund, which percentage is stated to be $1,860, be transferred by the Association to the proposed Memorial Fund.

6. That the proposed committee, through solicitation of members, libraries, historical societies, and other institutions and organizations, and through appeals to generously disposed individuals, undertake to increase the above sums to an amount the income of which will make the project self-sustaining.

7. That the committee to be appointed should review and revise the scope, policy, and format of *Writings*, supervise the expenditure of money to be derived from the proposed Jameson Memorial Fund, and have general direction of the publication. In this connection it was suggested that the committee at some time meet in conference a small group of historians, bibliographers, librarians, and teachers for the purpose of exchanging views on the needs of each profession which the publication is designed to serve. It was also hoped that, in view of the high and mounting cost of printing at the Government Printing Office, the proposed Memorial Fund would enable the committee to submit the printing of the bibliography to competitive bidding, thus making it possible to devote the entire governmental appropriation for printing to the expansion of the *Annual Reports*.

LEO F. STOCK, *Chairman.*

DECEMBER 15, 1937.

## OTHER REPORTS

### REPORT OF THE MANAGING EDITOR OF "THE AMERICAN HISTORICAL REVIEW"

With the October 1936 issue some changes were made in the format and organization of the *Review*. The small block of reviews on the front cover page was omitted; the old format had the disadvantage of imposing on the editorial office the invidious necessity of selecting a few reviews for special prominence. In making this change and in placing the names of authors after the titles of articles we are conforming to the general usage of historical journals, and the appearance of the cover page, we think, has been improved. The Historical News section was reorganized by removing from it brief notices of books of minor historical importance and lists of articles in periodicals, thus confining it more strictly to news proper. In this section, items are no longer signed or initialed. Reviews of 400 words in length or over come under the general heading of *Reviews of Books* (formerly they came under *Reviews*

*of Books* and *Shorter Notices*) ; notices of 300 words and less, and lists of articles, come under a new heading, *Notices of Other Recent Publications.* Articles are listed in tabular form, not run on, as formerly, and, as far as practicable, they are arranged chronologically. The former heading, *Shorter
Notices,* has been given up.

Volume XLII of the *Review* (October 1936–July 1937) carries 890 pages,
including an annual index of 25 pages, as compared with 877 pages in volume
XLI. Eleven major articles were published, including the *Presidential Address*
and an account of the *Annual Meeting of the Association at Providence* in
December; of these, six were in European history, two in American history,
and two (including the *Presidential Address*) in historiography. Six shorter
articles (*Notes and Suggestions*) were published, two in European history,
two in American history, one on opportunities for research in the Federal
Archives of New York City, and one on fictitious biographies in *Appletons'
Cyclopædia of American Biography.* Four documents or collections of documents were published, two in American history, one in European history, and
one in the field of Anglo-American relations. Volume XLII contains 241 reviews, as compared with 265 in volume XLI, and 249 notices, as compared with
238. The number of articles listed is 1,859, as compared with 1,087.

During the period covered by this report, 72 articles were submitted, including those suitable in subject and length for the *Notes and Suggestions* section.
Of these, 41 were in American history, 29 in European history, and 2 in Far
Eastern history. Of those in American history, 7 were accepted, 33 were rejected, and one is still under consideration; of those in European history, 8
were accepted, 20 were rejected, and one is still under consideration; of those
in Far Eastern history one was accepted and one was rejected. The most
interesting fact shown by these figures is the high death rate among the articles
in American history—80.5 percent as compared with 69 percent in the European
field. This does not necessarily imply that the former are inferior, on the
average, to the latter, though I have the impression that this is the case.
Occasionally an article in the American field which is up to our standards is
rejected on the ground that it would appear more appropriately in the pages
of one of the regional historical journals than in ours; a good many of our
rejections are eventually published elsewhere.

A comparison of the Macmillan Co.'s statement of profit and loss on account
of the *Review* for the period of July 16, 1936, to July 15, 1937, indicates in
comparison with that of the preceding 12 months a decrease in profit to the
Association of $244.89 (from $2,636.19 to $2,391.30). Macmillan's expenditures
on account of the *Review* for their 1936–37 year exceeded those for the previous
year by $561.52, the increase being accounted for by an unusually large pur-
chase of paper in anticipation of an increase in price and a purchase of cover
stock sufficient for at least two volumes, both items being included as expenditures for the year. There was no purchase of cover stock in the preceeding
year. We have been informed by the Macmillan Co. that these additional
expenditures amounted to $571.22, slightly more than the difference in the
total increase in their expenditures for 1936–37 over 1935–36.

Macmillan's statement shows a gratifying increase in the number of subscriptions to the *Review* (about 50) ; this is apart from the increase in the
membership of the Association. If receipts for the current year do not show
a decrease, it seems probable that their next statement will show a decided
increase in profit.

By action of the council, taken at its meeting at Providence last December,
$535 was transferred to the account of the *Review,* increasing its budget for

the fiscal year September 1, 1936, to August 31, 1937, from $6,000 to $6,535, and the budget for the current fiscal year was fixed at $6,500. This welcome action greatly relieved the embarrassment of the editorial office which I called to the attention of the council in my last *Annual Report*. It enabled the assistant editor to resume work on the 10-year index, which she had been compelled to discontinue, and I am glad to be able to report that the index has been nearly completed. It enabled us, also, to make far more satisfactory arrangements for office assistance. We have been fortunate in securing the full-time service of Miss Florence Miller, who has had graduate training in history and is an expert stenographer and typist, at an annual salary of $960. With $4,900 allocated to the salaries of the managing editor and assistant editor, this leaves $640 for all other expenses. As this is less by $10 than the amount estimated as necessary to cover irreducible expenditures for postage and express, stationery, telephone, honoraria to contributors of lists of articles, etc. (see my last *Annual Report*), it is evident that we shall have difficulty in balancing our budget for the current year. If there should be an increase in any of these items (for example, in the price of stationery), it would be seriously embarrassing.

As an alternative to asking for a slight increase in the regular appropriation for the *Review* for the current year, I recommend that the precedent of last year be followed, and that the money received by the Association for periodicals sold to the American Philosophical Society (since the sale in the summer of 1936) be transferred to the account of the *Review;* and in addition that the managing editor be authorized to sell at second hand (to the Columbia University Bookstore or others) the few books in the editorial office which are not to be sent to reviewers either because they have been reviewed in the office or because they are not suitable for review in our pages, and current issues of any periodicals in the office which the American Philosophical Society may not desire to purchase.

ROBERT L. SCHUYLER, Managing Editor.

OCTOBER 28, 1937.

### REPORT OF THE EDITOR OF THE "ANNUAL REPORT"

*Writings on American History, 1932* and *Proceedings* for 1933, 1934, and 1935 have been published since the last report.

*Writings* for 1933 is now in the bindery. *Proceedings* for 1936 is in page proof. *Writings* for 1934 is in galley proof. The first two are scheduled for publication before the close of the year; the third will appear early in 1938.

Dr. Bernard Mayo's *Instructions from the British Foreign Office to British Ministers in the United States, 1791–1812*, accepted for publication by the Publications Committee last June, and Miss Griffin and associates' *Writings* for 1935 are both well under way. The first manuscript will be delivered during the course of the winter and the second in June as usual.

The sum of $8,000 was allotted for the fiscal year beginning July 1, 1937. A book credit of $5,272.34 remains after providing for *Proceedings* for 1936. Final bills on *Writings* for 1933 and 1934 and on *Proceedings* for 1936 will, in all probability, exceed estimates by about $750. There will thus, apparently, be about $4,500 net available to cover other volumes. The editor proposes to employ this to bring out 1937 *Proceedings* and Mayo's *Instructions*. If the cost of the latter exceeds the credit remaining after 1937 *Proceedings* has been taken care of, the difference will be charged against the next allotment in the usual manner. Should there be a balance remaining after the Mayo estimate has been received, it can be applied on *Writings* for 1935. That volume will consequently be published very largely or entirely out of the next allotment.

With our printing credit currently set at $8,000 a year instead of the former $12,000, it would not be advisable to plan a third volume for either 1938 or 1939 (*Proceedings* is always Volume I; *Writings*, always Volume II). Some 50 pages of additional material could, however, readily be taken care of in each of the 1937 and 1938 *Proceedings* volumes. Instructions on the matter are requested from the Publications Committee.

LOWELL JOSEPH RAGATZ, *Editor.*

OCTOBER 30, 1937.

### REPORT OF THE EXECUTIVE BOARD OF "SOCIAL EDUCATION"

*Social Education* began publication in January 1937, in accordance with the plans reported a year ago. Nine issues will appear each year. A contract between the American Historical Association and the American Book Co. provides that the company will print and circulate the magazine and take responsibility, with the cooperation of the National Council for the Social Studies, for new subscriptions and renewals. An agreement with the National Council makes *Social Education* the official journal of that organization. The editor has assumed responsibility for the sale of advertising, the proceeds of which are allocated entirely to editorial costs.

The executive board has met twice during the past 12 months. The National Council for the Social Studies named as its two representatives Howard E. Wilson, to succeed himself, and Elmer Ellis, to succeed A. C. Krey. Ruth West succeeded Cecilia R. Irvine as a member of the advisory board. An effort will be made to hold meetings of the advisory board from time to time.

In accordance with the wishes of the executive board an editorial page has been maintained, a monthly review of periodical literature provided, the policy of an annual or biennial review article in American history, European history, economics, sociology, government, and education continued, and some articles and reviews of interest primarily to elementary school teachers and college or junior college instructors have been published.

The subscription list has built rapidly, the sale of advertising has increased, and it has been possible to decrease editorial costs somewhat. The resources of the magazine have been substantially supplemented through the allocation of the accumulated royalties from the Report of the Commission on the Social Studies, amounting to $7,190.55.

ERLING M. HUNT, *Chairman.*

OCTOBER 29, 1937.

### REPORT OF THE ASSOCIATION'S DELEGATE IN THE INTERNATIONAL COMMITTEE OF HISTORICAL SCIENCES

I beg to present the following report as delegate of the American Historical Association in the International Committee of Historical Sciences for the year 1937:

The International Committee of Historical Sciences has not held a general assembly in 1937, but a meeting of the bureau, attended by the American delegate as honorary counsellor, was held in Paris on May 28, 1937.

The treasurer presented a report for 1936 showing receipts of 31,641.87 Swiss francs, including dues from member countries aggregating 9,852.83 francs and payments from the subvention by the Rockefeller Foundation of 10,692.50

francs; and expenditures amounting to 29,710.87 francs; leaving a balance on hand of 1,931 francs.

Upon application, China, through the Academia Sinica, and Vatican City were admitted to membership in the International Committee, subject to ratification by the general assembly of 1938.

An application presented to the Rockefeller Foundation in March, for additional support in the amount of $19,500, to be available over a period of five years, is still (November 24) pending, but it is hoped that favorable action may be taken on it before the end of the year.

The plans for the International Congress of Historical Sciences, to be held in Zurich, August 28 to September 4, 1938, are well advanced, and have been announced in *The American Historical Review* and other American journals devoted to historical and related studies. By the end of May, the number of persons announcing their intention of attending the congress was 790, and the number of papers offered was 336. Of these, 26 Americans offered 13 papers.

The progress of the *International Bibliography of Historical Sciences* is satisfactory. Vols. I–X have now been issued, covering the years 1926–35, and the work progresses in a normal and regular manner. It is, however, absolutely necessary to secure a larger number of regular subscriptions if the *Bibliography* is to become self-supporting. At present, about 300 copies of each issue are sold, of which some 85 are sold in the United States. The regular sales must be increased to 800 and those in the United States must be doubled, if possible. Plans are well prepared, if the assistance from the Rockefeller Foundation for which application has been made is granted, for a thorough sales campaign, including the introduction of the *Bibliography* into countries in which at present no copies are sold.

Three issues of the *Bulletin*, the official organ of the Committee, have appeared thus far in 1937. Nos. 34–36 contain a large group of important contributions to the history of "enlightened despotism" and the proceedings of the Second International Congress of Literary History, held in Amsterdam, September 18–21, 1935. The circulation of the *Bulletin* is approximately 300 copies but should be increased to at least 500 in order to become self-supporting. There are no regular subscribers to it in the United States and a special effort must be made to improve this situation.

American scholars have been appointed to the various subcommittees of the International Committee as designated by the council of the American Historical Association and no additional appointments appear to be necessary at the present time. The organization of a new subcommittee on Far Eastern history should be noted. Its membership is not yet complete, but the American representative on it is Professor Kenneth S. Latourette of Yale University.

The Association's delegates in the International Committee for 1938 should be appointed (the present delegates are William E. Dodd and the undersigned), as should also be appointed special delegates to the International Congress at Zurich.

It has been customary to recommend that the American Historical Association appropriate funds for the payment of its annual dues, 300 Swiss francs ($72) and also $200 for the compilation of American titles to be included in the *International Bibliography*. I am prepared, however, for 1938, and without commitment as to later years, to assume responsibility for the compilation of titles of writings by American scholars on non-American history which will make it possible to reduce the appropriation on account of the *Bibliography* to $100.

WALDO G. LELAND, *Delegate.*

NOVEMBER 24, 1927.

REPORT OF THE REPRESENTATIVES OF THE ASSOCIATION ON THE SOCIAL SCIENCE RESEARCH COUNCIL

During the year 1937 the Social Science Research Council met in full session for 4 days, in April and in September. At the latter meeting it made a thorough review of past and current activities and, as a result, reasserted its primary function to be that of long-time planning in the social fields and the development of basic interrelations among them.

Lying closest to historians' interest are perhaps the Council's activities during the year in relation to (1) materials for research; (2) research personnel; and (3) plans for a more systematic exploration of comparative local American history.

(1) With the collaboration of a number of investigators a committee made an examination of what research had been undertaken, what materials gathered, and what research and materials are needed, on the social effects of the recent depression. The investigation resulted in the publication of 13 volumes concerned with various aspects of the subject: Religion, education, family, consumption, recreation, reading, crime, minorities, migration, rural life, health, relief, and social work. Among other activities of the Council having to do with the materials of research, there were the publication of a report covering the work of the committee on Government statistics and information services, appointed jointly with the American Statistical Association; the publication of a report by a committee (created jointly by the American Farm Economic Association and the Council's committee on agriculture) analyzing the various Federal censuses of agriculture with a view to indicating ways by which their value may be enhanced; and the publication by the committee on materials of research (appointed jointly with the American Council of Learned Societies) of a second edition of a manual on the reproduction of research materials.

(2) In relation to the development of research personnel the Council during the year maintained 8 predoctoral fellows in the first year of graduate study, and made 7 new appointments for 1937–38; maintained 7 predoctoral fellows in the second year of graduate study, all of whom had held Council fellowships during the first year of graduate work, and made 7 appointments for 1937–38 of holders of first-year fellowships in 1936–37; maintained 10 fellows for predoctoral field training, and made 19 new appointments for 1937–38; maintained 13 postdoctoral fellows, and made 2 renewals and 11 new appointments for 1937–38. In addition, special graduate training courses were continued in agricultural economics and rural sociology with course enrollments numbering 47. These courses, housed at times at American University and at the Brookings Institution, came to an end in June, after six and a half years. During that period there had been 517 registrations in advanced courses designed for improvement of personnel, particularly in branches of the public service. The Council also provided 40 grants-in-aid on a nation-wide basis to scholars of proved competence to assist in the completion of research of special significance, and made 43 new grants to be enjoyed in 1937–38. Finally, the Council awarded seven grants-in-aid for 1937–38 under geographical limitations to members of southern faculties.

(3) In order to stimulate interest in the field of comparative local social history, the Council financed a 3-day conference early in September under the chairmanship of Prof. Roy F. Nichols and attended by a dozen or so specialists in American history and related fields. The conference drew up a comprehensive report which has not yet been made public.

In relation to actual research, committees and staffs in the fields of social security and of public administration maintained active contact with Government officials, public and private agencies, and research workers, acting as a channel of communication among them, planning and in cases executing research that resulted in publications on the labor supply and regional labor markets, on industrial pension plans as affected by legislative acts and proposals, on population problems in relation to unemployment insurance in West Virginia, on administration of unemployment compensation in Wisconsin and New Hampshire, and on administration of old-age assistance in New York, New Jersey, and Massachusetts. In addition, the study of real estate financing as a part of the broader study of banking and credit in relation to economic stability was continued, and a first bulletin published by the National Bureau of Economic Research on national income and capital formation.

The Carnegie Corporation of New York, the General Education Board, the Rockefeller Foundation, the Julius Rosenwald Fund, and the Russell Sage Foundation have generously supported the operations of the Council. New grants made to the Council in 1936–37 totaled $515,250, of which $225,000 was for fellowships; $25,000 for national grants-in-aid; $78,750 for general administration; $105,000 for work in the field of social security; and $81,500 for work in the field of public administration.

A. M. Schlesinger.
Guy Stanton Ford.
Roy F. Nichols.

November 1, 1937.

### The Delegate of the Pacific Coast Branch

The Pacific coast branch is concerned regarding the status of its annual subvention from the American Historical Association. The officers have heard that the council voted to stop this subvention in 1937, but no formal statement of such an action has been sent to them.[1] Before taking final action, the council should consider the following points:

(1) The large majority of the members of the historical profession in the far west wish to remain within the American Historical Association, but can take no direct part in its activities except through a regional organization such as the Pacfic coast branch. The stopping of the subvention and the consequent

---

[1] In this connection it may not be inappropriate to call attention to the following letter from the executive secretary of the American Historical Association to Dr. John C. Parish, editor of *The Pacific Historical Review*. Dr. Parish and the executive secretary of the Association had been in personal conference on the subject of the Pacific coast branch during the summer of 1935:

JANUARY 17, 1936.

Dr. John C. Parish,
  University of California at Los Angeles,
      Los Angeles, Calif.

Dear Dr. Parish: I beg to transmit the following passage from the minutes of the meeting of the council of the American Historical Association at Chattanooga on December 27–28, 1935:

"At the request of Mr. E. E. Robinson, the council reconsidered its action of December 1 (cf. minutes of council December 1, 1935, p. 13) relative to an appropriation for the Pacific coast branch. Upon motion it was voted that instead of the appropriation approved December 1 ($100 a year for 4 years), an appropriation of $200 be made to the Pacific coast branch for the current fiscal year and $200 for the next fiscal year, but that thereafter all financial support for the Pacific coast branch from the American Historical Association should cease."

I don't know whether this should come to you or to someone else, but I will trust you to transmit it to the proper person.

Yours sincerely,

CONYERS READ, *Executive Secretary.*

No official action by the council relating to the Pacific coast branch has been taken since the action referred to in this letter. The council did not vote in 1937 to stop the subvention. The subvention stopped automatically in accordance with the action taken in 1935.

C. R.

disappearance of the Pacific coast branch would have the effect of excluding them from the Association. It is admitted that the American Historical Association can afford the loss of revenue involved, but the loss of good will through such an ill-considered action may be more serious. Even 50 resignations, and there might well be more, should not be regarded as an unimportant matter.

(2) If the relations with the American Historical Association were put on a permanent basis, the Pacific coast branch could take a more active part in membership campaigns. As long as the branch leads such a precarious existence, its officers cannot be successful in securing memberships in the American Historical Association from persons whose only direct contact with the Association must be through the Pacific coast branch. If the branch received a fixed proportion of each membership fee received from the far west each year, the result would be an increase in income for both the national and regional organizations.

(3) *The Pacific Historical Review* is no longer dependent financially on the Pacific coast branch, since the money it now receives from the branch is the equivalent of reductions in subscription rates made to members of the branch. If the council wishes these payments to stop, *The Pacific Historical Review* will not suffer, because the reduced rate will be discontinued.

No matter what decision is reached, the Pacific coast branch requests the council to inform the delegate of the result. It has been several years since the decisions of the council which may affect the branch have been communicated to the delegate or to the officers of the branch.

The statement which follows is not final; it is meant to inform the members of the council of the financial condition of the Pacific coast branch. The final statement will be sent to the Washington office early in January.

*Preliminary financial statement [1] of the Pacific coast branch, American Historical Association*

| | |
|---|---:|
| Balance, Jan. 1, 1937 | $66. 85 |
| Income: | |
| American Historical Association | 200. 00 |
| Sale of *Proceedings of the Pacific Coast Branch* | 10. 00 |
| Interest | 1. 87 |
| | 278. 70 |
| Expense: | |
| To *Pacific Historical Review* (tentative) | 150. 00 |
| Office supplies, assistance, postage | 26. 65 |
| Printing | 27. 55 |
| *Proceedings* purchased for resale | 5. 00 |
| Annual meeting (estimate) | 30. 00 |
| Estimated balance, Dec. 31, 1937 | 39. 50 |
| | 278. 70 |

[1] The final statement appears on p. 85.

NOTE.—The amount granted to *The Pacific Historical Review* is roughly equivalent to the total of the reductions in subscription rates given by the *Review* to members of the Pacific coast branch. The grant will not actually be made until after the annual meeting. The estimate for the expenses of the meeting (over the income from registration fees) is high; probably the deficit will be smaller.

## OFFICERS FOR 1938

PRESIDENT
### LAURENCE M. LARSON [1]
*University of Illinois, Urbana, Ill.*

FIRST VICE PRESIDENT
### FREDERIC L. PAXSON
*University of California, Berkeley, Calif.*

SECOND VICE PRESIDENT
### WILLIAM SCOTT FERGUSON
*Harvard University, Cambridge, Mass.*

SECRETARY
### DEXTER PERKINS
*University of Rochester, Rochester, N. Y.*

TREASURER
### SOLON J. BUCK
*The National Archives, Washington, D. C.*

ASSISTANT SECRETARY-TREASURER
### PATTY W. WASHINGTON
*740 Fifteenth Street NW., Washington, D. C.*

EDITOR
### LOWELL JOSEPH RAGATZ
*The George Washington University, Washington, D. C.*

EXECUTIVE SECRETARY
### CONYERS READ
*226 South Sixteenth Street, Philadelphia, Pa.*

COUNCIL
(Ex officio: The president, vice presidents, secretary, and treasurer)

Former Presidents

### ALBERT BUSHNELL HART
*Harvard University, Cambridge, Mass.*

### ANDREW C. McLAUGHLIN
*University of Chicago, Chicago, Ill.*

### GEORGE L. BURR
*The Library, Cornell University, Ithaca, N. Y.*

### WORTHINGTON C. FORD
*% Morgan and Co., 14 Place Vendome, Paris*

### EDWARD P. CHEYNEY
*R. F. D. No. 3, Media, Pa.*

### CHARLES M. ANDREWS
*424 St. Ronan Street, New Haven, Conn.*

### HENRY OSBORN TAYLOR
*135 East Sixty-sixth Street, New York, N. Y.*

---

[1] Died March 9, 1938.

EVARTS B. GREENE
*602 Fayerweather Hall, Columbia University, New York, N. Y.*

CARL BECKER
*Cornell University, Ithaca, N. Y.*

HERBERT E. BOLTON
*University of California, Berkeley, Calif.*

CHARLES A. BEARD
*New Milford, Conn.*

WILLIAM E. DODD
*Round Hill. Va.*

MICHAEL I. ROSTOVTZEFF
*Yale University, New Haven, Conn.*

CHARLES H. McILWAIN
*Harvard University, Cambridge, Mass.*

GUY STANTON FORD
*University of Minnesota, Minneapolis, Minn.*

Elected Members

DUMAS MALONE
*32 Quincy Street, Cambridge, Mass.*

WILLIAM L. WESTERMANN
*Fayerweather Hall, Columbia University, New York, N. Y.*

BESSIE L. PIERCE
*University of Chicago, Chicago, Ill.*

FREDERICK MERK
*Harvard University, Cambridge, Mass.*

CARL WITTKE
*Oberlin College, Oberlin, Ohio*

ISAAC J. COX
*Northwestern University, Evanston, Ill.*

EUGENE C. BARKER
*University of Texas, Austin, Tex.*

LAURENCE B. PACKARD
*Amherst College, Amherst, Mass.*

## PACIFIC COAST BRANCH OFFICERS FOR 1938

PRESIDENT
JAMES WESTFALL THOMPSON
*University of California, Berkeley, Calif.*

VICE PRESIDENT
HENRY S. LUCAS
*University of Washington, Seattle, Wash.*

## COMMITTEES FOR 1938

*Nominating committee.*—Violet Barbour, chairman, Vassar College, Poughkeepsie, N. Y.; Kent R. Greenfield, Johns Hopkins University, Baltimore, Md.; A. C. Krey, University of Minnesota, Minneapolis, Minn.; Frank Owsley, Vanderbilt University, Nashville, Tenn.; Edgar E. Robinson, Stanford University, Calif.

*Board of trustees.*—Thomas I. Parkinson, *chairman*, Equitable Life Assurance Society, New York, N. Y. (1942); Leon Fraser, First National Bank, New York, N. Y. (1938); Jerome D. Greene, Harvard University, Cambridge, Mass.; Stanton Griffis, 15 Broad Street, New York, N. Y.; Shepard Morgan, Chase National Bank, New York, N. Y. (1939).

*Executive committee of the council.*—James P. Baxter, III, *chairman*, Williams College, Williamstown, Mass.; Carlton J. H. Hayes, Columbia University, New York, N. Y.; Frederick Merk, Harvard University, Cambridge, Mass.; Laurence B. Packard, Amherst College, Amherst, Mass. *Ex officio:* Solon J. Buck, The National Archives, Washington, D. C.; Dexter Perkins, University of Rochester, Rochester, N. Y.

*Council committee on appointments.*—Bessie L. Pierce, *chairman*, University of Chicago, Chicago, Ill.; Eugene C. Barker, University of Texas, Austin, Tex. *Ex officio:* Dexter Perkins, University of Rochester, Rochester, N. Y.; Conyers Read, 226 South Sixteenth St., Philadelphia, Pa.

*Committee on program for the fifty-third annual meeting (1938).*—Louis R. Gottschalk, *chairman*, University of Chicago, Chicago, Ill.; Mrs. Pierce Butler, *secretary*, Newberry Library, Chicago, Ill.; A. E. R. Boak, University of Michigan, Ann Arbor, Mich.; Clyde L. Grose, Northwestern University, Evanston, Ill.; William J. Hail, Wooster College, Wooster, Ohio.; Samuel N. Harper, University of Chicago, Chicago, Ill.; William T. Hutchinson, University of Chicago, Chicago, Ill.; A. C. Krey, University of Minnesota, Minneapolis, Minn.; J. Fred Rippy, University of Chicago, Chicago, Ill. *Ex officio:* Frederic L. Paxson, President, American Historical Association, University of California, Berkeley, Calif.; Dorothy C. Barck, Secretary of the Conference of Historical Societies, New York Historical Society, New York, N. Y.; Dexter Perkins, Secretary, American Historical Association, University of Rochester, Rochester, N. Y.; Oscar C. Stine, Secretary of the Agricultural History Society, 1358 Independence Avenue SW., Room 304, Washington, D. C.

*Committee on local arrangements for the fifty-third annual meeting (1938).*— Tracy E. Strevey, *secretary*, Northwestern University, Evanston, Ill. (with power to appoint his associates).

*Committee on program for the fifty-fourth annual meeting (1939).*—E. N. Anderson, *chairman*, American University, Washington, D. C.

*Committee on local arrangements for the fifty-fourth annual meeting (1939).*— Dallas D. Irvine, *secretary*, The National Archives, Washington, D. C.

*Board of editors, "The American Historical Review."*—Robert L. Schuyler, *managing editor*, 535 West One Hundred and Fourteenth Street, New York, N. Y.; Dexter Perkins, University of Rochester, Rochester, N. Y. (term expires in 1943); Dumas Malone, 32 Quincy Street, Cambridge, Mass. (1939); Miss N. Neilson, Mount Holyoke College, South Hadley, Mass. (1940); A. E. R. Boak, University of Michigan, Ann Arbor, Mich. (1941); Preserved Smith, Cornell University, Ithaca, N. Y. (1941); William L. Langer, Harvard University, Cambridge, Mass. (1942).

*Committee on the George Louis Beer prize.*—Raymond J. Sontag, *chairman*, Princeton University, Princeton, N. J.; David Harris, Stanford University, Calif.; Alfred Vagts, Gaylordsville Post Office, Sherman, Conn.

*Committee on the John H. Dunning prize.*—Kathleen Bruce, *chairman*, Chesterfield Apartments, Richmond, Va.; Viola F. Barnes, Mt. Holyoke College, South Hadley, Mass.; Marcus L. Hansen, University of Illinois, Urbana, Ill.

*Committee on the Herbert Baxter Adams prize.*—Albert H. Lybyer, *chairman*, University of Illinois, Urbana, Ill.; Leona C. Gabel, 16 Washington Avenue, Northampton, Mass.; Walter C. Langsam, Columbia University, New York, N. Y.

*Committee on the Justin Winsor prize.*—Caroline F. Ware, *chairman*, American University, Washington, D. C.; Colin B. Goodykoontz, University of Colorado, Boulder, Colo.; Henry S. Commager, New York University, New York, N. Y.

*Committee on the Jusserand medal.*—Louis R. Gottschalk, *chairman*, University of Chicago, Chicago, Ill.; Howard Mumford Jones, Harvard University, Cambridge, Mass.; Frank Monaghan, Yale University, New Haven, Conn.

*Committee on the Carnegie revolving fund for publications.*—John D. Hicks, *chairman*, University of Wisconsin, Madison, Wis.; Kent R. Greenfield, Johns Hopkins University, Baltimore, Md.; Jakob A. O. Larsen, University of Chicago, Chicago, Ill.; William E. Lunt, Haverford College, Haverford, Pa.; Edward Whitney, Harvard University, Cambridge, Mass.

*Committee on the Albert J. Beveridge memorial fund.*—Roy F. Nichols, *chairman*, University of Pennsylvania, Philadelphia, Pa.; Arthur C. Cole, Western Reserve University, Cleveland, Ohio; James G. Randall, University of Illinois, Urbana, Ill.

*Committee on the Littleton-Griswold fund.*—Francis S. Philbrick, *chairman*, Law School, University of Pennsylvania, Philadelphia, Pa.; Charles M. Andrews, 424 St. Ronan Street, New Haven, Conn.; Carroll T. Bond, 1125 North Calvert Street, Baltimore, Md.; John Dickinson, Law School, University of Pennsylvania, Philadelphia, Pa.; Walton H. Hamilton, Yale University Law School, New Haven, Conn.; Richard B. Morris, College of the City of New York, New York, N. Y.; Thomas I. Parkinson, Equitable Life Assurance Society, New York, N. Y.; Charles Warren, Mills Building, Washington, D. C.

*Committee on historical source materials.*—T. R. Schellenberg, The National Archives, Washington, D. C. *Subcommittee on public archives.*—A. R. Newsome,

University of North Carolina, Chapel Hill, N. C.; Robert C. Binkley, Western Reserve University, Cleveland, Ohio; Francis S. Philbrick, Law School, University of Pennsylvania, Philadelphia, Pa. *Subcommittee on historical manuscripts.*—Julian P. Boyd, Historical Society of Pennsylvania, Philadelphia, Pa.; Theodore C. Blegen, University of Minnesota, Minneapolis, Minn.; Lester J. Cappon, University of Virginia, University, Va.

*Conference of historical societies.*—Dorothy C. Barck, *secretary,* New York Historical Society, New York, N. Y.

*Committee on publication of the "Annual Report."*—Leo F. Stock, *chairman,* 231 First Street NE., Washington, D. C.; Solon J. Buck, The National Archives, Washington, D. C.; Lowell Joseph Ragatz, The George Washington University, Washington, D. C.; St. George L. Sioussat, University of Pennsylvania, Philadelphia, Pa.

*Committee on "Writings on American History."*—Leo F. Stock, *chairman,* 231 First Street NE., Washington, D. C.; Samuel Flagg Bemis, Yale University, New Haven, Conn.; Waldo G. Leland, 907 Fifteenth Street NW., Washington, D. C.; St. George L. Sioussat, University of Pennsylvania, Philadelphia, Pa.

*Committee on "The Bibliography of American Travel."*—Frank Monaghan, *chairman,* Yale University, New Haven, Conn.; Julian P. Boyd, Historical Society of Pennsylvania, Philadelphia, Pa.; Harry M. Lydenberg, New York Public Library, New York, N. Y.

*Committee on membership.*—Elmer Ellis, *chairman,* University of Missouri, Columbia, Mo. (with power to appoint his associates).

*Committee on radio.*—Conyers Read, *chairman,* 226 South Sixteenth Street, Philadelphia, Pa.; Mrs. Evelyn Plummer Braun, 125 Bleddyn Road, Ardmore, Pa.; Felix Greene, American representative of the British Broadcasting System, New York, N. Y.; John A. Krout, Columbia University, New York, N. Y.; Walter C. Langsam, Columbia University, New York, N. Y.; Ralph S. Rounds, 165 Broadway, New York, N. Y.; Raymond Gram Swing, New York City; Elizabeth Y. Webb, 1028 Connecticut Avenue NW., Washington, D. C.

*Committee on Americana for college libraries.*—Randolph G. Adams, *chairman,* William L. Clements Library, University of Michigan, Ann Arbor, Mich.; Kathryn L. Slagle, *secretary,* William L. Clements Library, University of Michigan, Ann Arbor, Mich.; William W. Bishop, General Library, University of Michigan, Ann Arbor, Mich.; Julian P. Boyd, Historical Society of Pennsylvania, Philadelphia, Pa.; Conyers Read, 226 South Sixteenth Street, Philadelphia, Pa.; Thomas W. Streeter, Morristown, N. Y.; Lawrence C. Wroth, John Carter Brown Library, Brown University, Providence, R. I.

*Board of editors of "Social Education."*—Erling M. Hunt, *chairman,* 204 Fayerweather Hall, Columbia University, New York, N. Y.; Conyers Read, *secretary,* 226 South Sixteenth Street, Philadelphia, Pa.; Charles A. Beard, New Milford, Conn.; Phillips Bradley, Amherst College, Amherst, Mass.; Margaret A. Koch, Fieldston School, New York, N. Y.; Donnal V. Smith, State Teachers College, Albany, N. Y.; Ruth Wanger, South Philadelphia High School for Girls, Philadelphia, Pa.; Louis Wirth, University of Chicago, Chicago, Ill.

*Advisory Board of "Social Education."*—For a 3-year term beginning January 1, 1938: Marjorie Dowling Brown, Manual Arts High School, Los Angeles, Calif.; Merle Curti, Teachers College, Columbia University, New York, N. Y.; Elmer Ellis, University of Missouri, Columbia, Mo.; E. F. Hartford, duPont Manual Training High School, Louisville, Ky.; Howard C. Hill, University of Chicago, Chicago, Ill.; Ernest Horn, State University of Iowa, Iowa City, Iowa; Tyler Kepner, Public Schools, Brookline, Mass.; Allen Y. King, Public Schools, Cleveland, Ohio; D. C. Knowlton, New York University, New York, N. Y.; Martha

Layman, State Teachers College, Valley City, N. Dak.; Miles Malone, Phillips Academy, Andover, Mass.; L. C. Marshall, Johns Hopkins University, Baltimore, Md.; Myrtle Roberts, High School, Dallas, Tex.; Arthur M. Schlesinger, Harvard University, Cambridge, Mass.; Mabel Snedaker, University Elementary School, University of Iowa, Iowa City, Iowa. Continuing from 1937: Robert I. Adriance, High School, East Orange, N. J.; Julian C. Aldrich, High School, Webster Groves, Mo.; Howard R. Anderson, Cornell University, Ithaca, N. Y.; Nelle E. Bowman, Public Schools, Tulsa, Okla.; Mary E. Christy, North High School, Denver, Colo.; Harley S. Graston, Woodlawn High School, Birmingham, Ala.; Eugene Hilton, Allendale Schools, Oakland, Calif.; George J. Jones, Public Schools, Washington, D. C.; A. K. King, University of North Carolina, Chapel Hill, N. C.; Harrison C. Thomas, Richmond Hill High School, New York, N. Y.; Ruth West, Lewis and Clark High School, Spokane, Wash.

*Representatives of the American Historical Association in allied bodies: Social Science Research Council.*—Guy Stanton Ford, University of Minnesota, Minneapolis, Minn.; Roy F. Nichols, University of Pennsylvania, Philadelphia, Pa.; Arthur M. Schlesinger, Harvard University, Cambridge, Mass. (for a 3-year term, ending in 1939). *American Council of Learned Societies.*—Edward P. Cheyney, R. F. D. No. 3, Media, Pa. (term expires in 1938); W. S. Ferguson, Harvard University, Cambridge, Mass. (for a term of 4 years, ending in 1940). *International Committee of Historical Sciences, delegates.*—Waldo G. Leland, 907 Fifteenth Street N. W., Washington, D. C.; James T. Shotwell, Columbia University, New York, N. Y. *Subcommittee on archives.*—Robert D. W. Connor, The National Archives, Washington, D. C. *Subcommittee on diplomatic history.*—Samuel Flagg Bemis, Yale University, New Haven, Conn. *Subcommittee on chronology.*—John L. La Monte, University of Cincinnati, Cincinnati, Ohio. *Subcommittee on historical iconography.*—Leicester Holland, Library of Congress, Washington. *Subcommittee on historical geography.*—Charles O. Paullin, 1718 N Street NW., Washington, D. C. *Subcommittee on the "International Bibliography of Historical Sciences."*—Waldo G. Leland, 907 Fifteenth Street NW., Washington, D. C.

PROCEEDINGS OF THE
THIRTY-THIRD ANNUAL MEETING OF THE
PACIFIC COAST BRANCH
SEATTLE, WASHINGTON, DECEMBER 28–30, 1937

PROCEEDINGS OF THE THIRTY-THIRD ANNUAL MEETING OF THE
PACIFIC COAST BRANCH OF THE AMERICAN HISTORICAL ASSO-
CIATION

The thirty-third annual meeting of the Pacific coast branch of the American Historical Association was held in Seattle at the University of Washington, December 28–30, 1937. The program was prepared by a committee consisting of Professors Herman J. Deutsch (chairman), David K. Björk, Frederick E. Graham, and Harold C. Vedeler. Local arrangements were made by Professors Edith Dobie (chairman), C. Eden Quainton, and Charles M. Gates.

The opening session on Tuesday afternoon, presided over by Prof. Edward McMahon, was devoted to the following papers: *The Chancery and the Privy Seal, 1327–36*, by Prof. William A. Morris, of the University of California; *The Geneva Bible as a Political Document*, by Prof. Hardin Craig, Jr., of the California Institute of Technology; *Peter Chaadayev: His Conception of History*, by Dr. Anatole Mazour; and *The English Armament Industry and Navalism in the Nineties*, by Prof. Arthur J. Marder, of the University of Oregon. At the close of the session the members were entertained at tea by the courtesy of President Sieg, of the University of Washington.

President Joseph B. Lockey presided over the morning session on December 29, at which the following papers were read: *Foreign Intervention in the French Civil-Religious War of 1562–63*, by Dr. Bernerd C. Weber, of Stanford University; *The Panama Route to the Pacific, 1848–69*, by Mr. John Kemble, of Pomona College; *The Bulgarian Atrocity Agitation in England, 1876*, by Prof. David Harris, of Stanford University; and *The Partition of Samoa: A Study in Anglo-German-American Imperialism and Diplomacy*, by Prof. Joseph W. Ellison, of Oregon State College.

At the luncheon Prof. Julius P. Jaeger, of the College of Puget Sound, delivered an address on *The Historical Novel: Its Rights and Duties.*

The afternoon session, presided over by Prof. William A. Morris, was devoted to the following papers on frontier history: *The Russian State in the Siberian Fur Trade in the Seventeenth Century*, by Prof. Raymond H. Fisher, of Humboldt State College; *The Influence of the Army in the Building of a Western State*, by Prof. Merrill G. Burlingame, of Montana State College; *Turning the Tide of Emigration to Oregon Territory*, by Prof. Melvin Clay Jacobs, of Whitman College; and *The Clash Between North and South Idaho Over the Capitol Question*, by President Eugene Chaffee, of Boise Junior College. The paper by Professor Jacobs, who was unable to be present, was read by Prof. Percy W. Christian, of Walla Walla College.

At the annual dinner President Joseph B. Lockey addressed the members on *Pan-Americanism versus Imperialism.*

Prof. Dan E. Clark presided over the morning session on December 30, at which the following papers were read: *Some Aspects of the Economic Life of the Byzantine Empire*, by Dr. Solomon Katz, of the University of Washington; *Parliament and the English East African Companies, 1663–1714*, by Prof. E. E. Bennett, of Montana State University; and *The French Labor Movement, 1880–95*, by Prof. Harold E. Blinn, of Washington State College.

The business session followed, with President Lockey in the chair. After the report of the secretary-treasurer, Prof. R. C. Clark presented reports from Prof. Frederic L. Paxson, who acted as chairman of the board of editors of *The Pacific Historical Review* until April 30, 1937, and from the managing editor, Prof. Louis Knott Koontz.

The committee on nominations, consisting of Professors H. A. Hubbard, chairman, Francis J. Bowman, Harold W. Bradley, Merrill Jenson, and John H. Kemble, reported the following nominations, which were accepted: President, James Westfall Thompson, University of California; vice president, Henry S. Lucas, University of Washington; secretary-treasurer, Francis H. Herrick, Mills College. The council: the above officers and Herman J. Deutsch, Washington State College; David Harris, Stanford University; Joseph B. Lockey, University of California at Los Angeles; Rufus K. Wyllys, Arizona State Teachers College, Tempe. Board of Editors of *The Pacific Historical Review*, 1938–40: Thomas A. Bailey, Stanford University; Robert E. Pollard, University of Washington.

Committee on awards:

European history: William A. Morris, University of California, chairman; Andrew Fish, University of Oregon; O. H. Wedel, University of Arizona.

American history: Dan E. Clark, University of Oregon, chairman; George P. Hammond, University of New Mexico; F. W. Pitman, Pomona College.

Pacific history: H. H. Fisher, Stanford University, chairman; Ralph S. Kuykendall, University of Hawaii; W. Kaye Lamb, Provincial Archives, British Columbia.

The committee on resolutions, consisting of Monsignor Joseph M. Gleason, chairman, and Profs. E. E. Bennett and Hardin Craig, Jr., reported the following resolutions, which were adopted:

*Resolved,* That the Association express its grateful appreciation of the courtesy of the University of Washington, which has been its host in Seattle. Not only was Austin Hall placed at the service of the Association, thus providing in one beautiful building ample assembly rooms, lounges, and living quarters, but the comfort of the visiting historians was increased by the courtesy and kindly hospitality of the staff.

*Resolved,* That the Pacific coast branch send from Seattle its filial greetings to the American Historical Association now in session in Philadelphia to celebrate the Sesquicentennial of our National Constitution, and that we express hope that the publication of the papers read at Philadelphia may provide for the future a synthesis of historical wisdom on this great document.

Without presenting a formal resolution, the committee also expressed the views of the members present in congratulating the program committee and the individual members reading papers on the excellence of the formal sessions at the meeting.

On the motion of Prof. R. C. Clark, the secretary was instructed to send a letter to the Honorable Cordell Hull, Secretary of State, pointing out the importance of the series entitled *Foreign Relations of the United States,* and requesting that the volumes in arrears be printed as rapidly as they are prepared for publication by the Research Division of the Department. The secretary was also instructed to prepare copies of this letter to be sent to congressmen from western districts.

After a discussion of the relations between the American Historical Association and the Pacific coast branch and the possible withdrawal of financial support, the members accepted the motion of Prof. W. A. Morris authorizing the council to arrange to meet the expenses of the Pacific coast branch during 1938 without assessing a membership fee.

FRANCIS H. HERRICK, *Secretary-Treasurer.*

*Statement of the secretary-treasurer of the Pacific coast branch of the American Historical Association, 1937*

### INCOME

| | |
|---|---:|
| Balance in bank and in cash, Jan. 2, 1937 | $66.83 |
| American Historical Association subvention | 200.00 |
| Sale of *Proceedings of the Pacific Coast Branch of the American Historical Association*, 1926–1930 | 10.00 |
| Registration fees, annual meeting | 33.50 |
| Interest | 3.87 |
| | 314.20 |

### EXPENSE

| | |
|---|---:|
| Office supplies, clerical assistance, postage | 23.31 |
| *Proceedings* purchased for resale | 5.00 |
| *Pacific Historical Review*, compensation for reduced rate to members | 150.00 |
| Annual meeting—printing and expenses of committee on arrangements | 55.36 |
| | 233.67 |
| Balance, Dec. 31, 1937 | 80.53 |
| | 314.20 |

# THE CONFERENCE OF HISTORICAL SOCIETIES
## THIRTY-THIRD ANNUAL MEETING, PHILADELPHIA, DECEMBER 31, 1937

## MINUTES OF THE CONFERENCE OF STATE AND LOCAL HISTORICAL SOCIETIES, DECEMBER 31, 1937

The thirty-third annual conference of State and local historical societies, in joint session with the American Historical Association, was held at the Historical Society of Pennsylvania, 1300 Locust Street, Philadelphia, on Friday afternoon, December 31, 1937. Mr. Edward P. Alexander, Director of the New York State Historical Association, chairman of the conference, presided. In the absence of the secretary, Mr. Christopher B. Coleman, the chair appointed Miss Barck, of the New York Historical Society, as temporary secretary. The chairman expressed the conference's appreciation of the hospitality of the Historical Society of Pennsylvania.

The first paper on the program, *Philadelphia, Convention City of 1787*,[1] presented by Mrs. Elinor Schafer Barnes, of Philadelphia, described the city's appearance in that year, and the dress, business, social life, amusements, churches, and education of Philadelphians of that period.

Mr. Douglas C. McMurtrie, of Chicago, spoke on *The Record of American Imprints*,[2] stressing the importance to the historian of contemporary printed items, and telling of his having found valuable broadsides and pamphlets which threw light on the earliest history of printing in several States. He described the compilation of a catalog of imprints by the Historical Records Survey of the Works Progress Administration, which, when complete, will be available for reference at the Library of Congress. He explained that, unlike earlier bibliographies such as the one by Evans, this catalog would include the imprints of trans-Appalachian presses, and that the large number of workers made it possible for the first time thoroughly to examine widely-scattered and little-known repositories, as well as the large eastern libraries.

Mr. Alexander J. Wall, Director of the New York Historical Society, read his address on *The Place of the Historical Society in the United States and Elsewhere*, in which he pointed out that almost half of the museums in the United States are historical museums, and suggested that the public support which they have lacked in the past might be attracted to them by cooperation in educational work and by more spectacular exhibitions.

At the conclusion of the program the chairman opened the meeting for general discussion, in conformity with the custom prevailing at these conferences since 1904.

Mr. James A. Robertson, executive secretary of the Florida State Historical Society and Archivist of Maryland, commended Mr. McMurtrie's work in recording imprints and making the data available, and pointed out that imprints not of a region may contain material for the history of that region.

Dr. Luther H. Evans, National Director of the Historical Records Survey of the Works Progress Administration, said that the Survey was contemplating a place index of periodicals, and was about to study methods of procedure for such a work.

Dr. Alexander C. Flick, State Historian of New York, spoke of the many small historical museums which cannot play a real role in their communities

---

[1] Published in *The Social Studies*, November 1937.
[2] Published in this volume, pp. 107ff.

because of lack of leadership, and suggested that those present, being interested in such work, might provide the needed leadership in helping museums cooperate with local school programs. Dr. Flick asked Mr. McMurtrie whether his imprint catalog might not be condensed and published, for the more convenient use of scholars everywhere.

Mr. McMurtrie replied that useful, preliminary mimeographed lists of imprints, arranged by States, were to be sent out to libraries for corrections and additions, after which the final revised lists would be distributed. He reported that the preliminary list of *Missouri Imprints to 1840* had been issued, that those for Ohio, Minnesota, and Oregon were almost ready, and that lists for other States were well advanced.

Mr. J. Carroll Hayes, of the Chester County Historical Society, asked for suggestions for a name for historical collections. He said that the late Henry C. Mercer had called his wonderful collection at Doylestown, Pa., the "Tools of the Nation"—tools of hand and mind and eye—and had then revised his designation to "The Tools of the Old World," as they were not created here but were evolutionary, and brought from Europe by the early settlers.

Dr. Evans, referring to Dr. Flick's suggestion that leadership was needed in the field of small historical museums, said that the Works Progress Administration had competent women directing educational projects based on the whole museum structure of the States. He explained that the Works Progress Administration was prepared to furnish experts and children's exhibits, and suggested that anyone interested in advancing such work should get in touch with the local director of professional projects.

Dr. Herbert A. Kellar, of the McCormick Historical Association, urged historical societies to cooperate with the Works Progress Administration for a nation-wide program in the museum field. He congratulated Mr. McMurtrie on his valuable work in cataloging imprints, which would make the historian's work even more complicated.

Mr. Wall asked Dr. Evans what museums were entitled to aid from the Works Progress Administration, as he understood that privately-owned museums were excluded from such help. Dr. Evans replied that a city could sponsor a program and go to a privately-owned institution for cooperation, and so widen the service of the privately-owned museum by utilizing its facilities for the public good. He cited similar work done by the Historical Records Survey in private libraries, such as the calendar of material in the Historical Society of Pennsylvania.

At the close of this general discussion, the business meeting of the conference was held. The minutes of the last meeting and the secretary's financial statement were read and approved. The chairman, calling for nominations for the office of secretary, explained that that officer was the executive of the conference, and therefore really more important than the chairman. Upon motion by Dr. Flick, seconded by Dr. Kellar, it was voted that the chair appoint a committee of three with power to select the secretary for the ensuing year. (The chairman later appointed Mr. Wall, Dr. Kellar, and Dr. Augustus H. Shearer, of the Grosvenor Library, to this committee, and they selected Dorothy C. Barck to serve as secretary.)

Dr. Kellar moved the reelection of Mr. Edward P. Alexander as chairman. Dr. Flick took the chair, and the motion, seconded by Mr. Hugh M. Flick, was put to a vote and passed. Mr. Alexander resumed the chair and asked if there was any new business.

Upon motion by Dr. Kellar, seconded by Dr. Flick, it was resolved that the chair appoint a committee of three to cooperate with Dr. Evans, of the Works Progress Administration, respecting ways of rendering assistance to local and

State museums and historical societies. (The chairman appointed Dr. Kellar to head this committee, with power to select two associates.)

The chairman asked the pleasure of the meeting about reviving the former custom of mailing an account of the annual conference, within a short time, to all member historical societies, instead of depending upon the printed report of the American Historical Association, which does not appear for some months. Upon motion of Dr. Flick, it was voted that the conference order a mimeographed digest of the proceedings of the afternoon sent to members of the conference.

The chairman declared the meeting adjourned at half past four.

DOROTHY C. BARCK, *Secretary pro tem.*

*Conference of historical societies, financial statement, fiscal year Sept. 1, 1936–Aug. 31, 1937*

### RECEIPTS

| | |
|---|---:|
| 1936—Sept. 1. Balance on hand | $294.26 |
| Oct. 7. Received from Historical Society of Pennsylvania | 100.00 |
| Oct. 14. Received from New York Historical Society | 100.00 |
| Oct. 31. Received from Indiana Historical Society | 100.00 |
| Nov. 1. Interest on deposit | 2.85 |
| Deposit from 20 memberships | 20.00 |
| 1937—May 1. Interest | 2.67 |
| Proceeds from sales of *Handbooks* through the year | 377.31 |
| | 997.09 |

### EXPENDITURES

| | |
|---|---:|
| *1936*—Sept. 1. Gayle Thornbrough, assistance on *Handbook* | $46.90 |
| Sept. 15. Postage | 1.50 |
| Oct. 28. Western Union Telegraph Co | 3.35 |
| Dec. 1. Mailing programs to members | .36 |
| Dec. 7. N. C. Armstrong, assistance on *Handbook* | 25.00 |
| Dec. 14. Post cards, mailing notices, etc | 11.18 |
| Dec. 15. Mailing *Handbook* to members | 1.44 |
| Dec. 16. George Mayer & Co. for rubber stamp | .50 |
| Dec. 18. Postage | 8.00 |
| Dec. 18. Hendren Printing Co | 293.60 |
| Dec. 22. Beck Letter Service for multigraphing cards | 4.75 |
| Dec. 30. Gayle Thornbrough, clerical work | 11.30 |
| Dec. 31. Western Union Telegraph Co | 1.13 |
| Dec. 31. Postage | 1.50 |
| *1937*—Jan. 1. Cleta H. Robinson, clerical work | 50.00 |
| Jan. 7. Dorothy Riker, assistance on *Handbook* | 11.40 |
| Jan. 12. Copyright on *Handbook* | 2.05 |
| Jan. 28. Postage on *Handbook* | 8.00 |
| Feb. 3. Rubber stamp | 1.00 |
| Feb. 3. Postage on *Handbook* | 15.00 |
| March 16. National Library Bindery Co | 3.00 |
| Aug. 6. Postage | 10.00 |
| | $510.96 |

| | |
|---|---:|
| Total assets | $997.09 |
| Expenditures | 510.96 |
| *1937*—Balance, Sept. 1, 1937 | $486.13 |

C. B. COLEMAN, *Secretary.*

RECORDS OF THE UNITED STATES DISTRICT COURTS,
1790–1870, DEPOSITED IN THE COPYRIGHT
OFFICE OF THE LIBRARY OF
CONGRESS

BY

MARTIN A. ROBERTS

CHIEF ASSISTANT LIBRARIAN, LIBRARY OF CONGRESS

74920—39——8

RECORDS OF THE UNITED STATES DISTRICT COURTS, 1790–1870, DEPOSITED IN THE COPYRIGHT OFFICE OF THE LIBRARY OF CONGRESS [1]

The subject of my remarks are two long ranges of shelves in the Copyright Office filled with great folio record books, whose shredding sheepskin binding has for many years been gradually giving way to buckram. They are a tattered army, imposing from their size and number and ragged age. Every succeeding member of the staff of the Copyright Office has gazed at them with respect; their appearance immediately sets them off from the modern canvas-bound tomes in which the copyright entries are currently made. But this is not the source of the honor they receive; that arises from the fact that these volumes contain all the copyright records before 1870, before the date at which the Library of Congress became the registry of copyrights. These volumes are, so to speak, the ancestors; they connect the unrecorded past in which copyright records were nonexistent with the modern present in which copyright catalogers sometimes become presidents of bibliographical societies.

If such respect is exacted by these records even from their continuators, how much more should a bibliographer honor them! It is, therefore, a privilege to recount their unexciting history. In the preparation of this paper, besides the works cited in the text, I have drawn upon a study made by Mr. Verner W. Clapp, of the Library of Congress staff, of this phase of copyright history; also upon *Copyright Protection and Statutory Formalities*, by Thorvald Solberg, Washington, D. C., 1904; and *An Outline of Copyright Law*, by Richard C. De Wolf, Boston [c. 1925].

Statutory copyright dates only from the eighteenth century, and it is of interest to note that England was the only country to precede the United States in securing copyright legislation, the earliest French law coming into force only in 1791. The first American acts, those of Connecticut, Massachusetts, and Maryland, were all passed in 1783. The year previous Thomas Paine had written (in his *Letter to the Abbé Raynal*):

"The state of literature in America must one day become a subject of legislative consideration. Hitherto it hath been a disinterested volunteer in the service of the Revolution [one thinks of *Common Sense, The Crisis,* and the royalties they might have brought], and no man thought of profits; but when peace shall give time and opportunity for study, the country will deprive itself of the honor and service of letters and the improvement of science, unless sufficient laws are made to prevent depredations on literary property."

By 1786 all of the original States but Delaware had passed copyright laws. These were chiefly due, directly or indirectly, to the activity of one man—Noah Webster—who traveled from State to State urging the protection of author's rights. By the time that the Federal Convention met in Philadelphia to frame a new Constitution, therefore, the principle of statutory copyright was generally agreed upon, and its inclusion in the foundation document of our political structure gave rise to no difficulty. Article I, section 8, of the Constitution pro-

[1] Presented at the joint session of the American Historical Association and the Bibliographical Society of America, held in Philadelphia, December 30, 1937.

vides that "The Congress shall have power   *   *   *   to promote the progress of science and the useful arts by securing, for limited times, to authors and inventors the exclusive right to their respective writings and discoveries." Thus the United States was the first nation to include in its fundamental law a provision regarding the rights of authors. It is worthy of note, however, that it is the promotion of progress rather than the rights of the author which is the constitutional object, and the validity of any copyright act which could be shown not to promote the progress of science and the useful arts might immediately be called in question. It is worthy of remark, too, that unless the Constitution is amended Congress can never secure to authors an exclusive right to their writings for more than "limited times."

The constitutional provision still needed statutory expression, and this was given at the second session of the First Congress meeting in New York. The journals of Congress would seem to indicate incentives to such acts of legislation from a stream of petitions asking for exclusive rights in literary and other works. Among the petitioners we recognize Jedidiah Morse, Mrs. Hannah Adams, and David Ramsay. "An Act for the encouragement of learning, by securing the copies of maps, charts, and books, to the authors and proprietors of such copies, during the times therein mentioned," was approved on May 31, 1790, and was intended to take immediate effect. Its intentions were twofold: to confirm the rightful proprietors in the possession of literary property already published and to provide for copyright registration in the future prior to actual publication. Section 3 of the act read in part as follows:

   *   *   *   No person shall be entitled to the benefit of this act, in cases where any map, chart, book or books, hath or have been already printed and published, unless he shall first deposit, and in all other cases, unless he shall before publication deposit a printed copy of the title of such map, chart, book or books, in the clerk's office of the district court where the author or proprietor shall reside: And the clerk of such court is hereby directed and required to record the same forthwith, in a book to be kept by him for that purpose, in the words following, (giving a copy thereof to the said author or proprietor, under the seal of the court, if he shall require the same.) "District of                   to wit: *Be it remembered,* That on the                   day of                   in the year of the independence of the United States of America, A. B. of the said district, hath deposited in this office the title of a map, chart, book or books, (as the case may be) the right whereof he claims as author or proprietor, (as the case may be) in the words following, to wit: [here insert the title] in conformity to the act of the Congress of the United States, intituled 'An act for the encouragement of learning, by securing the copies of maps, charts, and books, to the authors and proprietors of such copies, during the times therein mentioned.' C. D. clerk of the district of                   ." For which the said clerk shall be entitled to receive sixty cents from the said author or proprietor, and sixty cents for every copy under seal actually given to such author or proprietor as aforesaid.   *   *   *

Other provisions of the act required that the claimant should exhibit his certificate of copyright by advertising it in one or more newspapers for 4 weeks within 2 months of registration, and that within 6 months of publication he should deposit a copy of the work with the Secretary of State, "to be preserved in his office."

[With the other aspects of copyright legislation we have here no concern. I may remark in passing, however, that the rights secured by this act were confined to citizens or residents of the United States; that the original term of 14 years could be extended by the author upon renewal of his registration for a similar period (the term of copyright has ever in this country been in multiples of the 7 years of the old royal patents); that copyright was expressly withheld from the work of foreigners; and that remedies for infringement were provided.]

The first work entered for copyright under the act was in the District Court of Pennsylvania on June 14 (exactly a fortnight after its approval). John Barry, master of the Free School of the Protestant Episcopal Church, registered as author "*The Philadelphia Spelling Book*, arranged upon a plan entirely new." No work by this title in this year has been discovered, but Evans has identified it (No. 22326) with *The American Spelling Book*, having otherwise the same title (Philadelphia: Printed by Carey, Stewart & Co., 1790), and even of this no copies are known to exist. Later editions (up to the tenth, 1812) having the original title are, however, in existence.

Four copyright entries had been made in the Pennsylvania court before one was made in Massachusetts, on July 10, 1790, in favor of the Rev. Jedidiah Morse (who, it will be remembered, had been a petitioner to Congress on the subject of copyright). Two works were cited in this first Massachusetts entry (thereby effecting a saving of $1.20—60 cents for registration and 60 cents for a copy of the certificate). These were *The American Geography* and *Geography Made Easy*. Both had been previously published and were to be often reprinted.

The District Court of Maine (not then a State) at Portland was the third (of which there is now record) to accept an entry for copyright registration. This was for Judge Samuel Freeman's *The Columbian Primer*, registered August 14, 1790. No copies of a Portland edition are known, although Evans (No. 22511) has attempted to identify one. The Boston Public Library has, however, a copy of a Boston, 1790, edition, and there were later editions. It is worthy of remark that the Maine court from the first had a printed form for the entry of copyrights, and for 15 years was unique in this respect. The use of this form made the earning of the fee a sinecure—but there is another side to the picture. Seventy-five years later the clerk of the court was still using the original stock of forms printed in 1790 (merely amended in 1802), and his entry consisted largely in crossing out the no longer applicable printed matter!

New York, now the publishing center of the United States, was late in effecting its first registration. This was also for a school book—Donald Fraser's *The Young Gentleman and Lady's Assistant*, entered on April 30, 1791. It was published by Thomas Greenleaf, New York, 1791, and copies are in existence (Evans, 23387).

Altogether, the whole recorded copyright business of the district courts for the first year from the passage of the act amounted to 33 titles. It must not be thought, however, from the samples given, that these were comprised wholly of textbooks. A classification of the titles entered shows the following:

| | Titles | | Titles |
|---|---|---|---|
| Schoolbooks | 10 | Religion | 2 |
| Geodetic and nautical tables | 5 | Almanacs | 1 |
| Maps | 3 | Agriculture | 1 |
| Music | 3 | Poems | 1 |
| Directories | 2 | Plays | 1 |
| Law | 2 | | |
| Medicine | 2 | | 33 |

Among the interesting registrations of this early period a few may be mentioned besides those already cited. The second Pennsylvania copyright (June 15, 1790) was the first play by an American author successfully produced upon the stage. This was Royall Tyler's *The Contrast, a Comedy* (Philadelphia: Pritchard & Hall, 1790, Evans 22948). The third Pennsylvania copyright was the Rev. John Churchman's *An Explanation of the Magnetic Atlas* (Philadelphia: James & Johnson, 1790, Evans 22406); A. J. Dallas' *Reports* (Philadelphia: For the reporter by T. Bradford, 1790, Evans 22445) was the fourth; and Samuel Sower (*sic*) registered, as proprietor, not author, *Das kleine [davidische] psalterspiel des kinder Zions* (Chestnuthill: Samuel Sauer, 1791, Evans 23197), the eighth Pennsylvania entry.

The second Massachusetts entry was in the name of Isaiah Thomas; this was for Samuel Deane's *The New-England Farmer; or, Georgical Dictionary* (Worcester: Isaiah Thomas, 1790, Evans 22450).

The fourth and fifth New York copyrights were entered on September 8, 1791, in the name of the Hon. Samuel Stearns, "doctor of physic and of the civil and canon laws, astronomer to the provinces of Quebec and New-Brunswick, also to the commonwealth of Massachusetts, and the state of Vermont in America." The titles which he registered were *The American Dispensatory* and *The American Oracle* (Evans 23794 and 23795). The first of these titles is particularly interesting, since it is that of an apparently "lost book." Evans gives no data of publication or location of copies, nor have I improved on his record. It is possible, of course, that *The American Dispensatory* may have become the author's *The American Herbal* printed at Walpole, N. H., in 1801. However this may be, this item brings up the question of lost books which is recurrent in connection with the old copyright records. You will recall that books were entered in them prior to publication, and in the period of 80 years which they cover a considerable number must never have reached the printer's stick.

You may perhaps remember Mrs. Hannah Adams as a petitioner to Congress in 1789 for exclusive rights in her *Alphabetical Compendium of the Various Sects* of which an edition had appeared in 1784. An entry for this work, as the sixteenth Massachusetts copyright, is found under the title *A View of Religions* (Boston [1791], Evans 23102). Again in 1798 our author copyrighted a book in the Massachusetts court, this time *A Summary History of New-England* (Dedham: Printed for the author, by H. Mann and J. H. Adams, 1799, Evans 35075), which was to involve her in controversy with the Rev. Jedidiah Morse.

We need not consider the various changes of the copyright laws from 1790 to 1870, save as these changes affected the records. The first amendment of the law of 1790 was enacted on April 29, 1802, and was effective from January 1, 1803. It added prints to the articles subject to the copyright laws. It also made a new requirement—that notice of copyright registration be printed in the article itself. The provision for the insertion of a notice of copyright in published copyright material has since become one of the most important articles of our copyright credo. It may be noted in passing that the practice was one which was adopted by the publishers without statutory compulsion and for their own protection. Some among the earliest books published under the act of 1790 (I may cite the *Kleine Davidische Psalterspiel* as an example) had on their title-pages the words "Published according to act of Congress." At least one early work, however, Churchman's *Explanation of the Magnetic Atlas*, bore on the verso of the title-page the full certificate as the law required it to be advertised in newspapers. The statutory provision doubtless grew out of this practice.

The law of 1802 did not, nevertheless, much affect the clerks of the district courts or the records they were making for posterity, save as it increased their copyright business by the addition of prints. The law of February 3, 1831, immediately effective, changed it considerably. This act was a complete revision of the copyright laws. It repealed those of 1790 and 1802. The changes which it effected as far as our present interest goes were as follows:

The terms of copyright were increased from 14 years for the original term and 14 years for renewal to 28 and 28 years, respectively. Within 3 months (instead of 6) the claimant was to deposit a copy of his work, not with the Secretary of State as formerly but with the clerk of the court. And, by section 4 of the act, the clerk's duties were extended:

\* \* \* It shall be the duty of the clerk of each district court, at least once in every year, to transmit a certified list of all such records of copyright including the titles so recorded, and the dates of record, and also all the several copies of books and other works deposited in his office according to this act, to the Secretary of State, to be preserved in his office.

The effect of this provision on the records will be seen at a glance. They were to be preserved thenceforth in duplicate.

The act of June 30, 1834, having immediate effect, provided that an assignment of copyright must be recorded in the court "where the original copyright is deposited and recorded." As a result of this, the clerks of many of the courts immediately set up registers of assignments separate from the original entries.

Up to the period at which we are now arrived, it will be noticed that the depository copies required by the law reverted to the Secretary of State, purely for purposes of preservation and legal record. It was now beginning to be realized, however, that the same machinery which was securing a copy for *record* might also secure copies for *use*. Now there were at this time two libraries of the Federal Government, each having in its own way claims to the title of the national library. These were the library of the Smithsonian Institution and the Library of Congress. Consequently, by an act approved August 10, 1846, it was provided that thereafter within 3 months of publication one copy of each copyright article should be delivered to the librarian of the Smithsonian Institution, and one to the Librarian of Congress "for the use of said libraries." An act of March 3, 1855, enabled such articles to be sent free through the mails. These acts are of particular interest, since the whole matter of copyright procedure was to be henceforth dependent upon the issue of the tug of war between the copy for record and the copy for use.

Meanwhile, if the libraries of the Federal Government were eagerly seeking copyright deposits, the Department of State was having a surfeit of them. With the growth of business of the Department, and its specialization in the field of foreign affairs, it lacked room and attention to give to these records of claim. It was felt that the Patent Office, whose functions were invoked by the same section of the Constitution which authorized the copyright laws, and which had a cognate guardianship in the preservation of models of patents, was the appropriate depository. Consequently, by a law approved February 5, 1859, all the records, deposits, and functions of the Department of State with regard to copyright were transferred to the Department of the Interior, of which the Patent Office was a unit. At the same time the law requiring copies to be deposited in the Smithsonian Institution and the Library of Congress was repealed.

In consequence a Copyright Library was organized in the Patent Office, with Edmund Flagg as the librarian, and the records and deposits of the Department of State were transferred to his care. Here they remained until 1870.

The act of March 3, 1865, signalized the arrival of a new art by extending the benefits of the copyright acts to photographs and their negatives. It also renewed the obligation to deposit a copy of every copyright article in the Library of Congress. The time for doing this was reduced to 1 month from the date of publication; the Librarian was required to give a receipt for the article, and if the article should not voluntarily be forthcoming from the publisher, the Librarian was empowered to demand it. Should it not be produced at his demand, the claimant would forfeit copyright.

This law meant only one thing: that the copy for use had suddenly assumed an importance equal if not superior even to that of the copy for record. No provision of law specifically voided copyright for failure to deposit a copy with the district clerk as this law did for failure to deposit with the Librarian of Congress. (Actually, however, the Supreme Court had ruled, in *Wheaton* v. *Peters*, 8 Peters 591, that the deposit of the copy for record was essential to the validity of a copyright, while in *Jollie* v. *Jacques*, 1 Blatchford 618, a United States Circuit Court had ruled that deposit of the copy for use was not essential. This was the reason for the specific penalty mentioned in this act.)

Another change wrought by the passage of time may be noted in this law. In 1865 the Smithsonian Institution was not renamed, as was the Library of Congress, a depository library. Since 1846 a differentiation of function had taken place; the Smithsonian had become more exclusively concerned in the formation of scientific collections, while the Library of Congress had become more nearly a National Library than at the earlier date. The very next year (1866) was to witness the Institution committing even its own library to the care of the Library of Congress, where it still remains as a separate unit, still receiving current accessions.

The provisions of the law of 1865 were strengthened, and certain loopholes closed by an act approved 2 years later (February 18, 1867). A penalty of $25 was provided for failure to transmit the depository copy within 1 month, and the depositor was given protection by authorizing him to exact a receipt from the postmaster into whose hands he committed it.

Thus the matter rested for 3 years. Meanwhile, there was a growing sentiment in favor of wholesale reform of the procedure. Matters of copyright were being handled in some 40 or 50 different offices—for the district courts had long ceased to be the original 13. Depository copies had to be sent to two places; copyright searches were troublesome, involved, and uncertain. At one stroke, therefore, by the act of July 8, 1870, all this business was concentrated. By the simple logic of sending the two depository copies—the one for record, the other for use—to the same official (the one interested in its use), and of giving him authority in all matters of registration and custody, the situation was rendered clear. The copy for use had won the day, and the Librarian of Congress was henceforth required "to perform all acts and duties required by the law touching copyrights." All records and deposits of copyright in the Patent Office and in the District Courts were to be transferred to his custody. It is sufficient to say that they were; that the deposits, numbering 23,070 volumes, were absorbed into the collections of the Library, and that the records are those which we now have under discussion.

Such, in brief (I am afraid not briefly enough), is the history of what may be termed the "ancestors" of the Copyright Office. Let me hasten to describe them.

The records, as a whole, number approximately 615 volumes. These are of five kinds: the original registers kept by the clerks of the District Courts, the copies certified by them to the Secretary of State or to the Secretary of the Interior pursuant to the law of 1831, the records of the Departments of State and of the Interior (Patent Office), the records of the depository libraries (Smithsonian Institution and Library of Congress), and, finally, miscellanea.

*1. The original registers.*—These comprise about 315 volumes; they vary considerably in completeness and uniformity. The records of the New York (later the New York Southern District), of the Pennsylvania (later Pennsylvania Eastern District), and of the Massachusetts District Court are unbroken from 1790 or 1791 to 1870, the records for New York comprising alone 112 volumes plus 3 volumes of assignments from 1834 to 1870. These and the records of other busy courts usually contain indexes in each volume. The titles of the articles submitted by claimants at the time of registration were often tipped in on the very page containing the entry. There are thus preserved to us many interesting specimens of typographic art, not only title pages of books not yet published, but patent-medicine labels, cigar-box linings, photographs, and all the other miscellanea which the copyright laws were called upon to protect.

There are certain important omissions. The Delaware records were said to be filed with the court's dockets and to be not in a condition for transmission to Washington. The Connecticut records, which would contain much early material of interest, lack all entries before No. 115. The Virginia records prior to 1865 are stated to have been destroyed in the fire of Richmond. Many of the States and territories had no records to send at all.

It is interesting to note the advance of the frontier in the date at which the records start in the various districts: Ohio, 1806; Illinois, 1821; Michigan, 1824; Missouri, 1857; California, 1851; Colorado, 1864.

2. *The copies of the original registers.*—From 1831 to 1870 the clerks of the courts were required by law to furnish at least once a year copies of their records to the Secretary of State, later the Secretary of the Interior. The volumes containing these records, nearly 300 in number, furnish a duplicate file from which many gaps in the originals can be closed. This is their whole importance, and beyond this they present no individual interest.

3. (a) *The records of the Department of State.*—The depository copies received in the Department of State from 1796 to 1842 are recorded in 11 volumes. Beginning with 1803 there are notations indicating that a certificate of receipt was issued by the Department. Beginning with 1819 the record is comprised of copies of these certificates on printed forms.

(b) *The records of the Department of the Interior (Patent Office).*—When the deposits of the Department of State were transferred to the Patent Office in 1859, these were recorded in a large ledger, chronologically by date of imprint, alphabetically within each year. There are 7,849 titles, covering copyrights from 1795 to 1858, but there are only 32 titles prior to 1816. Accessions from January 10, 1860, to July 5, 1870, were entered seriatim in two large ledgers numbered from 15001 to 43075.

4. *The records of the depository libraries.*—The accession registers of the Smithsonian Institution, showing the receipts of copyright deposits under the operation of the law from 1846 to 1859 were not among the records of which the transfer to the Librarian of Congress was required by the law of 1870. A disastrous fire in that Institution in 1865 destroyed many of their records up to that year. Similar registers for the Library of Congress are in existence, however, both for the period from 1846–52 and for the period 1865–70.

5. *Miscellanea.*—Here may be placed, for the time being, certain small groups of material which should really be sorted out and placed with the preceding. Among these are letters on copyright matters addressed to or from the District Courts, the Department of State, the Patent Office, and the Library of Congress at the time of the transfer, lists of clerks of the courts, title pages not entered in the registers at the time of original entry, etc.

\*        \*        \*        \*        \*        \*        \*

That these records contain a wealth of information fundamental to the bibliography of the United States needs no emphasis from me. They are the basic sources for a history of our literary and typographic arts for the period which saw those arts spring from the swaddling clothes of the eighteenth century to the giant stature of the nineteenth. At a rough estimate these records may contain 150,000 entries. And this wealth of material is substantially untouched. Evans, indeed, drew upon the single decade prior to 1800 for titles and annotations of entries for his monumental work. The records of the District Courts of Michigan from 1824 to 1870 have been published by Mr. William L. Jenks of Port Huron in the *Michigan History Magazine* from January 1927 to Winter 1931. The entries on accountancy were drawn off by Miss Ruth

S. Leonard for her and Mr. H. C. Bentley's *Bibliography of Works on Accounting by American Authors* (Boston, 1934–35). But of any further publication of the records I am unaware. And yet for more than half a century the crying need of American bibliography has been a complete account of the national literary production.

I should like to be able to tell you that the transfer of deposits from the Department of State to the Patent Office, and thence to the Library of Congress in 1870 was fully representative of the copyright business of the previous 80 years. It was not. At least with respect to the earlier registrations, it is often difficult to trace an identity between books now on our shelves and the original depository copies. When such pedigrees can be established they are interesting, however, and I will give you four examples, taking four well known books from three of the district courts.

Edgar Allan Poe's *The Raven* was registered in the Southern District Court of New York at New York City in the name of the author on November 12, 1845. The entry is found in volume 18, page 247 of the records of the court. A copy of the first edition now on our shelves (PS2609.A1 1845a) bears the endorsement of the district clerk on the title page, "Deposited in the clerk's office for t[he] So. Dist. of New York, Nov. 12, 184[5]." On the verso of the title-page is a number written in red pencil, "6307." This is the number of the entry in the "Register of Copyrights deposited in the United States Patent Office" covering the transfers from the Department of State on April 28, 1859. Finally, on the title-page is the impression of a rubber stamp, "Library of Congress * * * Copyright 1872," indicating its transfer from the Patent Office to its final resting place.

Nathaniel Hawthorne's *The House of the Seven Gables* was registered in the District Court of Massachusetts at Boston on March 1, 1851 (vol. 26, p. 79 of the court records). The Library has a copy of the first edition (PS1861.A1 1851) bearing on the title-page the endorsement "Dep[osite]d May 7, 1851. R[ec]orded Vol. 26 p. 79." I have not found this item in the register of transfers from the Department of State to the Patent Office. It nevertheless found its way eventually to the proper place. A second copy of the first edition bears on the title-page a green label bearing the words "Copyright Dec. 22, 1851." This signifies that this was the depository copy delivered to the Library of Congress under the act of 1846, and accordingly we find in the register of copies received in the Library under that act (p. 227) that a copy was received on that date.

*Uncle Tom's Cabin* was entered in the District Court of Maine at Portland on May 12, 1851 (vol. 1, p. 230 of the court records). I have not been able to find trace of the copy deposited with the clerk and presumably sent by him to the Department of State. However, both the other depository copies are in existence (PZ3.S89. Un. copies 1 and 2). The first volume of one of these bears on the title-page the green label signifying deposition in the Library of Congress, with the date May 26, [1]852, and the receipt of the volumes is recorded in the register under that date (p. 249). Of the other copy both volumes bear the stamp of the Smithsonian Institution.

With respect to another famous book, *The Courtship of Miles Standish*, I have been able to trace all three copies. The registration was made in the Massachusetts Court on October 4, 1858 (vol. 33, p. 566), and a copy was deposited there on October 14. We have this copy (PS2262.A1 1858 copy 2) bearing on the first front end leaf the endorsement of the clerk. I find no record of transfer to the Patent Office. Another copy (copy 3) has the green label indicating that it is the Library of Congress depository copy under the act of 1846, with the date of receipt October 25, 1858 (the register does not, however, come down so late), while a third copy (copy 1) has the Smithsonian Institution stamp on the title-page.

I have roughly estimated the entries in the records as 150,000, while only 23,070 volumes were turned over to the Library in 1870, representing the accumulated deposits of 80 years. The discrepancy surprised the authorities at that day but is susceptible of explanation. In the first place, the entries are in large part (as today) for articles other than books. Secondly, in many cases copyrighted items were never published. Thirdly, in many other cases the depository copy was never submitted, or, if deposited with the clerk of the court, never reached the Department of State or the Patent Office. Finally there were inevitable losses in all these places, due to a lack of personnel and space specifically devoted to the custody of the deposits, to war, fire, the removals over a period of almost a century. Chiefly they were due, perhaps, to a lack of interest in the deposits as mere deposits of record. A conserving interest could have been expected only from a custodian to whom the records would have also been of *use*. For all these reasons, then, the transfer of 1870 represents but a fraction of the whole. And this argues that the whole, which is represented only by the records themselves, should be given publication as soon as possible. They are a national heritage.

## A CHECK-LIST OF THE COPYRIGHT RECORDS PRIOR TO 1870

1. Registers of copyrights maintained by the clerks of the District Courts.

[A check list of the registers received by the Library of Congress is found on p. 3 of a volume filed with the registers, and entitled "Librarian of Congress. Record No. 1. Miscellaneous copyright." Quotations in the following list are from this volume]

California, San Francisco:
    1851–70 ------------------------------------------------------------ **2 v.**
    Assignments 1854–70 --------------------------------------------- **1 v.**
Colorado, Denver—1864–68 ----------------------------------------- **1 v.**
Connecticut, Hartford:
    1804–70 (begins with No. 115) ---------------------------------- **4 v.**
    Assignments ------------------------------------------------------ **1 v.**
Delaware, Wilmington. "Records w. Court Docket cannot be sent."
District of Columbia, Washington—1845–70 ------------------------ **2 v**
Georgia:
    Savannah—1845–70 (including separate volume for title-pages.) ----- **4 v.**
    Atlanta—1848–70 ------------------------------------------------ **1 v.**
Illinois:
    Chicago—1821–70 ----------------------------------------------- **7 v.**
    Springfield—1855–70 -------------------------------------------- **1 v.**
Indiana, Indianapolis—1822–70 (1841–53 wanting) ----------------- **3 v.**
Iowa, Dubuque—1868–70 -------------------------------------------- **1 v.**
Kansas, Topeka—Nos. 1–43, 1865–69 ------------------------ Unbound.
Kentucky, Louisville—1860–70 ------------------------------------- **1 v.**
Louisiana, New Orleans:
    1835 (1 entry) ------------------------------------------- Unbound.
    1851–70 (1856–63 wanting) -------------------------------------- **2 v.**
Maine, Portland—1790–1870 --------------------------------------- **2 v.**
Maryland, Baltimore—1831–70 ------------------------------------- **6 v.**
Massachusetts, Boston:
    1790–1870 ------------------------------------------------------ **45 v.**
    Assignments, 1834–70 ------------------------------------------- **4 v.**

Michigan:
    Detroit—1824–70_____ 5 v.
    Grand Rapids—1863–70_____ 2 v.
Minnesota, St. Paul—1858–70_____ 2 v.
Mississippi, Jackson—1850–70_____ 1 v.
Missouri:
    St. Louis—1857–70_____ 2 v.
    Jefferson City:
        1857–70_____ 1 v.
        Assignments_____ 1 v.
Nebraska, Omaha—1868–70_____ 1 v.
New Hampshire, Manchester—1848–70_____ 2 v.
New Jersey, Trenton—1846–70_____ 2 v.
New York:
    Buffalo—1813–70_____ 16 v.
    New York:
        1791–1870_____ 112 v.
        Assignments 1834–70_____ 3 v.
    Brooklyn:
        1865–70_____ 2 v.
        Assignments 1866–69_____ 1 v.
North Carolina: Cape Fear (Wilmington)—1865–70_____ 1 v.
Ohio, Cincinnati:
    1806–21, 1841–70_____ 10 v.
    Assignments, 1843–63_____ 1 v.
Pennsylvania:
    Philadelphia:
        1790–1870_____ 36 v.
        Assignments 1834–70_____ 2 v.
    Pittsburgh—1819–70_____ 5 v.
    Erie—1868–70_____ 1 v.
Rhode Island, Providence—1831–70_____ 2 v.
Tennessee:
    Nashville—1865–70_____ 1 v.
    Memphis—1865–70_____ 1 v.
Texas, Galveston—1867–70_____ 1 v.
Vermont, Burlington—1831–70_____ 1 v.
Virginia: Richmond—1867–70. "Prior to 1865 destroyed in Richmond
    fire"_____ 1 v.
    Norfolk—1837–70_____ 1 v.
Wisconsin, Milwaukee—1848–70_____ 1 v.

2. Copies of the Court records, and lists of the records and depository copies certified by the Clerks to the Secretary of State, later the Secretary of the Interior. They consist for the most part of printed forms filled out by the Clerks. Unless bound into volumes, these forms remain loose and unbound, tied up in bundles.

Alabama:
    Montgomery—1857–58_____ Unbound.
    Mobile—1858–59_____ Unbound.
Arkansas:
    Little Rock—1837, 1842, 1847, 1854, 1859, 1860, 1865_____ Unbound.
Connecticut, Hartford—1836–53_____ 2 v.
Delaware, Wilmington—1862–65_____ Unbound.
District of Columbia, Washington—1858–64, 1867–68, 1870_____ Unbound.

Illinois:
 Chicago—1861–70_____ Unbound.
 Springfield—1864–69_____ Unbound.
Indiana, Indianapolis—1853–66_____ Unbound.
Kentucky, Louisville—1859–69_____ Unbound.
Maine, Portland:
 1819–28, 1832–53_____ 3 v.
 1857–69_____ Unbound.
Maryland, Baltimore:
 1831–53_____ 2 v.
 1867–69_____ Unbound.
Massachusetts, Boston:
 1831–55_____ 13 v.
 1856–70_____ Unbound.
Michigan:
 Detroit:
  1856–59, 1861–65, 1869_____ 5 v.
  1870_____ Unbound.
  Lists 1857–67_____ Unbound.
 Grand Rapids—1863–66_____ Unbound.
Minnesota, St. Paul—1858–62_____ Unbound.
Missouri:
 St. Louis, 1856_____ Unbound.
 Jefferson City, 1860, 1865–67_____ Unbound.
New Hampshire, Manchester—1857–58, 1869_____ Unbound.
New Jersey, Trenton—1863–68_____ Unbound.
New York, Buffalo:
 1853–60_____ 3 v.
 1860–61_____ Unbound.
 Lists 1855–[62]_____ Unbound.
New York: New York:
 1831–59_____ 136 v.
 1859–68_____ Unbound.
 Indexes 1831–53_____ 2 v.
 Lists, etc_____ Unbound.
North Carolina: Edenton: 1856–59_____ Unbound.
Ohio:
 Cincinnati:
  1831–53_____ 2 v.
  1859–70_____ Unbound.
 Cleveland: 1859, 1861–68_____ Unbound.
Pennsylvania:
 Philadelphia:
  1831–35, 1836–38, 1842–46, 1850–59, 1861–69_____ 25 v.
  Index 1831–53_____ 2 v.
 Pittsburgh:
  1839–41_____ 1 v.
  1859, 1863–69_____ Unbound.
Rhode Island: Providence:
 1831–53_____ 1 v.
 1854–58, 1861–69_____ Unbound.
 Lists 1859, 1865–66_____ Unbound.

Tennessee:
    Nashville: 1848, 1854, 1857_____ Unbound.
    Knoxville: 1858–60__ _____ Unbound.
Vermont: Burlington:1831–53_____ 1 v.
Virginia:
    Richmond: 1867–70_____ 1 v.
    Norfolk: 1858–59_____ Unbound.
Wisconsin: Milwaukee: 1857, 1860–69_____ Unbound.

In addition to the foregoing there are three volumes and two binders containing miscellaneous copies and lists. Should these be sorted out they would somewhat augment the above list.

### 3. Records of Department of State.

Registers of copyrights received, 1796–1842_____ 11 v.
Copyright returns. Records of the returns made by the Clerks, 1853–68___ 1 v.

### 4. Records of Department of the Interior (Patent Office).

Registers of copyrights received, 1859–70_____ 3 v.
Index to copyrights [1]_____ 1 v.
Letter book. Copyright correspondence of the Commissioner of Patents,
    1859–70 [2]_____ 1 v.
Lists of books, prints, photographs, &c., cuttings of patterns, &c., *not*
    registered, taken for the Patent Office Library_____ 1 v.

### 5. Records of the Library of Congress.

Registers of copyrights received, 1846–52, 1865–70_____ 2 v.

[1] Prodromus.
[2] Covers wanting.

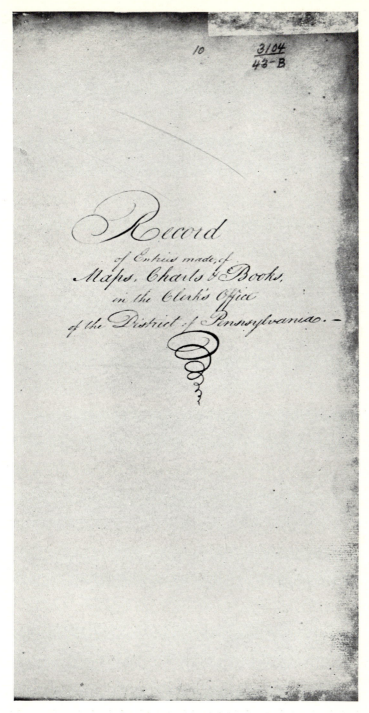

*Record<br>
of Entries made, of<br>
Maps, Charts & Books,<br>
in the Clerk's Office<br>
of the District of Pennsylvania. —*

The title-page of the first volume of the copyright records of the United States
District Court at Philadelphia.

*No. 1.*

District of Pennsylvania, to wit:

Be it remembered, that on the ninth day of June, in the fourteenth year of the independence of the United States of America, John Barry, of the said District, hath deposited in this office, the title of a book, the right whereof he claims as author, in the words following, to wit: — "The Philadelphia Spelling Book arranged upon a plan entirely new, adapted to the capacities of children, and designed as an immediate improvement in spelling and reading the English Language. The whole being recommended by several eminent teachers, as the most useful performance to expedite the instruction of youth. — By John Barry, Master of the Free School of the Protestant Episcopal Church." in conformity to the act of the Congress of the United States, entitled, "An act for the encouragement of learning, by securing the copies of Maps, Charts and Books, to the authors and proprietors of such copies during the times therein mentioned." —

Sam. Caldwell Clerk of the
District of Pennsylvania

*No. 2.*

District of Pennsylvania, to wit:

Be it remembered, that on the fifteenth day of June, in the fourteenth year of the independence of the United States of America, Thomas Wignell of the said District, hath deposited in this Office, the Title

Page 1 of the first volume of the copyright records of the United States District Court at Philadelphia, showing the first entry under the Copyright Act of 1790.

_District of Massachusetts, to wit:_

Be it remembered that on the tenth day of July in the fifteenth year of the Independence of the United States of America, the Rev.d Jedidiah Morse of the said District hath deposited in this Office the titles of two books the right whereof he claims as Author; of one in the words following, to wit: "The American Geography: or a view of the present situation of the United States of America illustrated with two Sheet maps; one of the southern the other of the Northern States, neatly & elegantly engraved & more correct, than any that have hitherto been publish'd. to which is added a concise abridgement of the Geography of the British, Spanish, French & Dutch Dominions in America & the West-Indies, of Europe, Asia & Africa" And of the other in the words following, to wit; "Geography made easy; being an abridgement of the American Geography; — to which is added a geographical Account of the European settlements in America & of Europe, Asia & Africa; illustrated with eight maps or Cuts, calculated particularly for the use & improvement of Schools in the United States. by Jedidiah Morse A.M. Minister of the Congregation in Charlestown near Boston" In conformity to the Act of the Congress of the United States intitled "An Act for the encouragement of learning, by securing the Copies of Maps Charts & books to the Authors & proprietors of such Copies during the times therein mentioned —

N. Goodale Clerk of the

District of Massachusetts

The first page of entries in the first volume of the copyright records of the United States District Court at Boston.

2

*District of Massachusetts — To wit:*

Be it remembered that on the thirteenth day of September in the fifteenth year of the Independence of the United States of America, Isaiah Thomas of the said District, hath deposited in this Office, the title of a Book, the right whereof he claims as Proprietor, in the words following to wit: "The New England Farmer; or, Georgical Dictionary, containing a compendious account of the ways & methods in which the most important Art of Husbandry, in all its various branches, is, or may be practised to the greatest advantage in this country. By Samuel Deane A. M. Fellow of the American Academy of Arts & Sciences — In conformity to the Act of the Congress of the United States, entitled "An Act for the encouragement of learning by securing the copies of maps, charts & books, to the Authors & Proprietors of such copies, during the times therein mentioned"

N. Goodale Clerk of the District of
Massachusetts

---

*District of Massachusetts, To wit:*

Be it remember'd that on the seventh day of October in the fifteenth year of the Independence of the United States of America, Isaiah Thomas & Ebenr. T. Andrews of the said District, have deposited in this Office, the title of a book, the right whereof, in Rhode island, New hampshire & Massachusetts, they claim as Proprietors, in three parts, in the words following to wit: "The American Spelling book, containing an easy standard of Pronunciation. — being the first part of a grammatical institute of the english language; — And of part the second "a grammatical institute of the english language; comprising an easy, concise & systematic method of education designed for the use of english Schools in America;

The second page of entries in the first volume of the copyright records of the United States District Court at Boston.

**DISTRICT OF MAINE—TO WIT:**

**DISTRICT CLERK'S OFFICE.**

BE IT REMEMBERED, That on the *fourteenth day of August AD. 1790* and in the *fifteenth* ———— year of the Independence of the United States of America, *Samuel Freeman* ———— of said District, has deposited in this office, the title of a *book*, the right whereof he claims as *author* ———— in the words following, to wit:

*"The Columbian Primer, on the School-Mistresses Guide to Children in their first steps to Learning. Part I. Containing Words of one & two Syllables. With an Appendix, containing Sundry Matters which Children may be taught to say by Heart. By Samuel Freeman, Esquire."*

In conformity to the act of the Congress of the United States, entitled "An Act for the encouragement of learning, by securing the copies of maps, charts and books, to the authors and proprietors of such copies, during the times therein mentioned:"

*D. Sewall, Clerk of the District of Maine*

---

**DISTRICT OF MAINE—TO WIT:**

**DISTRICT CLERK'S OFFICE.**

BE IT REMEMBERED, that on the *sixth day of December AD. 1791* and in the *sixteenth* ———— year of the Independence of the United States of America, *Rev. Elijah Kellogg* ———— of said District, has deposited in this office, the title of a *book*, the right whereof he claims as *proprietor*, in the words following, to wit:

*"A Discourse to Children. By the Reverend Moses Hemmenway D.D."*

In conformity to the act of the Congress of the United States, entitled "An Act for the encouragement of learning, by securing the copies of maps, charts and books, to the authors and proprietors of such copies, during the times therein mentioned:"

*D. Sewall, Clerk of the District of Maine.*

The first page of the first volume of the copyright records of the United States District Court at Portland, Maine, showing the earliest use of printed forms for this purpose.

*District of New York*. Be it remembered that on the thirtieth day of April in the Fifteenth Year of the Independence of the United States of America Donald Fraser of the said District hath deposited in this Office the title of a Book the right whereof he claims as Author in the words following towit

The
Young Gentleman and Lady's
Assistant;
Partly Original
But chiefly Compiled from the Works of
the most celebrated Modern Authors;
Calculated
To instruct Youth in the principles of
Useful Knowledge:
In five Parts viz,
Geography
Natural History
Elocution,
Poetry — and
Miscellany
To which is annexed — A short System of
Practical Arithmetic;
Wherein every example is wrought at Large,
and the whole
Including the Money of the United States,
rendered easy to the meanest Capacity.
This Work, is divided into small Sections
for the Convenience of Schools.
By Donald Fraser,
School — Master, New — York.—

The first page of entries in the first volume of the copyright records of the United States District Court at New York.

2

conformity to the Act of the Congress of the United States entitled "an Act for the encouragement of Learning by "securing the Copies of Maps, Charts and Books to the "Authors and Proprietors of such Copies during the times "therein mentioned."

*Robt Troup Clerk of the District*

District of New York ss. Be it Remembered that on the first day of June In the Fifteenth Year of the Independence of the United States of America William Linn D.D. of the said District hath deposited in this office the Title of a Book the right whereof he claims as Author in the Words following to wit

Sermons
Historical
and
Characteristical

By William Linn D.D.
One of the Ministers of the reformed Dutch Church In the City of New York

In conformity to the Act of the Congress of the United States entitled "An Act for the encouragement "of Learning by securing the Copies of Maps "Charts and Books to the Authors and Proprietors "of such Copies during the times therein mentioned"

*Robt Troup.*
*Clerk of the District*

---

The second page of entries in the first volume of the copyright records of the United States District Court at New York.

Southern District of New-York, ss.    No. 308

Be it Remembered, That on the *Twelfth*
day of *November* Anno Domini 1845,
*Edgar A. Poe* of the said
District, *hath* deposited in this Office the title of
a *Book*

the title of which is in the words following, to wit:

*The Raven*

*and other Poems.*

*By Edgar A. Poe.*

the right whereof *he* claims as *Author and Proprietor.*
In conformity with an act of Congress, entitled " An Act to amend the several Acts
respecting copy-rights."

*J. W. Metcalf*

Clerk of the Southern District of New-York.

Work deposited this *Twelfth* day of *November* 1845.

Facsimile of the registration of *The Raven,* 1845.

**District of Massachusetts...To wit:**

District Clerk's Office.

BE IT REMEMBERED, That on the *first*
day of *March* Anno Domini 185*1. Nathaniel
Hawthorne* of the said District, ha*s* deposited in this office the
Title of a *Book* the title of which is in the words following, to wit:

*The House*

*of*

*The Seven Gables,*

*A Romance.*

*By*

*Nathaniel Hawthorne.*

the right whereof he claim *s* as *Author* in conformity with an Act of
Congress, entitled "An Act to amend the several Acts respecting Copy-Rights."

*Clerk of the District.*

( *A Copy deposited May 7. 1851.* )

Facsimile of the registration of *The House of the Seven Gables,* 1851.

No 13

**DISTRICT OF MAINE**—TO WIT:

**DISTRICT CLERK'S OFFICE.**

BE IT REMEMBERED, That on the *twelfth day of May A.D. 1851.* and in the *Seventy fifth* year of the Independence of the United States of America, *Mrs H. B. Stowe* of said District, has deposited in this office, the title of a *Book* the right whereof he claims as title of which is in the words following, to wit:

"*Uncle Tom's Cabin, or Life among the Lowly; by Mrs H. B. Stowe.*"

*The right whereof she claims as Author in conformity with an Act of Congress entitled "an Act to amend the several Acts respecting Copy Rights"*

In conformity to the act of the Congress of the United States, entitled "An Act for the encouragement of learning, by securing the copies of maps, charts and books, to the authors and proprietors of such copies, during the times therein mentioned;" and also to an act, entitled "An Act supplementary to an act, entitled an act for the encouragement of learning, by securing the copies of maps, charts and books, to the authors and proprietors of such copies, during the times therein mentioned, and for extending the benefits thereof to the arts of designing, engraving and etching historical and other prints."

*Copy deposited April 1. 1852*

*Wm P. Preble*
Clerk of the District of Maine.

---

No 14

**DISTRICT OF MAINE**—TO WIT:

**DISTRICT CLERK'S OFFICE.**

BE IT REMEMBERED, That on the *twelfth day of May A.D. 1851.* and in the *Seventy fifth* year of the Independence of the United States of America, *Wm Hyde* of said District, has deposited in this office, the title of a *Book* the right whereof he claims as title of which is in the words following, to wit:

"*The Mother Rewarded and the Son Reclaimed; a Temperance Narration*
"*Many a hand that friendship plighted, Have I clasped with all delighted*
"*But more faithful none can be, Than my mother's hand to me. Montgomery*
"*Portland: William Hyde & Son. 1851*"

*The right whereof he claims as Proprietor in conformity with an Act of Congress entitled "An Act to amend the several acts respecting Copy Rights"*

In conformity to the act of the Congress of the United States, entitled "An Act for the encouragement of learning, by securing the copies of maps, charts and books, to the authors and proprietors of such copies, during the times therein mentioned;" and also to an act, entitled "An Act supplementary to an act, entitled an act for the encouragement of learning, by securing the copies of maps, charts and books, to the authors and proprietors of such copies, during the times therein mentioned; and for extending the benefits thereof to the arts of designing, engraving and etching historical and other prints."

*Copy deposited Oct 21. 1851.*

*Wm P. Preble*
Clerk of the District of Maine.

Facsimile of the registration of *Uncle Tom's Cabin*, showing the use in 1851 of the forms printed in 1790 and adapted for use in 1802 by the addition of three and a half lines of print.

# District of Massachusetts....To wit:

### District Clerk's Office.

BE IT REMEMBERED, That, on the *Fourth*
day of *October* Anno Domini 185*8*, *Henry Wadsworth*
*Longfellow* of the said District, has deposited in this Office the
Title of a *Book* the title of which is in the words following, to wit:

*The*

*Courtship of Miles Standish*

*And*

*Other Poems.*

*By*

*Henry Wadsworth Longfellow*

_____

the right whereof he claims as *Author* in conformity with an Act of
Congress, entitled, "An Act to amend the several Acts respecting Copyrights."

*J. P. Hallett* Clerk of the District.

(*A Copy deposited October 14, 1858.*)

Facsimile of the registration of *The Courtship of Miles Standish*, 1858.

# THE RECORD OF AMERICAN IMPRINTS

## By
## DOUGLAS C. McMURTRIE
### CHICAGO HISTORICAL SOCIETY

# THE RECORD OF AMERICAN IMPRINTS [1]

Insistence on almost exclusive dependence upon original sources appears to be the most significant trend in modern historical work. Original source material may be divided roughly into three classifications: Manuscripts, newspapers, and printed material in the form of books, pamphlets, or broadsides.

The value of manuscript material has long been recognized and much effort has been put into the discovery and record of existing manuscripts. A number of institutions have published finding lists or calendars of their holdings, and the Carnegie Institution has rendered a great service to American scholarship by preparing and issuing printed guides to manuscript material of American interest in overseas archives.

For years Dr. Clarence S. Brigham, the distinguished director of the American Antiquarian Society, has been seeking and recording American newspapers published before 1821. Single copies as well as files are comprehended in his exceedingly thorough bibliography. A number of historical societies have published lists of their newspapers, and university libraries, such as Yale and Duke, have provided a printed record of their newspaper holdings. Only recently was completed the monumental *Union List of Newspapers*, which supplements the Brigham record with a finding list of newspapers later than 1820.

A most important class of historical material, however, is represented by contemporary books, pamphlets, and broadsides. The very fact of their printing, at considerable effort and expense, bears testimony to the current importance of, and public interest in, the material presented. Most pieces of early printed matter carry in the lower portion of the title page or at the bottom of a single sheet, a note as to the place and date of printing and the name of the printer. These data are known collectively to the bibliographer as the "imprint." In consequence, pieces of printing produced at places and dates rendering them of special interest have come to be known as "imprints."

There were numerous sporadic efforts to list the issues of the early American press of the seventeenth and eighteenth centuries, but a major undertaking which dwarfs by comparison all other efforts in this field was the compilation and publication by Charles Evans of his *American Bibliography*. There have already appeared 12 substantial volumes of this important work covering the record of printing in English-speaking North America from its beginnings in Cambridge in 1639 down through the middle of the alphabet of authors of works printed in 1799. The arrangement is chronological, the imprints of each year being grouped together and arranged alphabetically by authors within any given year. Evans covered the holdings of the more important libraries and historical societies in the eastern portion of the country, giving full titles, collations, and pagination of such imprints as he saw personally or of which full record was contributed by others. His work has some minor faults, but we can only wonder at its thoroughness and magnitude when we consider that all

---

[1] Presented at the annual conference of historical societies, held in Philadelphia on December 31, 1937.

the work involved in its compilation was done by the hands of one man, unaided even by a clerk or secretary. Every title in these volumes was personally written out in pen and ink by Mr. Evans. Charles Evans is thus entitled to high honor by historians for the valuable contribution he has made to the record of source materials for American history.

Another pioneer in the field of American bibliography was Joseph Sabin, who undertook the compilation and publication of a monumental *Dictionary of Books Relating to America* which, after several delays, has now been carried to completion by several groups of successors. This work lists not only books printed in what is now the United States but also all books relating to both Americas without respect to the place or language of their publication. In spite of the breadth of its scope many American imprints of interest are found recorded "in Sabin."

There have been issued numerous excellent original lists of imprints, such as those for Pennsylvania by Hildeburn, for Maryland by Wroth, for Connecticut by Trumbull, and so forth. It is significant, however, that almost all of these lists deal with the issues of the press of the States along the Atlantic seaboard with the year 1800, or the year 1820, as their terminal date.

But American history in our present conception covers a wider field than the Atlantic seaboard. If we wish to understand fully and record adequately the history of the United States, we must deal also with that vast territory extending from the Alleghenies to the Pacific Ocean. Any bibliography taking 1800 as its terminal date automatically excludes most of the present area of the United States, for the reason that the printing press in the majority of the States had not begun to function by that date. It is manifest, therefore, that we must set up new date limits for the newer geographical areas. If we take 1800 as a logical terminal date for a bibliography of Boston, Philadelphia, or New York imprints, we must thus set up other and later dates for the Western States in order to take in a comparable range of historical material. There could be endless argument as to what terminal dates should be adopted, and one man's opinion is doubtless as good as another's in this field. For my own work in recording American imprints, however, in the effort to establish comparable dates, I fixed upon 1830, for example, for Ohio, West Virginia, and Kentucky; 1850 for Michigan, Indiana, Illinois, and Wisconsin; 1870 for Kansas and Nebraska; 1890 for most of the Rocky Mountain States; and 1876 for the three States bordering the Pacific Ocean. It has seemed to me that such date limits will insure inclusion of most issues of the press during the pioneer period when printing was an adventure rather than a business. Without going into too much detail, it can be said that up until a few years ago practically no efforts had been made to discover and record western imprints of historical importance.

The larger the book or pamphlet the better, it seems, has been its chance of preservation. The slender pamphlet, leaflet, or broadside was evidently subject to numerous hazards which have resulted, in some instances, in the destruction of almost all of the edition printed, and in other cases in the disappearance of every copy.

The historians who have so carefully inventoried manuscript materials in various institutions at home and abroad have for the most part ignored printed material, on the assumption that, being printed, it had a wide distribution and was therefore generally available for consultation in libraries throughout this country. But in many cases printed matter is just as rare as manuscript, being known in only a single extant copy. Any assumption to the contrary may result in our missing records which often prove of far greater importance than manuscripts in the same collection.

I think I can best demonstrate to you the rarity of printed material by telling you of a number of pamphlets and broadsides of vital historical interest which were once not known to exist at all and are now known only from a single surviving copy.

My first conviction that printed matter was often as rare as manuscript material was coincident with my first work in the field of American bibliography, which happened to concern Louisiana. In the summary at the back of the Evans volumes I read that the first printing in Louisiana was done in 1797, but when I came to consult imprints material at the New York Public Library, I found that the late Dr. Wilberforce Eames had found one New Orleans pamphlet of 1768 bearing the imprint of a specific printer and a clearly stated date. It was no wonder, however, that Mr. Evans missed this imprint in his round of the eastern libraries from Washington to Boston, for the two extant copies were only to be found overseas—one at Paris, the other at Seville. Other early Louisiana imprints were found scattered to the four winds, apparently unique copies of certain items being found in libraries in New York; Berkeley, Calif.; San Marino, Calif.; etc. During the course of more intensive work on these Louisiana imprints I was successful in turning up in New Orleans two pamphlets bearing the date of 1765 and finally a broadside of 1764 bearing a New Orleans imprint. Since during this latter year a local printer was known to have applied to the French authorities for exclusive license to print in Louisiana, I was apparently at the end of the trail and had found an imprint of the first year of printing in that colony.

My earliest interest was in the printing of the Western States, which had received so little attention at the hands of bibliographers, but fate threw into my hands some early printed materials for the Southern States which were of such importance that they could not be overlooked. For example, in reading the inventory of manuscripts of American interest in the Public Record Office at London, I ran across the listing of a letter from a colonial governor to the Board of Trade, at the end of which were added these two interesting words: "printed enclosures." I had these printed enclosures looked up and photostated, and found them to be imprints of the greatest significance, not only for the history of the press but also for the general history of the colony.

For some years South Carolina endeavored, without success, to persuade a printer to settle in Charleston. Finally, the legislature offered a bonus of £2,000, proclamation money, to be given any printer who would permanently settle there, print a newspaper, and publish the laws. Three printers arrived in Charleston in response to this offer, each claiming the proffered bonus. From the legislative records we know their names—Thomas Whitmarsh, Eleazer Phillips, and George Webb. The first named, who went there as a partner of Benjamin Franklin, began early in 1732 to print the successful *South-Carolina Gazette*, a practically full file of which has been preserved. Phillips is known to have begun publication early in 1732 of the *South-Carolina Journal*, but not a single copy of this newspaper has ever come to light, although it was published regularly for about 6 months. Its very existence is known only from a demand for payment of subscriptions for the period during which it was published. No record whatever had ever been found of the third printer applying for the bonus, George Webb.

When the photostats ordered arrived from London, I confess that I opened them with lively anticipation. This anticipation quickly turned into what is colloquially known as a "kick," when I found in the package photo-duplicates of four South Carolina imprints of 1731, a year earlier than any printing had previously been known to have been done in that colony. But that was not all, for one of the four, a pamphlet of six pages, bore at the bottom of the last page the clear and explicit imprint, "Charles-Town: Printed by George Webb," so the record of our three printers was now complete, and we were for the first time in position to make quite specific statements regarding the beginnings of printing in South Carolina.

I could go on for a long time reporting on the discovery of hitherto unknown printed material in the most surprising places, but time forbids.

A new approach to the bibliography of historical source material is now being made by one activity of the Works Progress Administration—the American Imprints Inventory, which is now functioning on a nation-wide scale. This work forms part of the program of the Historical Records Survey, under the able direction of Dr. Luther H. Evans, who has asked me to provide the technical direction for the imprints work. I am thus happy to report to you that work is now under way in many States, recording imprints which will be compiled into State or regional lists and made available in mimeographed form. It is as yet too early to make any promises, but what work is being done is being done well. I am personally confident that this program under Works Progress Administration auspices will go far toward filling the present need for an adequate record of American imprints.

# LIST OF MANUSCRIPT COLLECTIONS RECEIVED IN THE LIBRARY OF CONGRESS, JULY 1931 TO JULY 1938

COMPILED BY

## C. PERCY POWELL

# CONTENTS

# PREFATORY NOTE

*A List of Manuscript Collections in the Library of Congress to July, 1931,* compiled by Curtis W. Garrison, was printed in the *Annual Report* of the American Historical Association for 1930. The collections were presented according to six chronological periods of American history. This method of presentation proved to be satisfactory and has been used in listing the collections acquired since 1931. In a like manner, many features of the prior list have been adopted.

The entries in the following list were selected from information recorded on the accession cards in the Manuscripts Division. No account was taken of accessions containing fewer than twenty-five (25) pieces, unless they were deemed exceptional. Certain other materials, such as printed matter, political posters, transcripts, and Oriental manuscripts were not included.

Persons interested in using manuscript collections should keep in mind such variables as size and restrictions. A collection contained in a single box may be supplemented and shortly appear in a series of bound volumes. Restrictions are constantly added, removed, and altered. The term "restricted" in a specific entry will be explained upon request.

Help in preparing this list was given me by Mr. J. J. de Porry, Mr. D. H. Mugridge, and my wife.

C. PERCY POWELL.

THE LIBRARY OF CONGRESS, *July 1938.*

## LIST OF MANUSCRIPT COLLECTIONS RECEIVED IN THE LIBRARY OF CONGRESS, JULY 1931 TO JULY 1938

### I. PERIOD OF EXPLORATION AND COLONIZATION, 1492–1774

Account Books: Account books of iron works, etc., Maryland, 1745–1835. 6 vols.

Allen, Ethan. *Author.* "Synodalia," or Records of Clergy Meetings in Maryland Between 1695 and 1773. Compiled by Ethan Allen, 1864. Photostats. c. 260 pages.

America. British Colonies. Photostats of the Vice-Admiralty Court Records of North Carolina, 1728–58 (except the year 1738). 4 vols. 389 pages. Photostats of the Minutes of the Vice-Admiralty Court of Charleston, S. C., 1716–63. 9 ms. boxes.

Amory Family. Correspondence of Thomas Amory (1682–1728), dated from 1697 to 1739. c. 166 pieces, half in Portuguese. Five letterbooks, dated 1711–28. Scrapbook relating to Rebekah Holmes Amory, 1723–44. Correspondence of Thomas Amory (1762–1823), dated 1802–04, about 358 pieces. A letterbook of Thomas Amory (1762–1823), dated 1798–99.

Asylum Company. Pennsylvania. Minutes of Proceedings, April 23, 1794, to June 7, 1797. 1 vol.

Ball, Joseph. Letterbook for the years 1743 to 1759. In the same volume is the letterbook of Rawleigh Downman for the years 1760 to 1780.

Briggs, Isaac. A volume of miscellaneous letters dated from 1691 to 1886. Restricted.

Carroll, Charles of Annapolis, Father of Charles Carroll of Carrollton. Eighty-seven pieces dated 1661–1771. 1 vol. Catalogued.

Charles, Duke of Marlborough. Commission by George II, King of Great Britain, dated March 30, 1738.

Conway, George R. G. Nine bound volumes of typewritten transcripts and translations of manuscripts in Mexican archives and in the library of Mr. Conway. Jews in Mexico, 1625–49. Don Rodrigo de Vivero, 1597–1673. Diaries of Padre Miguel de la Campa and Padre Benito de la Sierra. Also four volumes relating to (1) Don Tristan de Luna y Arrellano, (2) Elizabethan sailors and the Mexican Inquisition Auto de Fe, 1574, (3) Martin Lopez Ossorio, 1624, (4) British subjects in Spanish possessions, 1660–1786.

Copley, John Singleton (1738–1815). *Painter.* Miscellaneous papers, dated 1767–99. About 45 pieces.

Downman, Rawleigh. See Ball, Joseph.

Fitzgerald, John. Fifty-two pieces dated from 1756 to 1797. Commercial. Alexandria, Virginia. Catalogued.

Franklin, Benjamin (1706–90). *Statesman. Diplomat.* Photostats of original manuscripts in the Pierpont Morgan Library. 1 ms. box. Restricted.

Germany. Two ordinances relating to the minting of money. One is by Kurfurst Moritz of Saxony, dated March 27, 1549; the other by Charles V, dated July 24, 1550. German script. Apparently contemporary copies.

Graffenried, Baron de (1661–1743). Narrative of Christopher, Baron de Graffenried's voyage to America, dated mainly 1711. Recent copy and preface. (In German and French, resp.).

Gregg Collection 1716–1916. Miscellaneous papers of Andrew Gregg, David McMurtrie Gregg, Joseph Hiester, and others, dated from 1716 to 1916. Several accounts of military marches and the autobiography [copy] of Conrad Weiser are included. Letterbook, D. M. Gregg, 1863–64. 2 bound volumes and 2 ms. boxes. Catalogued.

Hanschurst, Sarah. Letterbook, dated 1762, at Sterling, N. Y., to persons in New York. 1 vol.

Journals & Diaries. (1) [Diary of Captain John Evans kept on a trip from South Carolina to the Indian Country in 1708.] 1 vol. (2) Diary [Samuel Fisher] kept during operations around Lake George, 1758. 12 pages. Photostat. (3) Journal relating to the navigation of the Mississippi River, with descriptions of adjacent territories. Date c. 1770. 1 vol. (4) Diary of Lieut. Spaulding describing activities near Lake George [July] 30 to Nov. 2, 1758. Film negative and prints. 17 pages. (5) Journal of James Wolfe, Major General, British Army, May 10–Aug. 7, 1759. 22 pages. Photostat. Descriptive notes by E. L. Judah. 1 page mimeograph.

Louisiana & Texas. Hand-written transcripts of important documents relating to boundaries. Letters of Talamantes and documents of Pichardo. 1630–1812. 1,551 pages. Catalogued.

Meneses, Sebasteaõ Cesar de. Eleito Bispo de Coimbra. Summa politica. Offrecida ao Principe Dn. Theodosio de Portugal. 1650. 1 vol.

Mexico. See Conway, George R. G.

Moore, James (1667–1740). *Speaker of the Assembly of South Carolina.* Mainly drafts of messages of the Governor, dated Jan.–April 1721. 30 pieces.

New Jersey. Rolls of the Swedish troops stationed in Swedish forts on the Delaware River in New Sweden, 1637–55. Photostats. 35 pages.

North Carolina. Vice-Admiralty Records. See America, British Colonies.

Orderly Books. (1) Book kept by a provincial officer in the forces of General Amherst at Lake George, July 27 to Aug. 4, 1759. 1 vol.

Pinckney Family of South Carolina. Papers, dated 1744–1825. c. 570 pieces in 8 ms. boxes. Deposit. Restricted.

Rolland, Nicolaus Adrianus. Philosophia seu Phisica tradita. 1 vol.

Sandys, Edwin (Sir, 1561–1629). *Statesman.* Photographs of some 20 letters written to him between 1619 and 1621.

Thatcher, Herbert. Collection of miscellaneous material on American Colonial History. Typewritten copy, "Causes of American Revolution." Bibliographical notes. Photostats of maps and other documents in the British Public Record Office. 14 ms. boxes.

Virginia, Alexandria.   (1) Proceeding of Board of Trustees of Alexandria, Virginia, dated from 1749 to 1767.  55 pages.   (2) Fairfax County land records, court orders, deeds, dated 1742–73.  3 vols.  Copy.

Wolfe, James.   See Journals & Diaries.

Zuendt zu Kenzingen, Ernst Anton.   Letters, documents, plays, poems, press clippings, photographs, etc., relating to the Zuendt and Fugger families, dated 1697–1899.  64 pieces.

## II. THE REVOLUTIONARY AND CRITICAL PERIOD, 1774–1789

Account Books.   (1) "Account Book for the Estate of The Right Honble. Thomas Lord Fairfax, dece'd.  Entered in another Book" dated Dec. 9, 1781–May 13, 1786.  A. D. 1 vol.   (2) Parkinson & Burr, May 26 to Aug. 4, 1787. 1 vol.   (3) Account books of James and Henry Ritchie and James Ritchie & Co., Essex County, Va., dated 1771–77.  12 pieces.   (4) Time Oar Coal Iron Book, dated 1774–76, 1779–80.  1 vol.   (5) Account books of iron works, etc., Maryland, 1745–1835.  6 vols.   (6) Personal accounts of Seth and Aristachus Griffin, farmers of Granby, Conn., 1789–1819.  Typewritten carbon.  36 pages.

Alaska.   Papers of the Russian Church in Alaska for the period preceding the purchase of Alaska by the United States, dated 1772 to about 1867.  702 ms. boxes.

Appleton, Nathaniel.   *Merchant.*   Papers relating to the transportation of paper money, etc., 1779–92.  57 pieces.

Black, Joseph (1728–99).   Lectures on Chemistry.  1 vol.  Contemporary copy [c. 1785].

Briggs, Isaac.   One volume of letters and documents ranging in dates from 1691 to 1886.  Restricted.

[Bruce, Alexander.]   "A Discovery Relative to War, Etc."  A. D. 1 vol.

Collins, Stephen, & Son.   *Philadelphia Merchants.*   (a) Memoranda of accounts, 1770–72.  1 vol.   (b) Account book and letterbook combined, 1772–74.  1 vol. (c) Miscellaneous papers, 1772–1814.  40 pieces.

Dunlop Family (1775–1872).   James Dunlop, II, 1775–85; James Dunlop, III, 1793–1872; Robert P. Dunlop.  Papers contained in 2 ms. boxes and 9 packages.

Filhiol, Juan, and his descendants.   Documents, letters, pamphlets, and map relating to grant of land including Hot Springs, Ark., dated 1783–1904.  c. 60 pieces.  Deposit.

Fitzerald, John.   Fifty-two pieces dated from 1756 to 1797; mainly commercial and relating to Alexandria, Va.  Catalogued.

Gallatin, Gaspard-Gabriel, Baron.   Narrative of the voyage of Rochambeau's army from Brest, France, to Rhode Island, 1780–81, A. D. 3 vol.  Also a journal of the siege of Yorktown.  A. D. 1 vol.

Gregg Collection 1716–1916.   Miscellaneous papers of Andrew Gregg, David McMurtrie Gregg, Joseph Hiester, and others, dated from 1716 to 1916.  Several accounts of military marches, and the autobiography of Conrad Weiser [copy] are included.  2 vols., 2 ms. boxes and a letterbook for 1863–64.  Catalogued.

Hazard, Arnold.   Account of expenditures on voyages in the brig *Hope*, dated 1773–78.  1 vol. unbound.

Hemsley, William.   Papers relating to the tobacco business, etc., dated 1784–86. 40 pieces.

Henry, Patrick (1736–99).   *Statesman.*   Miscellaneous papers, dated 1762–1801. 47 pieces.

Huie, Reid, & Company.   Letterbook kept at Dumfries, Va., from Dec. 25, 1788, to April 7, 1791.  Fragmentary.

Hunt, William.   Books kept by William Hunt, Assistant Commissary of Issues at Watertown, Mass.  3 vols.  2 daybooks and 1 journal, dated 1775–78.

Jefferson, Thomas (1743–1826).   *Third President of the United States.*   Catalogue cards for the papers (1767–1826) of Thomas Jefferson in the Massachusetts Historical Society.  136 pages of photostats.

Jones, John Paul (1747–92).   *Naval Officer.*   Documents mainly relating to charges of assault brought by Katerina Stepanova against John Paul Jones, 1788–89.  25 pages.  Photostats.  Also English translation.

Journals & Diaries. (1) Journal kept by William Alexander (Lord Stirling) from Jan. 1 to April 17, 1779. 1 vol. (2) Diary of Samuel Vaughan, a London merchant, kept on a tour to Fort Pitt, thence through Virginia, Maryland, and Pennsylvania, dated June 18 to Sept. 4, 1787. Photostat. (3) Philadelphischer Calender auf das Jahr 1775. Printed book filled with pages of manuscript (diary, Jan. 1–Dec. 12, 1775) in German script. 1 vol.

Lafayette, Marquis de (1757–1834). *French Statesman and Soldier.* Letters written between 1779 and 1834. 63 pieces. Photostats. Catalogued. Restricted.

Lowndes, William (1782–1822). *Congressman from South Carolina.* Papers of William Lowndes and other members of his family, dated 1787–1842. 1 ms. box.

Madison, James (1750–1836). *Fourth President of the United States.* Papers of, or relating to, James Madison and Dolly Payne Madison, dated from 1779 to 1852. 57 pieces.

Mason, Kender. Statement of money received from Great Britain for victualling troops, vessels, and rebel prisoners in East Florida from 1778 to 1780. Parchment roll about 13 feet long.

Mersereau, Joshua. Account book of Joshua Mersereau, Deputy Commissary of Prisoners, for expenses incurred in conveying of prisoners from Burgoyne's Army from Saratoga to Cambridge, dated Dec. 2, 1777 to Feb. 1779. 1 vol.

McHenry, James (1753–1816). *Secretary of War, 1796–1801.* Correspondence and miscellaneous papers. c. 50 pieces. Photostats.

Morris, Gouverneur (1752–1816). *Statesman. Diplomat.* Collection of 52 items. Included are: 2 vols. legal memoranda prior to 1776, bankbook 1782–88, 13 vols. of his diary, 14 vols. of his letters, miscellaneous account books, cash books, etc. Restricted. List made by D. H. Mugridge.

Orderly Books. (1) Orderly book of Captain Jeremiah Marston, dated June 24 to Nov. 2, 1762.

Paterson, William. Notes covering "Mr. Randolph's Proposition 29 May 1787" and "Col. Hamilton's Plan" for a constitution. Typewritten. 47 pages. Photostats.

Pinckney, Thomas (1750–1828). *Soldier. Diplomat. Governor of South Carolina.* Correspondence of members of the Pinckney, Horry, Huger, Motte, and Rutledge families, dated 1751–1847. 2 ms. boxes.

Pinckney Family of South Carolina. Additional papers, dated 1744–1825. c. 570 pieces in 8 ms. boxes. Deposit. Restricted.

Shippen Family. Additional papers, dated 1773–93. 1 ms. box.

Society of the Cincinnati. Papers of the Society, dated 1784–1936. c. 399 pieces. Deposit. Restricted. Listed. Minute book of the Standing Committee of the Society, 1872–1938. A. Ds. S. and typewritten Ds. S. 1 vol. Deposit. Restricted.

Stoddert, Rebecca Lowndes (Mrs. Benjamin Stoddert). Letters dated 1766–1840. 40 pieces.

Strachey, Henry (Sir) 1736–1810. *Politician.* Letters to and from Sir Henry Strachey, dated 1776–83. 16 pieces.

Teall, Oliver. Narrative of the Life of Oliver Teall, Revolutionary Soldier, written by Himself. A copy by his son, Harry Teall. 4 pages.

Thacher, James. Collection of 32 letters, 1780–83, 1804–42. Photostats.

Thornton, Sir Edward. Memoirs, mainly 1766–93. 1 vol.

Tilghman, Tench (1744–86). *Soldier.* Washington's aide-de-camp. Diary and accounts relating to services for the Indian Commission dated from July 28, 1775 to Dec. 5, 1775. 36 pages. Also diary and accounts relating to operation at Yorktown dated from Sept. 22, 1781 to Oct. 18, 1781. 20 pages. Photostats.

Tong, William. Autobiography of William Tong, soldier in Maryland militia during the War of the American Revolution. Typewritten. 5 pages.

Turner, Peter. *Surgeon.* Letters, diaries, accounts, etc., dated 1772–89. c. 100 pieces.

United States. Constitution. Broadsides relating to the U. S. Constitution, dated 1787–90, 1794. Positive photostats of 43 pieces. Transferred from the U. S. Constitution Sesquicentennial Commission.

Van Schaak, Peter (1747–1832), and Others. Collection of Peter Van Schaak, Henry, and David Van Schaak, dated 1776–1841. 53 pieces.

Wadsworth, Jeremiah (1743–1804). *Soldier. Congressman from Connecticut.* Miscellaneous letters, 1777–1833. c. 90 pieces. Photostats.

Washington, George (1732–99). *First President of the United States.* Photostats of original letters and documents now in the possession of various libraries and individuals. In virtually every instance copies of the original as made by Washington exist in the Papers of George Washington in the Library of Congress.

Washington, Martha. Twelve letters, 1774–97. Photostats from the originals in the Henry E. Huntington Library.

Wilson, James (1742–98). Papers relating to the Federal Convention of 1787. 42 pages. Photostats.

### III. PERIOD OF ESTABLISHMENT AND ADJUSTMENT, 1789–1815

Account Books. (1) Phineas Brown account book dated 1785–1818. 1 vol. (2) Day book of the Cumberland Forge, Maryland, 1802. 1 vol. (3) Day book of Samuel Davidson of Georgetown, D. C. 1801–10. 1 vol. (4) Account book of Isaac Grubb, dated 1772–90. 1 vol. (5) Account book of the Manufacturing Society of Philadelphia, dated Nov. 12, 1788 to Mar. 29, 1790. 1 vol. (6) Accounts of the executors of the estate of Christopher Smith, dated 1804–11, Louisa County, Virginia. 1 vol. (7) Accounts of a tanyard, dated 1796–1805. Louisa County, Virginia. 1 vol.

Alaska. Papers of the Russian Church in Alaska for the period preceding the purchase of Alaska by the United States, dated 1772 to about 1867. 702 ms. boxes.

Amory Family. Correspondence of Thomas Amory (1682–1728), dated from 1697 to 1739. c. 166 pieces, one-half in Portguese. Five letter-books, dated 1711–28. Scrapbook relating to Rebekah Holmes Amory, dated 1723–44. Correspondence of Thomas Amory (1762–1823), dated 1802–04. c. 358 pieces, and a letterbook dated 1798–99.

Bartlett, Josiah, Jr. (1768–1838). *Physician.* Papers, dated 1790–1838. 22 ms. boxes.

Bradley, Stephen Row (1754–1830). *Jurist.* William C. Bradley, Mark Richards, and others. Collection of letters dated from 1777 to 1881. c. 500 pieces.

Briggs, Isaac. Book of letters dated from 1691 to 1886, to Isaac Briggs and others from Thomas Jefferson and others. Deposit. Restricted.

Campbell, George Washington (1769–1848). *U. S. Senator. Secretary of Treasury.* 77 pieces, dated 1793–1844. Catalogued.

Collier, John Payne. Notes by Collier in shorthand on the 9th and 12th lectures of Samuel T. Coleridge on William Shakespeare. 37 pages. Photostats.

Collins, Stephen, & Son. *Philadelphia Merchants.* (a) Memoranda of accounts dated 1770–72. 1 vol. (b) Account book and letterbook combined, dated 1772–74. 1 vol. (c) Miscellaneous papers, dated 1772–1814. 40 pieces.

Copley, John Singleton (1738–1815). *Painter.* Miscellaneous papers dated 1767–99. c. 45 pieces.

Cox, James, Jr. Miscellaneous letters received, dated 1780–1857. c. 108 pieces.

Croghan Family. Papers of William Croghan, William, Jr., John, George, and Charles, dated 1789–1848. 2 ms. boxes.

Denison, Gideon. Letterbooks concerning the business of Gideon Denison, merchant in Savannah, Georgia, dated 1789–94. 2 vols.

Dunlop Family. James Dunlop, II, 1775–85, James Dunlop, III, 1793–1872, Robert P. Dunlop. Papers contained in 2 ms. boxes and 9 packages.

Ellicott, Andrew (1754–1820). *Surveyor and Mathematician.* Correspondence dated 1796–1800. 3 vols.

Filhiol, Juan, and his descendants. Documents, letters, pamphlets, and map, relating to the grant of land including Hot Springs, Ark., dated 1783–1904. c. 60 pieces. Deposit.

Foster, Augustus John (Sir). Notes on the United States of America collected in the years 1804 to 1812. 5 vols.

Georgia. Papers relating to the Yazoo land grants of the State of Georgia, dated from 1790 to 1815. 46 pieces. Catalogued.

Gerry, Elbridge (1744–1814). *Statesman.* Letterbook for Sept. 21, 1797 to Jan. 20, 1801. 1 vol. Photostats. Restricted.

Gregg Collection 1716–1916. Miscellaneous papers of Andrew Gregg, David McMurtrie Gregg, Joseph Hiester, and others, dated from 1716 to 1916. Several accounts of military marches and the autobiography [copy] of Conrad Weiser are included. 2 vols., 2 ms. boxes and a letterbook of D. M. Gregg for 1863–64.

Hall, Elihu and Washington Hall. Business and financial records dated 1777–1849. Baltimore, Md. 12 vols.

Hamilton, Alexander (1757–1804). *Statesman. Secretary of Treasury.* Letters and documents relating to financial matters, dated 1789–1802. 17 pieces.

Harrison, William Henry (1773-1841). *Ninth President of the United States.* Miscalleous papers, dated from 1735 to 1860. c. 70 pieces. Catalogued.

Homer, Arthur. Bibliography of books and pamphlets, etc., relating to the slave trade & African Company trading to the West Indies. A. D. 1 vol.

Jefferson, Thomas (1743–1826). *Third President of the United States.* (a) Account book, Jan. 1, 1791–Dec. 28, 1803. (b) Account book, Jan. 1, 1804–June 25, 1826. Photostats. (c) Catalogue cards for the papers (1767–1826), of Thomas Jefferson in the Massachusetts Historical Society. 136 pages. Photostats.

Jesup, Thomas Sidney (1788–1860). *Soldier.* Papers, dated 1810–59. 17 letter file boxes, 7 ms. boxes, 2 vols. of letterbook for 1846–47.

Journals & Diaries. (1) Journal of a cruise on board the U. S. S. *President,* of 44 guns, Commodore S. Barron, Commander, Cape Henry to Tripoli, July–Nov. 1804. A. D. 1 vol. (2) Journal of Major Lewis Bond covering June 1812 to May 1813, recording the Battle and Massacre of River Raisin. 1 vol. (3) Diary of John Brown, of Lewiston, Penn., dated Dec. 10, 1794 to July 30, 1795. Typewritten copy. 38 pages.

Kentucky. Opinions of the Court of Appeals, 1790–1800. Cont. copy. 1 vol.

Lafayette, Marquis de (1757–1834). *French Statesman and Soldier.* Letters written between 1779 and 1834. 63 pieces. Photostats. Restricted. Catalogued.

Lear, Tobias. Accounts kept as secretary to George Washington, dated 1789–91. Typewritten. 26 pages.

Lowndes, William (1782–1822). *Congressman from South Carolina.* Papers of William Lowndes and other members of the family, dated 1787–1842. 1 ms. box.

McHenry, James (1753–1816). *Secretary of War, 1796–1801.* Correspondence and miscellaneous papers. c. 50 pieces. Photostats.

Madison, James (1750–1836). *Fourth President of the United States.* Papers of, or relating to, James Madison and Dolly Payne Madison, dated 1779–1852. 57 pieces.

Marcy, William Learned (1786–1857). *Governor of New York. Secretary of State. Secretary of War.* Notes relating to the career of Marcy and his papers prepared by H. B. Learned. 5 ms. boxes.

Marshall, John (1755–1835). *Chief Justice of U. S.* Letters, dated 1776–1835. 3 vols. Account book. 1783–95. 2 vols. Letters of Mrs. Edward Carrington, 1793–1823. 1 vol. Photostats. 1 ms. box.

Mitchell, John. *American Agent at Halifax During the War of 1812.* Miscellaneous papers, dated 1809–99. 4 vols. Catalogued.

Morris, Gouverneur (1752–1816). *Statesman. Diplomat.* Collection of 52 items. Included are: 2 vols. legal memoranda prior to 1776, bank book 1782–88, 13 vols. of his diary, 14 vols. of his letters, miscellaneous account books, cash books, etc. Restricted. List made by D. H. Mugridge.

Palmer, Alexander S., and Nathaniel Brown Palmer (1799–1877). *Sea Captain.* Papers, dated 1797–1900. 10 ms. boxes.

Perry, Christopher Raymond (1761–1818). *Naval Officer.* Journal covering four cruises on board the U. S. Frigate *President,* dated from June 20, 1812 to Feb. 19, 1814. 1 vol.

Philippine Islands. Narrative of a journal in 1802, by General Alava. Also treatises on the Togal language. 1 vol.

Pinckney, Thomas (1750–1828). *Soldier. Diplomat. Governor of South Carolina.* Correspondence of members of the Pinckney, Horry, Huger, Motte, and Rutledge families, dated 1751 to 1847. 2 ms. boxes.

Pinckney Family of South Carolina. Additional papers, dated 1744–1825. c. 570 pieces in 8 ms. boxes. Deposit. Restricted.

Sever, James. *U. S. Naval Officer.* Papers, dated 1794–1801. c. 80 pieces. Photostats. 1 vol.

Shippen Family of Pennsylvania. Deeds, indentures, and family documents, dated 1693–1854. Thomas Lee Shippen account books, 1759–97. Miscellaneous manuscripts and memoranda, 1772–1804. 5 ms. boxes. Deposit. Restricted.

Smith, Samuel (1752–1839). *Soldier. Statesman.* Correspondence, dated from 1793 to 1832. 26 pieces.

Story, Joseph (1779–1845). *Jurist.* Papers, dated 1807–53. c. 780 pieces.

Tappan, Benjamin (1773–1857). *U. S. Senator. Jurist.* Papers, dated from 1799 to 1852. c. 55 pieces. Restricted.

Thacher, George (1754–1824). *Congressman. Jurist.* Letters to his wife, dated 1790–92. 33 pieces. Copies.

Turner, Daniel (1782– ). Papers of Dr. Turner of Rhode Island, a physician in St. Marys, Georgia, dated 1792–1808. 65 pieces.

Turner, John. Papers of John Turner of Alexandria, Va., dated 1793–1804. 32 pieces.

Van Schaak, Peter (1747–1832), and Others. Collection of Peter Van Schaak, Henry, and David Van Schaak, dated 1776–1841. 53 pieces.

Wadsworth, Jeremiah (1743–1804). *Soldier. Congressman from Connecticut.* Miscellaneous letters, 1777–1833. c. 90 pieces.

Wayne, Anthony (1745–96). *Soldier.* Papers relating to Ohio River forts, dated 1792–97. 25 pieces.

Welles, Gideon (1802–78). *Secretary of the Navy.* Papers relating to Welles compiled by H. B. Learned, dated 1828–98. 3 ms. boxes.

### IV. PERIOD OF EXPANSION AND DIVERSIFICATION, 1815–50

Aberdeen, George Hamilton Gordon (1784–1860). Fourth Earl of. Selections from correspondence, 1838–69. 5 vols. Printed.

Account Books. (1) Accounts with members of the 29th and 30th Congresses for copies of documents procured from the Office of the Public Printer. 1 vol. (2) Account book of Capt. Jonathan Chase, of Waldoborough, Maine, relating to voyages to Charleston, Havana, Liverpool, etc., between 1834 and 1842. 1 vol. (3) Account book of Elk Mills, Maryland, dated April 1820 to April 1830. 1 vol. (4) Account book of house expenses from June 25, 1825 to July 6, 1830, kept by J. M. Forbes. 1 vol. (5) Record book of Hopeton Plantation. Account of Cotton Picked, 1818–41. Photostat. (6) Account book of Peter Lenox showing rentals in Washington, D. C., dated 1821–33. 1 vol. (7) Medical account book dated at Kingston, Ohio, Feb. 1831 to Sept. 1833. 1 vol. (8) John A. Moon, Chattanooga, Tenn. Oct. 1, 1832 to Mar. 30, 1835. 1 vol. July 1, 1860 to Nov. 30, 1862, and June 3, 1874 to Aug. 2, 1879. 1 vol. (9) Judge Turner Reavis, Alabama, account book dated 1842–90, includes accounts paid for slaves. 1 vol.

Bartlett, Josiah, Jr. (1768–1838). *Physician.* Papers, dated 1790–1838. 22 ms. boxes.

Birney, James Gillespie (1792–1857). *Anti-slavery Leader.* Papers, dated 1830–50. 1 ms. box. 3 volumes of his dairy and 1 volume of anti-slavery notes. Deposit.

Blair, Gist. Collection of papers of the Blair and Woodbury families, dated 1785–1923. Levi Woodbury, Sec. of Navy, 1831–34, and Sec. of the Treasury, 1834–41; Montgomery Blair (1813–83), Postmaster General under Lincoln; Francis Preston Blair, prominent political journalist. c. 160 ms. boxes. Also scrapboods, ledgers, printed matter. Restricted in part.

Buford, Charles, Sr., *of Kentucky and Illinois.* Correspondence, dated 1842–65. 28 pieces. Catalogued.

Bradley, Stephen Row (1754–1830). *Jurist.* William C. Bradley, Mark Richards, and others. Collection of letters dated from 1777 to 1881. c. 500 pieces.

Cameron, Simon (1799–1889). *U. S. Senator from Pennsylvania. Secretary of War.* Papers, dated 1738–1919. Correspondence, speeches, newspaper clippings, accounts, and diary for 1862. 36 ms. boxes. Deposit. Restricted.

Campbell, George Washington (1769–1848). *U. S. Senator. Secretary of Treasury.* 77 pieces, dated 1793–1844. Catalogued.

Clay, Henry (1777–1852). *Statesman. Secretary of State.* Journal of the National Clay Club, July 1842. 1 vol.

Colfax, Schuyler (1823–85). *Vice-President of the U. S.* Correspondence, dated 1839–80. 112 pieces.

Cox, James, Jr. Miscellaneous letters received, dated 1780–1857. 108 pieces.

*Constitution* (whaler). Log book of the whaler *Constitution*, Nantucket, Mass., dated May 10, 1840 to April 17, 1842. 1 vol.

Cushing, Caleb (1800–79). *Statesman.* Correspondence, early notebooks and essays, literary and legal papers, dated 1817–79. 300 ms. boxes. Journal of U. S. Mission to China, 1844. Official documents relating to convention between U. S. and Columbia, 1868. Diaries, 1829–30, 1835.

Custis Family Bible. The Custis family Bible and some genealogical notes. Deposit. Restricted.

Davidson, Lewis Grant, *of Georgetown.* Letters received, bills, receipts, dated 1810–62. 70 pieces.

Draper, Isaac, Jr. W. F. Draper, and William Preston. About 132 pieces, mainly letters of W. F. Draper, dated 1861–63.

Dunlop Family. James Dunlop, II, 1775–85; James Dunlop, III, 1793–1872; Robert P. Dunlop. Papers contained in 2 ms. boxes and 9 packages.

Eld, Henry. *Naval Officer.* Letters to his parents, 1831–49. Some written from the sloop *Peacock*, which was in Commodore Wilkes' squadron. c. 150 pieces.

Ewell, Richard Stoddert (1817–72). *Soldier.* Letters and documents dated 1838–96. c. 88 pieces. Also group of 68 pieces. Restricted.

Filhiol, Juan and his descendants. Documents, letters, pamphlets, and map relating to grant of land including Hot Springs, Ark., dated 1783–1904. c. 60 pieces. Deposit.

Forbes, J. M. (1) Account book of house expenses from June 25, 1825 to July 6, 1830. (2) Letterbook for July 25, 1817 to Aug. 1, 1818.

French, Benjamin Brown. *Commissioner of Public Buildings under Lincoln.* Papers, dated 1826–70 and 1885. 7 vols. Restricted.

Frost, Edward. Papers, dated 1826–66. 5 ms. boxes. Deposit. Restricted.

Gales, Joseph (1786–1860). *Journalist.* William Winston Seaton (1785–1866). *Journalist.* Miscellaneous papers, dated from 1806 to 1867. 148 pieces.

Gibbes, Lewis R. *Biologist.* Originals and copies of letters to and from Lewis R. Gibbes. 59 pieces. Dated 1828–83.

Granger, Francis (1792–1868). *Political Leader.* Letters written by Granger, mainly to Thurlow Weed, during the years 1825, 1827–38. 1 vol.

Greenhow, Mary (Mrs. Hugh Lee). Diary written in Washington, D. C., from Sept. 4, 1837 to March 1838. 39 pages. Diary written at Winchester, Va., from Mar. 11 to Sept. 3, 1862, Mar. 9, 1863 to November 16, 1865. 222 pages. Film negatives with enlargement prints.

Hall, Elihu, and Washington Hall. Business and financial records dated 1777–1849. Baltimore, Md. 12 vols.

Hamilton, John, and William Hamilton. Letters from John Hamilton dated 1838–55. Letters of William Hamilton and others dated 1862–65. 2 vols.

Harrison, William Henry (1773–1841). *Ninth President of the United States.* Miscellaneous papers, dated from 1735 to 1860. c. 70 pieces. Catalogued. Also 41 pages of copies.

Hayden, Levi (1813–——). Journal of a voyage from Boston to Manila in the ship *Eben Preble*, begun June 26, 1840. 1 vol. Autobiographical notes. 1 vol.

Indians. Boundaries. Notes of the boundary lines between the Sioux and Chippeway Nations of Indians. Certified by J. L. Bean and J. A. Clarke, 1835. 2 vols.

Irvine, Callender. *Commissary General of U. S.* Account book, dated Mar. 31, 1817 to Nov. 8, 1822. 1 vol.

Jackson, Andrew (1767–1847). *Seventh President of the United States.* Letterbook, dated Feb. 15, 1829 to Aug. 27, 1831. 1 vol.

Jackson, Thomas Jonathan (1824–63). *Confederate General.* Papers, dated 1845–60. 109 pieces. Photostats.

Jesup, Thomas Sidney (1788–1860). *Soldier.* Papers, dated 1810–59. 17 letter file boxes, 7 ms. boxes, and letterbook for 1846. 2 vols.

Johnson, James (1774–1826). *Army officer.* Collection of James Johnson, dated May 6 to Dec. 1, 1819. Mainly copies. 102 pages.

Johnston, Albert Sidney (1803–62). *Soldier.* Papers, dated 1822–61. 27 pieces. Photostats.

Journals & Diaries. (1) Journal of a voyage from Fort Vancouver, Columbia, to (York) factory in Hudson Bay, 1841. Typewritten. 58 pages. (2) "A Gallop through the Willamette, November 1841." Typewritten. 10 pages. (3) Journal in Mexico by Lieutenant Colonel William Preston of the Fourth Kentucky Regiment of Volunteers, dated from Nov. 1, 1847 to May 25, 1848. Typewritten copy. 1 vol. (4) Journal kept by Daniel H. Smith on a voyage from Newbury Port, Mass., to San Francisco, Calif., in the Brig *Ark*, from Oct. 31, 1849 to May 25, 1850. 1 vol. (5) Diary of Richard Wigginton Thompson (1809–1900), Congressman from Indiana and Secretary of the Navy, kept in Washington, D. C., from Jan. 1, 1842 to Mar. 22, 1842. 1 vol. (6) "Trips in Sandwich Islands," Mar. 2–4, 1848. Typewritten. 6 pages. (7) Journal kept by Daniel W. Lord on a trip from Baltimore to Savannah and return, 1824. A. D. 1 vol.

Latrobe, John Hazlehurst Boneval (1803–1891). *Lawyer. Inventor.* Letters received from Mathew Carey, Amos Kendall, Samuel F. B. Morse, and Richard Rush, dated 1828–50. 27 pieces.

Leavitt, Joshua (1794–1873). Correspondence of Joshua Leavitt, Roger Hooker Leavitt, and other members of the family, dated c. 1812 to 1871. 1 ms. box. Deposit. Restricted.

Loper, R. F. *Transport Agent of the U. S. War Department.* Papers, dated 1846–54. c. 350 pieces. Deposit.

McHenry, James (1753–1816). *Secretary of War, 1796–1801.* Correspondence and miscellaneous papers. c. 50 pieces. Photostats.

McKim, Charles Follen (1847–1909). *Architect,* and John Askin. Nine looseleaf binders containing correspondence, notes, memoranda, 1810–1928. 8 ms. boxes of material relating to American Academy in Rome, 1894–1918. 19 letterbooks, 1891–1910. Several ms. boxes of miscellaneous items including material dated 1888–89, relating to Boston Public Library. Also printed volume of Burton Historical Records, "John Askin Papers, 1796–1820."

Marcy, William Learned (1786–1857). *Governor of New York. Secretary of War. Secretary of State.* Correspondence, including a diary and official diplomatic letterbooks, 1808–57. 79 vols. Notes relating to the career of Marcy and his papers prepared by H. B. Learned. 5 ms. boxes.

Marshall, John (1755–1835). *Chief Justice of the United States.* Letters, dated 1776–1835. 3 vols. Account book, 1783–95. 2 vols. Letters of Mrs. Edward Carrington, 1793–1823. 1 vol. Photostats. 1 ms. box.

Mason, Charles (1804–82). *Jurist.* "Life and Letters of Judge Charles Mason of Iowa, 1804–82." Typewritten. 17 vols.

Mexico. Plana Mayor de exercito, Manual de Cargo, . . . Mexico. Enero 2 de 1840. (Military accounts.) A. D. 1 vol.

Mitchell, John. *American Agent at Halifax During the War of 1812.* Miscellaneous papers, dated 1809–99. c. 500 pieces. Catalogued.

Monroe, James. *Fifth President of the United States.* Diary, dated Feb. 11, 12, and 14, 1825. 4 pages. Autobiography, 9 pages. Memorandum relating to the papers. Photostats.

Nicollet, Joseph Nicholas (1786–1843). *Explorer. Mathematician.* Photostats. 69 pages. Dated 1832–42.

Palmer, Alexander S., and Nathaniel Brown Palmer (1799–1877). *Sea Captain.* Papers, dated 1797–1900. 10 ms. boxes. Additional papers, dated 1824–92. c. 205 pieces. Accounts, 1858–61, 1873, 1875. A. D. 1 vol.

Perry, Matthew Calbraith (1794–1858). *Naval Officer.* Book containing letters, notes, and journal, dated June 9 to Aug. 14, 1838. 1 vol.

Pierce, Franklin. *Fourteenth President of the United States.* Letters to and from Asa Fowler, dated 1838–42, 1845, and undated. Several letters of H. H. Carroll. c. 150 pages. Photostats.

Plitt, George. Sixty-eight photostats of letters exchanged with James Buchanan and J. W. Forney, 1836–59. Restricted.

Postel, Karl (*Pseud. Charles Sealsfield, 1793–1864*). *Novelist.* "Nathan le Squatter ou le Premier American au Texas." French translation from the English.

Preston, William. See Draper, Isaac.

Randolph, "John Randolph of Roanoke" (1773–1833). *Statesman.* Autograph copies of letters written by John Randolph and James M. Garnett, 1806–1832. 1 vol. Catalogued.

Riggs Family. Papers, dated 1813–62. c. 250 ms. boxes. Strictly commercial. R. & E. Riggs Co. Riggs & Aertsen & Co., Riggs, Son & Paradise. Riggs, Taylor & Co. Corcoran & Riggs. Riggs & Co.

Ritchie, Thomas (1778–1854). *Journalist. Politician.* Family correspondence, 1830–52. 1 ms. box. Deposit. Restricted.

Sealsfield, Charles. See Postel, Karl.

Seaton, William Winston. See Gales, Joseph.

Sewall, Frederick, and Joseph Sewall. Civil War and military papers of Colonel Frederick D. Sewall. Records of the Custom House at Bath, Maine, while Joseph Sewall was collector, 1834–41. 11 ms. boxes.

Shakers. "A General Statement of the Holy Laws of Zion. Introduction by Father James." 1840. 1 vol.

Shippen Family of Pennsylvania. Deeds, indentures, and family documents dated 1693–1854. Thomas Lee Shippen account books, 1759–97. Miscellaneous manuscripts and memoranda, 1772–1804. 5 ms. boxes. Deposit. Restricted.

Smith, Samuel (1752–1839). *Soldier. Statesman.* Correspondence, dated from 1793 to 1832. 26 pieces.

Snowden, Nathaniel Randolph (1770–1851). Autobiographical sketch. 1 page. Reminiscences. 19 pages. Notes on the Mississippi Valley, dated 1837–38. 7 pages. Photostats.

Starr, Nathan. Mainly letters received, dated 1813–51. 66 pieces.

Stephens, Alexander Hamilton (1812–83). *U. S. Congressman. Vice-President of the Confederacy.* Papers, dated 1831–83. 67 ms. boxes. Autobiography and journal, dated April 14, 1834 to Jan. 26, 1837. A. D. 1 vol.

Story, Joseph (1779–1845). *Jurist.* Papers, dated 1807–53. 7 vols. Additional group of 40 pieces, dated 1804–35.

Taney, Roger Brooke (1777–1864). *Chief Justice of the U. S.* Letters of Taney, Amos Kendall, Thomas Ellicott, William P. Fessenden, and others, dated 1829–67. 102 pieces.

Tappan, Benjamin (1773–1857). *U. S. Senator. Jurist.* Papers, dated from 1799 to 1852. c. 55 pieces. Restricted.

Tappan, Lewis, & others. Photostats of 54 letters written by Lewis Tappan, Joel Parker, and Arthur Tappan between 1828 and 1872. Diary of Lewis Tappan dated 1816–53. 9 vols. Restricted.

Taylor, Jeremiah H. "Sketches of Religious Experiences" [in and near New York City, 1811 to 1858.] 1 vol.

Taylor, Zachary (1784–1850). *Twelfth President of the United States.* Letters written to Thomas S. Jesup, dated 1817–40. 16 pieces. Photostats.

Thacher, James.  Collection of 32 letters dated 1780–83 and 1804–42.  Photostats.

Thorn, Herman.  Papers relating to court martial of Herman Thorn, and papers relating to the disputes between naval officers, 1813–43.  1 vol.

United States.  (1) Scrapbook of newspaper clippings, etc., relating to the history of the United States, 1770–1846.  1 vol.  (2) Library of Congress.  Letterbooks, 1843–99.  Letters received, 1897–99.  c. 45 vols.  (3) War Department.  Official documents pertaining to the construction of the Cumberland Road.  Quarterly returns from various forts.  Meteorological and topographical records, letterbooks, etc.  Transferred from the War Department in 1932–33.  Several large wooden boxes and about 100 ms. boxes.

Walker, Robert John (1801–69).  *U. S. Senator.  Secretary of Treasury.  Governor of Kansas Territory.*  Papers.  1815–1936.  4 vols.  Deposit.  Restricted.  Also 2 scrapbooks.  2 vols. of pamphlets.

Ward Family.  Papers of the Ward family of Richmond County, Va., dated 1830–65.  c. 573 pieces.  Additional papers deposited and restricted.

Washington, Martha (1732–1801).  Photostats of some 120 pieces relating to the estate of Martha Washington, dated between 1800 and 1826.  Catalogued.

Weed, Thurlow (1797–1882).  *Journalist.  Politician.*  Letters to and from Thurlow Weed, dated 1823–82.  130 pieces.  Many by Francis Granger.

Welles, Gideon (1802–78).  *Secretary of the Navy.*  Papers relating to Welles compiled by W. H. Learned, dated 1828–98.  3 ms. boxes.

Whitney-Burnham.  *Cotton Merchants.*  Papers of Israel Whitney and W. A. Burnham, New Orleans, dated mainly 1839–46.  9 ms. boxes.

Wright, Elizur (1804–85).  *Reformer.*  Papers, dated 1817–87.  8 ms. boxes.  Drafts of writings.  5 ms. boxes.  An account book for 1828–32.  1 vol.  A bound volume of clippings.

Wright-Stephenson Collection.  Papers of Nathaniel Wright, Reuben H. Stephenson, Nathaniel Wright Stephenson, and others, dated 1812–1900.  c. 50 ms. boxes.  Several bundles.  Deposit.

## V. PERIOD OF EXPANSION AND CONFLICT, UP TO THE WITHDRAWAL OF THE TROOPS FROM THE SOUTH, 1850–1877

Account Books.  (1) Judge Turner Reavis of Alabama, account book dated 1842–90; includes amounts paid for slaves.  (2) Mitchell and Purroy families.  8 vols. Dated from 1847 to 1894.  Deposit.  (3) "Freedom at Elijah Watson's," Jan. 1 to Sept. 13, 1866.  A. D. 14 pages.

Anderson and Moler Families.  Papers of the Anderson and Moler families dated 1854–95.  c. 84 pieces.  Catalogued.

Anti-slavery Papers.  Minute Book of Western Anti-Slavery Society, 1845–57.  1. vol.  Also anti-slavery album.  1 vol.

Allen, Elisha Hunt (1804–83).  *Chief Justice and Chancellor of Hawaii.*  Papers, dated 1846–82.  13 ms. boxes.

Arnold, John Carvel.  Papers of John Carvel Arnold, Company I, 49th Reg. Penn. Inf., and other members of the family, dated 1856–95.  1 ms. box.  Typewritten copies of 40 additional pieces.

Bailey, Orra B.  Letters from a private soldier in a Connecticut regiment to his wife, dated 1862–64.  74 pieces.

Bancroft, George (1800–91).  *Historian.  Diplomat,* and Alexander Bliss.  Correspondence, dated 1848–89.  c. 125 pieces.  Additional papers, dated from 1847–89.  c. 135 pieces.  Catalogued.

Barstow, Wilson.  *Soldier.*  Letters, dated 1861–69.  53 pieces.

Bayard, Thomas Francis (1828–98).  *Secretary of State.  Diplomat.*  Papers, dated 1844–98.  c. 200 ms. boxes.  Also a number of scrapbooks and letterbooks.  Restricted.

Black, Jeremiah Sullivan (1810–83).  *Attorney General.  Secretary of State.*  Scrapbooks of newspaper clippings, dated 1857–1900.  Deposit.  4 vols.

Blair, Gist.  Collection of papers of the Blair and Woodbury families, dated 1785–1923.  Levi Woodbury, Secretary of the Navy, 1831–34, and Secretary of Treasury, 1834–41.  Montgomery Blair (1813–83), Postmaster under Lincoln.  Francis Preston Blair, prominent political journalist.  c. 160 ms. boxes.  Also scrapbooks, ledgers, and printed matter.  Restricted in part.

Bledsoe, Albert Taylor (1809–77). *Editor. Author.* Collection of 34 letters written by famous persons and dated between 1858 and 1894. Photostats. Catalogued.

Bloomfield, Alpheus S. Letters from Alpheus S. Bloomfield, private, Battery A, 1st Reg., Ohio Vol. Light Artillery, to his family dated Sept. 24, 1861 to July 16, 1865. 324 pages. Photostats.

Booth, Junius Brutus (1796–1852). *English Actor.* Papers relating to Booth and his family, dated 1817–91. 24 pieces.

Bourland, James A. Papers relating to the Red River Border (Texas-Oklahoma), dated 1837–67. c. 175 pieces.

Bradford, William M. "Journal kept by Judge William M. Bradford during the extra session of the General Assembly of the State of Tennessee in 1861, and other miscellaneous material." Typewritten copy. 1 vol.

Bristow, Benjamin Helm (1832–96). *Secretary of the Treasury.* Papers, dated 1839–1932. 15 ms. boxes. 3 scrapbooks, 14 letterbooks. One letterbook is limited to the Whiskey Frauds of 1875. Deposit. Restricted.

Brown, John (1800–59). *"Old Brown of Osawatomie."* Letters, documents, etc., mainly addressed to Henry A. Wise, dated 1851–1928. c. 208 pieces.

Bruce, Charles (1798–1879). *Planter.* Plantation accounts for Staunton Hill, Charlotte County, Va. c. 500 pieces, dated during the Civil War and after.

Butler, Benjamin Franklin (1818–93). *Governor of Massachusetts.* Papers, dated 1836–95. c. 260 ms. boxes. Also military letter books, account books, and ledgers.

Cameron, Simon (1799–1889). *U. S. Senator from Pennsylvania. Secretary of War.* Papers, dated 1738–1919. Correspondence, speeches, accounts, diary for 1862, and newspaper clippings. 36 ms. boxes. Restricted. Deposit. Lincoln letters listed.

Campbell, Given. Memorandum of a journal kept daily during the last march of Jefferson Davis, kept by Captain Given Campbell, dated April 15–May 10, 1865. 9 pages. Photostat.

Cannon, William R. Collection of 15 letters written to Colonel William R. Cannon by well-known persons between the years 1849 and 1863. Catalogued.

Carnegie, Andrew (1835–1919). *Manufacturer. Philanthropist.* Papers, dated 1834–1920. c. 160 ms. boxes. Arranged by topics. Indexed in part. Restricted.

Caton, John Dean (1812–95). *Jurist.* Papers, dated 1826–78. c. 29 ms. boxes. 9,000 pieces. Deposit.

Chamberlain, Joseph Lawrence (1828–1914). (1) Accounts for Maine Soldiers' Relief Association, June 17, 1862 to Feb. 6, 1867, A. D. 1 vol. (2) Accounts, Sept. 9, 1867 to July 14, 1871. A. D. 1 vol. (3) List of books belonging to senior library, Bowdin College. A. D. 1 vol.

Chandler, Joseph Ripley (1792–1880). *Journalist. Congressman from Pennsylvania.* Letter-press copy book for Dec. 4, 1850 to August 8, 1851.

Chandler, Zachariah (1813–79). *U. S. Senator.* Papers, dated 1854–99. 7 vols.

Chittenden, Lucius Eugene (1824–1902). *Author.* Notes of debates in the Peace Conference at Washington, D. C. February 16–21, 1861. 1 vol.

Clowry, Robert C. Military papers of Captain Robert C. Clowry, Assistant Quartermaster, U. S. A., dated 1862–71. 73 pieces. Letterbook from Mar. 3, 1864 to Aug. 15, 1865.

Colfax, Schuyler (1823–85). *Vice-President of the United States.* Correspondence, dated 1839–80. 112 pieces.

Columbia, South Carolina. (1) The Burning of Columbia, by Col. James G. Gibbs. Typewritten copy, 23 pages. (2) Narrative of the Burning of Columbia, Feb. 17, 1865, and Journey to Fayetteville, N. C. with Sherman's Army, Feb.–Mar. 1865, by Harriette C. Keatinge, A. D. 55 pages. (3) Notes relating to burning of Columbia, by Joseph Le Conte. copy. 6 pages.

Confederate States of America. *Army.* Discharge Book of 1st Corps, Army of the Potomac, dated at Fairfax Court House, Flint Hill, Leesburg, etc. August 12–Oct. 21, 1861.

Croghan Family. Papers of George, John, and William Croghan, Sr., dated 1789–1848. 2 ms. boxes.

Cuba. Puerto Principe. Description of Puerto Principe by Joseph A. Springer, 1874. A. D. 1 vol. Drawings and photographs.

Cushing, Caleb (1800–79). *Statesman.* Correspondence, early notebooks and essays, literary and legal papers, dated 1817–79. c. 300 ms. boxes.

Dahlgren, John Adolphus (1809–70). *Inventor of the Dahlgren Cannon. Naval Officer.* Papers, 47 vols. Material for the most part in the Civil War period.

Davidson, Lewis Grant, *of Georgetown.* Letters received, bills, receipts, dated 1810–62. 70 pieces.

Dawes, Henry Laurens (1816–1903). *Congressman and Senator from Massachusetts.* c. 75 ms. boxes. Deposit. Restricted.

Denison, George Stanton. Letters and documents, dated 1854–1921. c. 95 pieces.

Depew, Chauncey Mitchell (1834–1928). *U. S. Senator from New York. Lawyer. Railway President.* Papers, dated 1865–1926. 1 ms. box. Photostats.

Dickinson, Anna Elizabeth (1842–1932). *Author. Lecturer.* Papers, dated 1860–1932. 28 ms. boxes. 27 transfer cases.

Dodge, Mary Abigail (Pseud. Gail Hamilton, 1833–96). *Author.* Collection of her letters, about 20 pieces, dated 1856–77, and 2 scrapbooks of clippings.

Doolittle, Lucy. *Teacher.* Memoranda of Mrs. Lucy Doolittle beginning: Dec. 18th 1865. Commenced teaching in the industrial school in Georgetown for the N. Y. National Freedman Relief Association. A. D. 1 vol.

Downing, Samuel. Thirty-one pieces dated 1840–85, relating to Samuel Downing of Lancaster Court-House, Va.

Draper, William Franklin (1842–1910). *Soldier. Diplomat.* "Letters from the Front, 1861–64." Typewritten copy. 1 vol.

Early, Jubal Anderson (1816–94). *Confederate General.* Papers, dated 1829–1911. 15 vols. Diary for 1865. 1 ms. box.

Eaton, Margaret L. O'Neill (*Mrs. John H. Eaton, 1796–1879*). Manuscript of autobiography as dictated in 1873. 149 pages. Deposit.

Elliott, James Thomas. Orders and miscellaneous papers of James T. Elliott, Major, Enrolling Officer, 4th Div., Dist. of Arkansas, C. S. Army, dated 1859–95. 1 ms. box.

Enslow, Charles Calvin. Excerpts of letters written by Enslow to his wife during the years 1861–65. Typewritten. 100 pages.

Ewell, Richard Stoddert (1817–72). *Soldier.* Letters and documents, dated 1838–96. c. 88 pieces. Also group of 68 pieces. Restricted.

Ewing, Thomas (1789–1871). *Secretary of the Treasury. Secretary of the Interior.* Letters to Ewing, dated 1858–60. 1 ms. box. Memoranda by Gen. Thomas Ewing recording incidents of 1865 as related by his father. Memorandum on the Bank Charter, 1841. Extracts from periodicals.

Fish, Hamilton (1808–93). *Secretary of State.* Papers, dated 1831–93. c. 250 ms. boxes. Also scrapbooks and printed matter. Deposit. Restricted.

Fowler, Joseph Smith (1820–1902). *U. S. Senator.* An undated notebook.

French, Benjamin Brown. *Commissioner of Public Buildings under Lincoln.* Papers, dated 1826–70 and 1885. 7 vols.

Frost, Edward. Papers, dated 1826–66. 5 ms. boxes. Deposit. Restricted.

Garfield, James Abram (1831–81). *Twentieth President of the United States.* Collection of letters, dated 1857–81, written to B. A. Hinsdale. 2 ms. boxes.

Gibbes, Lewis R. *Biologist.* Originals and copies of letters to and from Lewis R. Gibbes. 59 pieces, dated 1828–83.

Gillette, James (1838–81). *Army Officer.* Twenty-one letters written by Lieut. Gillette, 3rd Md. Inf., between Jan. and Sept. 1862. Typewritten copies.

Gist, Branford P. Letters of William H., Mary, Richard I., and Branford Gist, dated 1852–65. c. 80 pieces.

Godfrey, Edward Settle (1843–1932). *Army Officer.* Papers relating to the Battle of Little Big Horn River and to Custer's last battle, dated mainly 1876 and 1892. 5 ms. boxes. Military scrapbook, 1 vol.

Gould, William J. *Soldier.* Thirteen pieces, including four small diaries, 1864–65.

Gourdin, Henry. Letters addressed mainly to Gourdin, of the firm of Gourdin, Mathiesen & Company, Charleston, S. C., dated 1860–61. 38 pieces.

Gregg Collection, 1716–1916. Miscellaneous papers of Andrew Gregg, David McMurtrie Gregg, Joseph Hiester, and others, dated from 1716 to 1916. Several accounts of military marches and the autobiography [copy] of Conrad Weiser are included. 2 vols., 2 ms. boxes. Letterbook of D. M. Gregg, 1863–64. Catalogued.

Gresham, Walter Quinton (1822–95). *Postmaster General. Secretary of State.* Papers, dated 1857–96, including a letterbook for 1893–95. 8 ms. boxes. A series of 14 volumes containing letters to and from Gresham during 1883–84.

Gwin, William McKendree (1805–85). *Politician.* Memoirs on history of the United States, Mexico, and California. 175 pages. Photostats.

Halpine, Charles Graham (1829–68). *Humorous Writer.* Scrapbooks of newspaper clippings dated 1861, 1863–67. 4 vols.

Hamilton, John, and William Hamilton. Letters of John Hamilton, dated 1838–55. Letters of William Hamilton and others, dated 1862–65. c. 218 pieces.

Hardee, William Joseph (1815–73). *Confederate General.* Letters written by Hardee during the years 1861 and 1862. 29 pieces.

*Harrison* (ship, of San Francisco). Log Book of the ship *Harrison* on voyages to Carmen Island, Bellingham Bay, Melbourne, etc., 1862–65. A. D. 1 vol.

Hay, John Milton (1838–1905). *Journalist. Diplomat.* Newspaper clippings relating mainly to the Spanish-American War, international politics and diplomacy, etc., dated 1860–1905. 73 vols. Deposit.

Hewitt, Edward Lukens. *U. S. Navy.* Technical notes and drawings relating to steam navigation in the U. S. Navy during the period of the Civil War, prepared on board the U. S. S. *Mahaska.* 1 vol.

Hoppe, Albert Friedrich. (1828—). *Author.* "Lebenslauf von Albert Friedrich Hoppe." A. D. 22 pages.

Howe, Hiram P. Letters of Hiram P. Howe, private in a Missouri regiment in the Union Army, dated 1861–64. c. 76 pieces.

Howe, Julia Ward (1819–1910). *Author. Reformer.* Papers dated 1861–1917. 10 ms. boxes.

Ingersoll, Robert Green (1833–99). *Lawyer. Lecturer.* About 500 pieces of correspondence, dated 1871–99. 34 scrapbooks. Printed matter. 24 ms. boxes. 1 large flat box.

Jesup, Thomas Sidney (1788–1860). *Soldier.* Papers, dated 1810–59. 7 ms. boxes. 17 letter file boxes. Letterbook, 1846–47, 2 vols.

Journals and Diaries. (1) Journal of William E. Bernard, dated at Thetford, Vt., and Dartmouth College, Hanover, N. H., Feb. 29, 1851 to May 29, 1853. 1 vol. (2) Diary of August Ripley Burbank kept on a journey from Illinois to California in 1849, and later experiences in Oregon, etc., dated 1849 to 1880. 1 vol. (3) Memorandum of a journal kept during the last march of Jefferson Davis, kept by Captain Given Campbell, dated April 15 to May 10, 1865. 9 pages. Photostat. (4) Notes of travel from the diary of the late Isaac Draper, Jr., M. D., dated from Sept. 29, 1853 to July 31, 1855. 1 vol. Typewritten. (5) Journal of D. B. Gardner covering trip from Middleport, Ill., to California, March to July 1850. 1 vol. A second copy of the journal contains entries for April 1851. Deposit. (6) "A Journal of My Life and Experience as a Soldier," by H. Graham, dated Oct. 27, 1862–Sept. 1, 1863. 1 vol. (7) Journal kept by Albert Janin from Feb. 12 to June 12, 1868. (8) "Notes by the Way," from the diary of E. E. Johnson, Co. B, 18th Reg., Ind. Vol., dated Jan. 24 to April 21, 1862. Typewritten copy, 19 pages. (9) Diary of Edwin F. Ludwig (1839–84), telegraph operator at Charleston, S. C., entries date from Jan. 1 to June 7, 1861. (10) Diary of a Michigan cavalryman dated June 23, 1863 to Dec. 31, 1864. 1 vol. (11) Diary of Josiah W. Ripley, Co. C, 18th Reg. Mass. Vol. Militia, May 16–Aug. 21, 1862. (12) Journal of E. Paul Reichhelm, Sergeant major, 3rd Inf. Mo. Vol. U. S. A., describing the expedition to Vicksburg and the battles of Chickasaw Bayou and Arkansas Post, dated Dec. 20, 1862–Jan. 11, 1863. 1 vol. (13) Diary and notes of O. M. Dorman, Jan. 4, 1864–Jan. 21, 1886. A. Ds. 7 vols. Also a volume containing copies of 6 letters and a fragment.

Jameson, Robert Edwin. *Surgeon.* Correspondence, dated 1857–65. 14 pieces. Diary, kept while in the Union Army, dated June 14–Aug. 13, 1863. 1 vol.

Kautz, August V. "Reminiscences of the Civil War." Typewritten carbon. 1 vol.

**Larned, Daniel Reed.** Papers of Daniel Reed Larned, private secretary to Gen. A. E. Burnside, dated Dec. 9, 1861–May 11, 1865. c. 350 pieces.

**Lee, Robert Edward** (1807–70). *Confederate General.* Approximately 700 letters. With the exception of 200 letters written mostly by Mrs. Lee, they are all written by General Lee. An invoice book of Daniel Parke Custis, 1749–57. General Lee's letterbooks, 1865–66, and 1866–70, 2 vols. Mrs. Lee's reminiscences of the War, 1 vol. Agnes Lee's Journal, 1852–58. 1 vol. Deposit. Restricted.

**LeGendre, Charles William** (1830–99). *Soldier. Diplomat.* Collection of 74 volumes (50 of the volumes are in manuscript and 24 of the volumes are printed in English, French, and Oriental languages). Manuscript volumes are mostly official documents and scientific accounts. A few volumes of correspondence, dated 1868–92.

**Librarians' Convention, 1853.** Papers relating to the biographies of delegates to the Convention in New York City, Sept. 15–17, 1853. 58 pieces.

**Lincoln, Abraham.** *Sixteenth President of the United States.* (1) Biography of Abraham Lincoln by Emanuel Hertz. Typewritten manuscript and proof sheets. "What Were Lincoln's Purposes? What Did Lincoln Say at Gettysburg?" by Emanuel Hertz. Typewritten document. (2) Poem, "My childhood-home I see again." A. D. 4 pages. Statement relating to the "relocation" of road between Sangamon town and the town of Athens, with note by Lincoln, enclosing a map. 2 pieces. Originals. (3) Several photostats including the speech delivered from a window of the White House, Nov. 10, 1864, and the letter written to Major General Reynolds on Jan. 20, 1865.

**Long, Crawford Williamson** (1815–78). *Anaesthetist. Surgeon.* Papers of Dr. Long and others relating to the first use of anaesthetic in surgical cases, dated from 1837 to 1930. c. 110 pieces. Also miscellaneous pamphlets and photographs. c. 25 pieces.

**McNeill, Jesse C.** Narrative of the capture of the Union generals, Crook and Kelly, by the Confederate lieutenant, McNeill, in Cumberland, Maryland, Feb. 21, 1865. Typewritten carbon. 15 pages.

**Mahan, Alfred Thayer** (1840–1914). *Naval Officer.* Papers, 7 miscellaneous notebooks, 3 scrapbooks of clippings for 1909–10, contained in 3 ms. boxes and 2 folio volumes. Additional papers, 9 ms. boxes. Deposit. Restricted.

**Marble, Manton Malone** (1835–1917). *Editor. Publisher.* Eighty-seven pamphlet cases of letters received, letters sent, and drafts of articles, dated c. 1853–1917. In process of mounting and binding.

**Markland, Absalom H.** *Superintendent of Mails, U. S. Army.* Collection of miscellaneous papers, dated 1860–1908. c. 170 pieces.

**Mason, Charles** (1804–82). *Jurist.* "Life and Letters of Judge Charles Mason of Iowa, 1804–82." Typewritten. 17 vols.

**Maynard, Edward** (1813–91). *Inventor.* Papers relating to the invention and manufacture of firearms, dated 1845–58. 103 pieces.

**McKim, Charles Follen** (1847–1909). *Architect,* and John Askin. Nine loose-leaf binders containing correspondence, notes, memoranda, dated 1810–1928. 8 ms. boxes of material relating to American Academy in Rome, 1894–1918. 19 letterbooks, 1891–1910. Several ms. boxes of miscellaneous items including material dated 1888–89, relating to Boston Public Library. Also printed volume of Burton Historical Records, "John Askin Papers, 1796–1820."

**Moore, Charles** (1855–    ). *Author. Member D. C. Fine Arts Commission.* Letters, clippings, photographs, pamphlets, etc., dated 1745–1937. c. 12 ms. boxes and 2 vols.

**Morgan, John Hunt** (1825–64). *Confederate General.* Dispatches concerning a raid in July 1863, received by Captain John F. Oliver. 17 pages.

**Morrill, Justin Smith** (1810–98). *U. S. Senator.* Additional papers, 4 ms. boxes, dated 1855–97.

**Myer, Albert James** (1829–80). *Army Officer.* Papers, dated 1851–1933. c. 200 pieces. Printed matter, 80 pieces. Photographs, 38 pieces.

**Negro Papers.** Miscellaneous papers dated 1830–1930. c. 590 pieces.

**Ommanney, Erastus.** *British Navy.* Letterbrook of Captain Ommanney, commanding H. M. S. *Brunswick,* 1857–60. 1 vol. contemporary copy.

**Oregon.** Jackson County. Records of mining claims, 1860 and 1869–72. 2 vols.

Osborne, J. Bloomfield. *Union Soldier.* Letters written from 1861 to 1865. 40 pieces.

Palmer, Alexander S., and Nathaniel Brown Palmer (1799–1877). *Sea Captain.* Papers, dated 1797–1900. 10 ms. boxes. Additional papers, dated 1824–92. c. 205 pieces. Accounts, 1858–61, 1873–75. A. D. 1 vol.

Pearce, James H. Letterbook, dated 1867–74. 1 vol.

Pierce, Franklin. Twenty-seven pieces of correspondence including two letters from Jefferson Davis, dated from 1848 to 1868.

Plummer, William Laurens (1824–74). Narrative of visits to Oregon, California, Hawaiian Islands, Manila, Batavia, St. Helena, etc., and six pieces of correspondence.

Porter, David Dixon (1813–91). *Naval Officer.* "Memorials of Rear Admiral David D. Porter, U. S. N., and the Mississippi Fleet in the War of 1861–65. 1899." 1 vol. "Journal of Occurrences during the War of the Rebellion," including copies of five letters dated 1862–71. 2 vols.

Remey, George Collier (1841–1928). *Naval Officer.* "Life and Letters of Rear Admiral George Collier Remey." 16 vols. "A Supplement to the Reminiscences of Rear Admiral George Collier Remey." 1 vol. In addition a deposit of 43 pieces, dated 1862–1930.

Riggs Family. Papers, dated 1813–62. c. 250 ms. boxes. Strictly commercial. R. & E. Riggs Co. Riggs & Aertsen & Co. Riggs, Son & Paradise. Riggs, Taylor & Co. Corcoran & Riggs. Riggs & Co.

Roosevelt, Robert Barnwell (1829–1906). *Political Reformer. Writer.* Scrapbook containing letters dated 1862.

Schoonmaker, Marius (1811–94). Miscellaneous papers, deeds, patents, indentures, dated 1707–1894. 4 ms. boxes. Deposit.

Sewall, Frederick, and Joseph Sewall. Civil War and military papers of Colonel Frederick D. Sewall. Records of the Custom House at Bath, Maine, while Joseph Sewall was collector, 1834–41. 11 ms. boxes.

Sheppard, Eli T. *Consul at Tientsin, China.* Correspondence, dated 1872–79. 2 ms. boxes.

Signor, Leslie E. Scrapbook of newspaper clippings, mostly poems, dated 1840–59.

Starr, George H. "Jottings Abroad," by Colonel G. H. Starr, dated 1864–1910. 2 vols. of newspaper clippings.

Stephens, Alexander Hamilton (1812–83). *U. S. Congressman. Vice-President of the Confederacy.* Papers, dated 1831–83. 67 ms. boxes. Descriptive lists.

Stevens, Charles. Letters and extracts of letters of Charles Stevens, emigrant from Princeton, Ill., to Astoria, Oreg., and of Frances E. Stevens, dated 1837–95. Typewritten copies. 1 ms. box.

Stickney, Frank L. Miscellaneous papers including much family material, dated 1840–1934. 13 ms. boxes. Several scrapbooks. Restricted in part. Account book, 1883–1901. 1 vol.

Strong, James (1822–94). *Biblical Scholar.* Collection of James Strong and others, dated 1867–1922. 2 ms. boxes.

Tappan, Lewis, and others. Photostat negatives of 54 letters written by Lewis Tappan, Joel Parker, and Arthur Tappan between 1828 and 1872.

Townsend, George Alfred (1861–1920). *Journalist.* Scrapbook of letters, newspaper clippings, memoranda, pictures, etc., dated 1865–99.

United States. (1) Army. Commissary Department. Letterbook with orders, accounts, etc., of the Commissary Dept., at Helena Island and Folly Island, S. C., Scranton, Penn., etc., dated May 3–31, 1862, and Mar. 7–Aug. 26, 1863. (2) Library of Congress. Letterbooks, 1843–99. Incoming letters, 1897–99. c. 45 vols. (3) War Department. Letters, documents, photographs, pamphlets, and cartoons. c. 1,000 pieces.

Wade, Benjamin Franklin (1800–78). *U. S. Senator from Ohio.* Papers, dated 1832–98. 22 ms. boxes.

Walker, Robert John (1801–69). *U. S. Senator. Secretary of the Treasury. Governor of Kansas Territory.* Papers, dated 1815–1936. 4 vols. 2 scrapbooks and 2 volumes of pamphlets. Deposit. Restricted.

Wallis, George. Journal of George Wallis, May 14, 1853–Aug. 21, 1853. 2 vols.

Wells, David Ames (1828–98). *Economist.* Papers, dated 1864–94. 10 ms. boxes. Descriptive list.

Ward Family. Papers of the Ward family of Richmond County, Va. 1830–65. 573 pieces. Additional papers deposited and restricted.

Weed, Thurlow (1797–1882). *Politician. Journalist.* Letters to and from Thurlow Weed, dated 1823–82. 130 pieces.

Weeks, Benjamin Franklin. *Army Officer.* Military papers, mainly invoices, returns, etc., 1861–65. 450 pieces.

Welles, Gideon (1802–78). *Secretary of the Navy.* Papers relating to Welles, compiled by H. B. Learned, dated 1828–98. 3 ms. boxes.

Wheeler, John Hill (1806–82). *Lawyer. Diplomat.* Papers, dated 1854–81. 21 vols. 19 of the volumes are diaries, 1 volume of newspaper clippings, and 1 volume of papers relating to North Carolina.

Wigfall Family. Papers, dated 1858–1909. 518 pieces, dated chiefly during the years 1858–74. Deposit.

Wise, Henry Alexander (1806–76). *Governor of Virginia.* Correspondence of Governor Wise, Lieutenant Wise, and Beverly Tucker, dated 1851–57. 37 pieces. Catalogued.

Wright, Elizur (1804–85). *Reformer.* Papers, dated 1817–87. 8 ms. boxes. Drafts of writings. 5 ms. boxes. Account book, 1828–32. 1 vol. Bound volume of clippings.

Wright-Stephenson Collection. Papers of Nathaniel Wright, Reuben H. Stephenson, Nathaniel Wright Stephenson, and others, dated 1812–1900. c. 50 ms. boxes. Several bundles. Deposit.

## VI. The Modern Era, 1877 to the Present

Account Books. (1) Mitchell and Purroy families. 8 volumes dated from 1847 to 1894. Deposit. (2) Judge Turner Reavis of Alabama, account book dated 1842–90; includes amounts paid for slaves.

Ahern, George P. Correspondence between Major Ahern, Director of Forestry, Manila, P. I., and Ngan Han, Chief Forester of China, dated 1911–32. Typewritten copies. 34 pieces.

Ainsworth, Fred Crayton (1852–1934). *Army Officer.* Correspondence, dated 1901–28. 1 ms. box.

Alaska. Papers of the Alaskan Engineering Commission, 1915–24, and of the Alaska Railroad and River Boat Service, 1923. Transferred from the Department of the Interior. 12 ms. boxes.

Aldrich, Nelson Wilmarth (1841–1915). *Statesman. Financier.* Notes of Prof. N. W. Stephenson on the papers of Aldrich. 23 ms. boxes.

Allen, Elisha Hunt (1804–83). *Chief Justice and Chancellor of Hawaii.* Papers, dated 1846–82. 13 ms. boxes.

Amberg, Emil (1868———). Correspondence of Emil Amberg, M. D. 4 vols.

American Historical Association. Papers of the American Historical Association, 1882–1934, including papers pertaining to 1735–1802, 1815, and 1847. Descriptive list. Deposit.

Anderson and Moler Families. Papers of the Anderson and Moler families, dated 1854–95. c. 84 pieces. Catalogued. Also a group of 60 pieces which contain genealogical data of the Bealmear and Duckett families.

Arnold, Samuel Bland. "Lincoln Conspiracy and Its Conspirators." A volume of clippings as published in 1902.

Arthur, Chester Alan (1830–86). *Twenty-first President of the United States.* Ninety pieces of correspondence dated mainly 1878–84. Deposit. 1 ms. box.

Associated Survivors of the Sixth Army Corps of Washington, D. C., and Union Ex-Prisoners of War Association. Letters, clippings, pamphlets, bankbook, record books, etc., dated 1883–1926. 250 pieces.

Astor, William Waldorf (1848–1919). *Journalist. Capitalist.* Correspondence, dated 1904–10. 45 pieces. Restricted.

Babine, Alexis V. *Author.* Five manuscript stories by A. V. Babine, 2 type-written stories by other persons, several miscellaneous manuscripts, 27 note-books of a literary character, with some notes on the Russian Revolution of 1917.

Baldwin, Evelyn Briggs (1862–1933). *Explorer.* Collection of miscellaneous papers contained in one large wooden box.

Bancroft, George (1800–91). *Historian. Diplomat,* and Alexander Bliss. Additional papers, dated from 1847 to 1889. c. 260 pieces. Catalogued.

Barker, Wharton (1846–1921). *Financier.* Papers, dated 1879–1920. 22 letter file boxes and 5 ms. boxes. 6 letterbooks, 1879–88. Several scrapbooks.

Bayard, Thomas Francis (1828–98). *Secretary of State. Diplomat.* Papers, dated 1844–98. c. 200 ms. boxes. Also a number of letterbooks and scrapbooks. Restricted.

Benjamin, Marcus (1857———). *Editor.* Collection of 25 letters dated from 1894 to 1928. Also collection of programs and invitations to unveiling of statues in Washington, D. C. c. 30 pieces.

Berlepsch, Hans von (Count). Papers of Count Hans von Berlepsch, concerned primarily with neo-tropical birds, dated 1879–1913. 3 ms. boxes. Minutes of the Council of the American Ornithologists' Union, 1883–93, 1902–32. 3 vols. Deposit.

Bingham, Theodore Alfred. See White House.

Bixby, M. H. Original sketches and tracings of British turrets. 1 vol. Lectures on sea fortifications, delivered at U. S. Naval War College, 1886. 1 vol.

Blaine, James Gillespie (1830–93). *Secretary of State.* Letters received, 1859–92. 3 vols. Also ms. of "Twenty Years in Congress."

Blatch, Harriot Stanton. Letters, newspaper clippings, etc., relating to the woman suffrage movement, chiefly in New York, dated 1908–15. 12 vols. Restricted.

Bledsoe, Albert Taylor (1809–77). *Editor. Author.* Collection of 34 letters written by famous persons and dated between 1858–94. Photostats. Catalogued.

Bliss, Tasker Howard (1853–1930). *Army Officer.* Papers, dated 1870–1930. 209 ms. boxes. Indexed. Descriptive list prepared by Miss Dorothy Vastine.

Bolton, Henry Carrington (1843–1903). *Chemist.* Exercises in chemistry, contained in 17 envelopes.

Booth, Junius Brutus (1796–1852). *English Actor.* Collection of documents relating to Booth and his family, dated 1817–91. 24 pieces.

Bristow, Benjamin Helm (1831–96). *Secretary of the Treasury.* Papers, dated 1839–1932. 15 ms. boxes. 3 scrapbooks. 14 letterbooks. One letterbook is limited to the Whiskey Frauds of 1875. Deposit. Restricted.

Bryan, William Jennings (1860–1925). *Secretary of State.* Miscellaneous papers, dated 1883–1931. 175 pieces.

Butler, Benjamin Franklin (1818–93). *Governor of Massachusetts. Army Officer.* Papers, dated 1836–95. c. 260 ms. boxes. Also military letterbooks, account books, and ledgers.

Cale, Howard. *Lawyer.* Forty-five items including about 10 letters from President Benjamin Harrison.

Call, Annie Payson. *Author.* "How to Live Quietly." 34-page typewritten document.

Cameron, Simon (1799–1889). *Secretary of War. U. S. Senator from Pennsylvania.* Papers, dated 1738–1919. Correspondence, newspaper clippings, speeches, accounts, diary for 1862. 36 ms. boxes. Deposit. Restricted.

Carnegie, Andrew (1835–1919). *Manufacturer.* Papers, dated 1834–1920. c. 160 ms. boxes. Arranged by topic. Partly indexed. Restricted.

Carter, Thomas Henry (1854–1911). *U. S. Senator from Montana.* Papers, dated 1895–1911. 34 letter file boxes. Scrapbooks. Notebooks.

Castle Family. Papers relating to the genealogy of the Castle family. Also "Dorothy and Martains," by Marie L. Castle. Typewritten copy. 4 ms. boxes.

Caton, John Dean (1812–95). *Jurist.* Papers, approximately 9,000 pieces. Deposit.

Chandler, Zachariah (1813–79). *U. S. Senator.* Papers, 1854–99. 7 vols.

Chase, Wilfrid Earl. "Sayings by Wilfrid Earl Chase," A. D. 96 pages. Also "Additional Sayings by Wilfrid Earl Chase," A. D. 30 pages. Deposit.

Clark, Paul H. *Army Officer.* Secret letters written to General Pershing during 1918 and 1919. Contained in small handbag. Carbon copies. Deposit. Restricted.

Clemens, Cyril. Collection of about 50 pieces, mostly copies of letters written to Cyril Clemens by well-known persons. Catalogued.

Conn, Edward. Typewritten copies of five poems by Edward Conn.

Cushman, William H. *Engineer.* Letters and papers relating to the sinking of the Confederate cruiser *Alabama,* June 19, 1864, by the U. S. man-of-war *Kearsage.*

Dawes, Henry Laurens (1816–1903). *U. S. Senator and Congressman.* Papers contained in seven large wooden boxes. Deposit. Restricted.

Denison, George Stanton. Letters and documents, dated 1854–1921. c. 95 pieces.

Depew, Chauncey Mitchell (1834–1928). *U. S. Senator from New York. Lawyer. Railway President.* Letters received, 1865–1926. 1 ms. box. Photostats. Originals in the library of George Washington University.

Dewey, George (1837–1917). *Naval Officer.* Papers, dated 1880–1917. Deposit. Restricted. c. 30 transfer cases. Letterbooks. Diaries.

Dickinson, Anna Elizabeth (1842–1932). *Author. Lecturer.* Papers, dated 1860–1932. 28 ms. boxes. 27 letter file boxes.

Dickinson, Charles Monroe (1842–1924). *Newspaperman. Diplomat.* Collection of about 1,000 pieces dated 1886 to 1924. Deposit.

Dickinson, Donald McDonald (1846–1917). *Postmaster-general.* Correspondence, dated 1885–99. 316 letters. 3 letter-press copy books.

Doolittle, James Rood (1815–97). *Senator from Wisconsin.* Letters and newspaper clippings, dated 1884–1913. 26 pieces.

Dutton, Joseph. One volume of letters and photographs relating to the life and work of Joseph Dutton, Molokai, Hawaii, dated 1919–21. Catalogued.

Early, Jubal Anderson (1816–94). *Confederate General.* Papers, dated 1829–1911. 15 vols. 1 ms. box.

Elliott, Charles Burke (1861–1937). *Supreme Court of the Philippine Islands.* 20 pieces, dated 1910–12. Diaries. Letterbooks. Scrapbooks. Restricted.

Ellsworth, Harry Alanson. *U. S. Marines.* "One Hundred Eighty Landings of United States Marines, 1800–1934." Mimeographed copy. 2 vols.

Emerson, Ralph Waldo. A volume of newspaper clippings from the Emerson Centenary number of the Boston Advertiser, May 25, 1903.

European War (World War 1914–18). Scrapbooks of letters, newspaper clippings, broadsides, etc. 3 vols.

Ewell, Richard Stoddert (1817–72). *Soldier.* Letters and documents, dated 1838–96. c. 88 pieces. Also group of 68 pieces. Restricted.

Fish, Hamilton (1808–93). *Secretary of State.* Papers, dated 1831–93. c. 250 ms. boxes. Also several scrapbooks and much printed matter. Deposit. Restricted.

Ford, Worthington Chauncey (1858–    ). *Historian.* Notebooks covering the searches made in the British Museum and Public Record Office in London, and the Bibliothèque Nationale, in Paris, for materials relating to the history of America. 1923. Five autograph volumes.

Fornaris Ochoa, Modesto de (1848–1933). Papers relating to the part played by General Modesto de Fornaris Ochoa in the Ten Years War and the War for Independence of Cuba. c. 25 pieces.

Foulke, William Dudley (1848–1935). *Civil Service Commissioner. Reformer.* Papers, dated 1885–1935. 8 letter file boxes. 8 ms. boxes.

Godfrey, Edward Settle (1843–1932). *Army Officer.* Papers relating to the Battle of Little Big Horn River, and to Custer's Last Battle, dated mainly 1876 and 1892. 5 ms. boxes. 1 scrapbook.

Goebel, Julius (1857–1931). Papers, dated 1873–1931. Papers, dated 1873–1930. 7 cardboard filing boxes. Restricted in part.

Goethals, George Washington (1858–1928). *Engineer. Soldier.* Papers, dated 1890–1927. Small transfer cases numbered 1–78. 2 ms. boxes of letters to his son, 1890–1927. 6 ms. boxes misc. documents. Deposit. Restricted.

Gresham, Walter Quintin (1822–95). *Postmaster-general. Secretary of State.* Papers, dated 1857–96, including a letterbook for 1893–95. 8 ms. boxes. A series of 14 volumes containing letters to and from Gresham for the years 1883–84.

Guiney, Louise Imogen (1861–1920). *Essayist. Poet.* Papers, dated 1885–1920. c. 1,000 pieces, including nine sonnets. Two volumes of letters written to Louise C. Moulton during the years 1884 to 1908. Typewritten copies of originals in the papers of Louise Chandler Moulton.

Hamlin, Charles Sumner (1861–1938). *U. S. Federal Reserve Board.* Scrapbooks of newspaper clippings, 1871–1926. 156 vols. Index to scrapbooks, 9 vols. Deposit. Restricted.

Harding, Warren Gamaliel (1865–1923). *Twenty-ninth President of the United States.* Photostats and typewritten copies of about 25 letters dated from 1909 to 1925. Restricted.

Harrison, Francis Burton (1873–    ). *Congressman from New York. Governor of the Philippines, 1913–21.* Letters, press clippings, etc., relating to the Philippine Islands, dated mainly 1927–31. One folder. Restricted.

Hay, Eugene Gano (1853–    ). *Jurist.* Newspaper clippings dated from 1876 to 1901. 3 vols.

Hay, James. Letters to and from James Hay, dated 1909–30. 18 pieces. Nine letters from Woodrow Wilson.

Hay, John Milton (1838–1905). *Journalist. Diplomat.* Key to printed edition of the letters and diaries of John Hay. Photostats. 1 vol. Newspaper clippings relating mainly to the Spanish-American War, international politics and diplomacy, etc. 73 vols. Deposited by Hon. James W. Wadsworth. Restricted.

Hayes, Rutherford Birchard. (1822–93). *Nineteenth President of the United States.* Film negatives of 29 pieces relating to Alabama politics, dated 1876–80. Negatives relating to Virginia politics, dated 1876–81. About 340 negatives relating to Louisiana for the years 1868–95, and to the Inter-Oceanic Canal, 1878–88. Originals in the Hayes Memorial Library. Miscellaneous papers dated 1856–91. c. 75 pieces.

Hillman, H. Poems. A. D. 1 vol. Also typewritten copies of other poems.

Holmes, Georgiana Klingle. Scrapbook of clippings, manuscripts, and typewritten material, dated from 1909 to 1930. Correspondence and miscellaneous manuscripts dated from 1909 to 1934. c. 500 pieces. Restricted.

Holmes, Oliver Wendell (1809–94). *Essayist. Poet.* Poem, "To Corinna." A. D. 1 page.

Hoover, Irwin Hood. Papers, dated mainly 1909–33. 11 ms. boxes. 24 volumes relating to affairs at the White House. Restricted.

Howe, Julia Ward (1819–1910). *Author. Reformer.* Papers, dated 1861–1917. 10 ms. boxes.

Hughes, Charles Evans (1862–    ). *Jurist. Chief Justice U. S. Supreme Court.* Virtually all his papers to date. Deposit. Restricted.

Ingersoll, Robert Green (1833–99). *Lawyer. Lecturer.* Correspondence dated 1871–99. 34 scrapbooks. Printed matter. 24 ms. boxes and 1 large flat box.

Jacoby, Henry S. *Professor.* A text-book on descriptive geometry.

Jameson, John Franklin (1859–1937). *Historian.* Miscellany of letters, transcripts, photostats, etc., pertaining to, or originating with the Carnegie Institution of Washington. 5 ms. boxes.

Journals & Diaries. (1) Diary of the World War, 1917–18, Ralph M. Brown, D. S. V. 515, with the French Army. Typewritten carbon. 1 vol. (2) Diary of Augustus Ripley Burbank kept on a journey from Illinois to California in 1849, and later experiences in Oregon, etc., dated 1849 to 1880. 1 vol. (3) Diary of Heber Percy kept on a journey in the United States and western Canada from June 1 to Dec. 23, 1878. 1 vol. (4) Diary of Samuel S. Dale dated 1887–1929, in 3 vols. Restricted. (5) Diaries, recipes, and memoranda of Mrs. Louisa A. Withee, of La Crosse, Wis., dated 1890–1918. 23 vols. (6) Diary of a research expedition to Europe, July–Sept. 1931. Typewritten documents. c. 157 pages.

Kennan, George (1845–1924). *Explorer. Author.* Additional papers contained in 2 ms. boxes. Restricted.

Klyce, Scudder (1879–1933). Papers, dated 1911–33. 22 ms. boxes. They are concerned with philosophy, education, ethics, religion, and science.

Kunz, George Frederick (1856–1932). *Gem Expert.* The Geology of the Hudson River and Its Relation to Bridges and Tunnels. Correspondence and newspaper clippings. c. 102 pieces.

Kunz, Opal Logan. Miscellaneous pieces. "Notes—Miss Brown's Lectures," by Bessie H. Kunz. A. D. 1 vol. Papers relating mainly to biography of Charles Lewis Tiffany, dated 1898, 1900, 1916, 1928. Invitations, menus, certificates, and broadsides. c. 250 pieces.

La Follette, Robert Marion (1855–1925). *U. S. Senator from Wisconsin.* Papers relating to the Conference for Progressive Political Action, the La Follette-Wheeler Campaign, and the Progressive Movement, dated 1924–25. 7 ms. boxes.

Lamb, H. E. Scrapbook of obituaries and biographies of eminent persons, dated 1885–94. 1 vol.

Lampson, E. C. Black Passions. An Historical Narrative of the Sons of Liberty of 1859. 356 pages. Typewritten. Unpublished.

Laughlin, James Laurence (1850–1933). *Economist.* Several hundred pieces of correspondence, dated 1910–32. Printed matter. 15 ms. boxes.

Lee Family. Collection of Miss Sarah Lee. Small wooden box containing correspondence of Thomas Sim Lee and other members of the family. Deposit. Restricted.

LeGendre, Charles William (1830–99). *Soldier. Diplomat.* Collection of 74 volumes. (50 of the volumes are in manuscript and 24 of the volumes are printed in English, French, and Oriental languages.) Manuscript volumes are mostly official documents and scientific accounts. A few volumes of correspondence dated 1868–92.

Logan, Mary S. and Mary Logan Tucker. Correspondence, 1880–1905. 9 letter file boxes.

Long, Crawford Williamson (1815–78). *Anaesthetist. Surgeon.* Documents relating to the first use of anaesthetic in surgical cases, dated from 1837 to 1930. c. 110 pieces. Also miscellaneous pamphlets and photographs. c. 25 pieces.

Mahan, Alfred Thayer (1840–1914). *Naval Officer.* Additional papers. 9 ms. boxes.

Marble, Manton Malone (1835–1917). *Editor. Publisher.* Eighty-seven pamphlet cases of letters received, drafts of articles, and letters sent, dated from c. 1853 to 1917. In process of mounting and binding.

Markland, Absalom H. *Superintendent of Mails, U. S. Army.* Collection of miscellaneous papers, dated 1860–1908. c. 170 pieces.

McElroy, Robert. *Author.* Manuscript of five chapters of Cleveland biography. Copies of letters exchanged between Cleveland and Andrew Carnegie.

McGee, William John (1853–1912). *Geologist.* Papers, dated 1877–1916. c. 50 ms. boxes. 17 letterbooks. Scrapbooks. Deposit. Restricted.

McKelway, Alexander Jeffrey, and St. Clair McKelway. Papers, dated 1860–1932. Correspondence of Secretary for the Southern States of the National Child Labor Committee, 1905–12. Correspondence of A. J. McKelway, 1901–18. Original and notes of St. Clair McKelway biography. 14 ms. boxes. Deposit. Restricted in part.

McKim, Charles Follen (1847–1909). *Architect,* and John Askin. Nine looseleaf binders containing correspondence, notes, memoranda, 1810–1928. 8 ms. boxes of material relating to the American Academy in Rome, 1894–1918. 19 letterbooks, 1891–1910. Several ms. boxes of miscellaneous items including material dated 1888–89, relating to B. P. L. Also printed volume of Burton Historical Records, "John Askin Papers, 1796–1820."

McKinley, William (1843–1901). *Twenty-fourth President of the United States.* Papers, dated 1847–1902. The major portion is dated 1896–1901. 86 bound vols. 95 ms. boxes. Approximately 100 letterbooks for the years 1894–1901. 34 scrapbooks. Restricted.

McLaurin, John Lowndes (1860——). *U. S. Senator from South Carolina.* Scrapbooks of newspaper clippings, dated 1888–1935. 2 vols.

Mearns, Edgar Alexander (1856–1916). *Naturalist.* A volume of letters written by Mearns between June 18, and Sept. 15, 1898; a group of miscellaneous pieces dated 1892–98. 29 pieces.

Michener, Louis T. *Lawyer. Indiana Politician.* Correspondence, dated 1880–1924. 2 ms. boxes.

Miller, Hunter (1875———). *Historian.* Documents pertaining to the Peace Conference of Paris, 1918–19. Printer's copy of "My Diary at the Conference of Paris, with Documents." 5 metal cases with 4 drawers each. Guide cards. Restricted.

Miller, Harriet Mann (Pseud. Olive Thorne Miller, 1831–1918). *Author.* Letters, dated 1900–09. 28 pieces. Her diary for Dec. 1904–April 1905, and some daguerreotypes, are on deposit.

Moler Family. See Anderson and Moler Families.

Moody, William Henry. (1853–1917). *Secretary of the Navy.* Papers, dated mainly 1902–04. 7 ms. boxes.

Moore, Charles (1855———). *Author. Member D. C. Fine Arts Commission.* Letters, clippings, photographs, pamphlets, etc., dated 1745–1937. c. 12 ms. boxes and 2 vols. Restricted.

Moore, Harry H. Letters, memoranda, pamphlets, etc., dated 1912–32. c. 70 pieces.

Morrill, Justin Smith (1810–98). *Congressman and Senator from Vermont.* Additional papers, dated 1855–97. 4 ms. boxes.

Mulholland, Lynette E. Book of clippings supplementary to the "Survey of the White Press of Washington, D. C., Mar. 8–May 8, 1931." Also typewritten document. 2 vols.

Myer, Albert James (1829–80). *Army Officer.* Collection of about 200 pieces dated 1851–1933. Printed matter. 80 pieces. Photographs. 38 pieces.

National Child Labor Committee. See McKelway, Alexander J.

National League of Women Voters. Papers of the National League of Women Voters, dated 1920–30. 58 packages. Deposit.

National Society for the Promotion of Industrial Education (later known as the National Society for Vocational Education). Papers, dated 1906–18. 41 ms. boxes.

Negro Papers. Miscellaneous papers, dated 1830–1930. c. 560 pieces.

Ogden, Robert Curtis (1836–1913). *Merchant.* Collection of documents, dated 1906–13. c. 129 pieces.

Olney, Richard (1835–1917). *Attorney General. Secretary of State.* Additional papers relating to his official life and later, dated 1892–1925. c. 67 vols.

Opium Papers. Documents relating to the international traffic in opium and other drugs, dated 1919–33. Mimeographed and printed.

Owen, Mrs. H. S. Miscellaneous programs, invitations, photographs, badges, newspaper clippings, pertaining to official U. S. functions from 1891 to 1925. c. 160 pieces.

Palmer, Alexander S., and Nathaniel Brown Palmer. Additional papers, dated 1824–92. c. 205 pieces. 1 volume of accounts, 1858–75.

Perthuisot, Fernande. Letters, postcards, and photographs sent from France, 1917–23, by Fernande Perthuisot and Marthe Perthuisot. 49 pieces.

Petersen, Josef. "Argonauterne." Typewritten carbon. 23 pages. English translation.

Philbrick, Francis S. Correspondence of Professor Philbrick relating to biographies being prepared for the Dictionary of American Biography, dated 1927–29. 1 ms. box.

*Philippine* (Schooner). Official log-book. Mercantile Marine of the United States. A. D. 1 vol. Dated May 23, Aug. 5–22, 1911.

Porter, Horace (1837–1921). *Soldier. Railroad Executive. Diplomat.* Papers, contained in 9 ms. boxes.

Post, Louis Freeland (1849–1928). *Writer. Reformer.* Collection of letters dated 1880–1922. c. 115 pieces. Catalogued.

Pulitzer, Joseph (1847–1911). *Journalist.* Papers, dated 1870–1924. 25 vols. 4 ms. boxes.

Putnam, Frederick Wallace. "Five Early Medical Colleges. Compiled by Frederick W. Putnam, 1930." 1 vol.

Putnam, Frederick Ward (1839–1915). *Archeologist. Naturalist.* Miscellaneous letters, dated 1898–1932. 114 pieces. Catalogued.

Quay, Matthew Stanley (1833–1904). *U. S. Senator from Pennsylvania.* Correspondence, dated 1871–1927. c. 170 pieces. Photostats and typewritten copies.

Rainey, Henry Thomas (1860–1934). *Congressman from Illinois. Speaker of the House.* Papers, dated 1899–1935. 18 ms. boxes and 7 letter file boxes. Restricted.

Realf, Richard (1834–78). *Poet.* Collection of George S. Cottman documents relating to Richard Realf. c. 100 pieces, dated 1878–98.

Remey, George Collier (1841–1928). *Naval Officer.* "Life and Letters of Rear Admiral George Collier Remey." 16 vols. "A Supplement to the Reminiscences of Rear Admiral George Collier Remey." 1 vol. In addition, a deposit of 43 pieces consisting of manuscripts, clippings, and photographs, dated 1862–1930.

Remey, Mary Josephine Mason. "Life and Letters of Mary Josephine Mason Remey." 17 vols. Typewritten copy.

Riggs, Elisha Francis (1851–1910). *Banker.* Ledgers, journals, cash books, etc. 25 vols. Correspondence, 12 ms. boxes. Deposit. Restricted.

Root, Elihu (1845–1937). *Statesman. Lawyer.* Additional papers, dated 1900–30. 177 pieces. Deposit. Restricted.

Rose, John Carter (1861–1927). *Jurist. Author.* Newspaper clippings of articles by John C. Rose. 2 vols.

Rusk, Jeremiah McClain (1830–93). *Secretary of Agriculture.* Correspondence, dated 1888–92. 23 typewritten pages.

Russia. Clippings, maps, letters, photographs, pamphlets, dated 1864–1908. 3 ms. boxes.

Schoonmaker, Marias (1811–94). Miscellaneous documents, deeds, patents, indentures, dated 1707–1894. 4 ms. boxes. Deposit.

Scott, Hugh Lenox. (1853–1934). *Army Officer.* Papers, dated c. 1885–1934. 129 ms. boxes.

Sherman, John (1823–1900). *U. S. Senator from Ohio.* A collection of original letters and photostats acquired through the efforts of Dr. Jeannette Nichols.

Simons, Edward F. "Life of Abraham Lincoln." Ten-page autograph document.

Smalley, George Washburn (1833–1916). *Journalist.* Letters from Smalley to Millicent, Duchess of Sutherland, dated from July 26, 1895 to February 24, 1902. 56 pieces. Catalogued.

Society of the Cincinnati. Papers of the Society, dated 1784–1936. c. 399 pieces. Deposit. Restricted. Listed. Minute book of the Standing Committee of the Society, 1872–1938. A, Ds. S. and typewritten Ds. S. 1 vol. Deposit. Restricted.

Spring, Everett. Typewritten copies of articles, scrapbooks of clippings, printed volumes. 6 ms. boxes of articles. 5 scrapbooks. 5 printed vols.

Starr, George H. "Jottings Abroad," by Colonel G. H. Starr, dated 1864–1910. 2 vols. of newspaper clippings.

Stevens, Charles. Letters and extracts of letters of Charles Stevens, emigrant from Princeton, Ill., to Astoria, Oreg., and of Frances E. Stevens, dated 1837–95. Typewritten carbon copies. 1 ms. box.

Stickney, Frank L. Miscellaneous personal and family papers, dated 1840–1934. 13 ms. boxes. Several scrapbooks. Restricted in part. Account book, 1883–1901. 1 vol.

Strong, James (1822–94). *Biblical Scholar.* Collection of James Strong and others, dated 1867–1922. 2 ms. boxes.

Thayer, William Wilde (1829–1896). Autobiography of William Wilde Thayer. A. D. 151 pages. Also a narrative written by his daughter to complete the autobiography. 4 pages.

Thomas, John Robert (1846–1914). *Congressman from Illinois.* Eighty pieces, mostly letters written to Thomas between 1880 and 1912.

Thormeyer, Paul. Philosophisches Worterbuch von Dr. Paul Thormeyer. 1930. 34 pages. German script.

Tillman, Benjamin Ryan (1847–1918). *Governor of South Carolina. U. S. Senator.* Papers, contained in 7 cardboard (florist) boxes. Deposit. Restricted.

Townsend, George Alfred (1861–1920). *Journalist.* Scrapbook of letters, newspaper clippings, memoranda, pictures, etc., dated 1865–99.

Tucker, Mary Logan. See Logan, Mary S.

United States. (1) President's Research Committee on Social Trends. Newspaper clippings dated Jan.–Apr. 1933, mounted in 10 vols. (2) Recent Social Trends. Social statistics of population of the United States, mainly 1910–30. 13 ms. boxes. (3) Materials used for chapter on education by Charles H. Judd. 1 ms. box. (4) Navy. Log-book of the U. S. S. *Harvard,* dated April 23–Aug. 30, (1898). A. D. 1 vol.

Wade, Benjamin Franklin (1800–78). *U. S. Senator from Ohio.* Papers, dated 1832–98. 22 ms. boxes.

Walker, Francis Amasa (1840–97). *Educator.* Group of letters received between 1878 and 1896. 37 pieces. Deposit.

Walsh, Thomas James (1859–1933). *U. S. Senator.* Papers (entire). Deposit. Restricted.

Wells, David Ames (1828–98). *Economist.* Papers, dated 1795–1898. 13 ms. boxes. Descriptive list.

Wheeler, John Hill (1806–82). *Lawyer. Diplomat.* 19 volumes of his diary, 1 volume of newspaper clippings, and 1 volume of papers relating to North Carolina. The collection covers the years from 1854 to 1881.

White House. Programs, newspapers, badges, records, etc., relating to official festivities and ceremonies at the White House and elsewhere during the years 1897 to 1903. Bingham Collection.

Whitlock, Brand (1869–1934). *Writer. Diplomat.* Papers, dated 1895–1934.

Wildman, Edwin (1867–1932). *Editor. Author,* and Rounsevelle Wildman. Manuscripts, newspaper clippings, pamphlets, photographs, etc., relating to the conquest of the Philippine Islands by the United States, and to the Boxer troubles in China. c. 860 pieces.

Willcox, Walter F. Source material for a study of the growth in the population of the earth and of the continents since 1650. Typewritten papers, manuscripts, and photographs. 1 ms. box.

Williams, John Sharp (1854–1932). *Congressman and Senator from Mississippi.* Papers, dated 1906–23. c. 200 ms. boxes.

Willis, Clarence P. Notes relating to the density of planets, electricity, etc., dated 1923–34. 16 vols.

Witbeck Collection. Documents on Louisiana and several other States contained in 1 ms. box and dated 1833–1933.

Woman Suffrage Political Source Material. Letters, newspaper clippings, etc., relating to the woman suffrage movement, chiefly in New York, dated 1908–15. 12 vols. Restricted.

Women's Organization for National Prohibition Reform. Letters to Mrs. E. W. Root, Director of Research, dated 1896–1933. 1 ms. box.

Wood, Henry Clay. *Assistant Adjutant General.* Papers, dated 1838–1907. Mounted in 3 vols.

Wood, Leonard (1860–1927). *Army Officer.* Papers contained in 2 large wooden boxes. Deposit. Restricted. Also 3 scrapbooks of newspaper clipping relating to the candidacy of General Wood for president in 1920, collected by P. G. McDonnell.

Woodward, Mary Alethea. Letters, poems, and newspaper clippings dated from 1926 to 1929. 1 vol.

Wright, Elizur (1804–85). *Reformer.* Papers, dated 1817–87. 8 ms. boxes. Drafts of writings, 5 ms. boxes. Account book, 1828–32. 1 vol. 1 bound volume of clippings.

Wright-Stephenson Collection. Papers of Nathaniel Wright, Reuben H. Stephenson, Nathaniel Wright Stephenson, and others, dated 1812–1900. c. 50 ms. boxes. Several bundles. Deposit.

Zuendt zu Kenzingen, Ernst Anton.  Letters, documents, plays, poems, press clippings, photographs, etc., relating to the Zuendt and Fugger families, dated 1697–1899.  64 pieces.

## VII. OTHER GROUPS

### A. LITERATURE

Ethiopia.  A book on witchcraft, in Amharic, the language of Ethiopia.

German prayerbook, dated 1732, with inscriptions dated 1846 and 1863.  Also German religious cards, illustrated, 16 pieces.

Langland, William (c. 1332–1400).  "Piers Plowman," by William Langland. 220 pages.  Photostats.  Original in Henry E. Huntington Library.

Montgomery, James (1771–1854).  *Poet.*  An account of the life and works of James Montgomery, Scotch poet and hymn-writer.  Typewritten document. 193 pages.

Geoffrey of Monmouth.  "Historia Regum Brittanniae," by Geoffrey of Monmouth (Welsh chronicler, c. 1100–1154).  Photostats.  10 vols.

### B. SCIENTIFIC MATERIAL

Hewitt, Edward Lukens.  Technical notes and drawings on steam navigation in the United States Navy during the period of the Civil War, prepared on board the U. S. S. *Mahaska*.  1 vol.

### C. MATERIAL RELATING TO THE STUDY OF LANGUAGE AND TO COUNTRIES OTHER THAN EUROPE

Indian Languages.  Maya Society Publications; No. 3.  Codex Ixtlan.  No. 4. Codex Meixueiro.  No. 5.  Codex Abraham Castellanus.  Facsimiles on linen.

Indian languages.  Six Aztec dramas.  For the most part English translations.

Orientalia.  7 vols.  (1) Abdu-al-Rahman Jami.  (2) Aja 'ib al-Makhu-kat wa-athar al-bilad.  (3) Abd-al-Rohman.  (4) Abu Saud ibn Mohammad al Imadi. (5) Jula-ul-deen As Soyuty.  (6) Hippocrates, The Aphorisms.  (7) Al-Ketabi Majales-al-Mumeniu.  Purchased from Kirkor Minassian.

Orientalia.  Treaties on astrology in Persian.  Arabic manuscript attributed to Ali al-Mourtadha.

Orientalia.  History of Solunan I.  Turkish ms. 1 vol. by Mufti K'ara Tschelebizade A'bdela'zez Efendi.

Pacific Islands.  Vocabularies of languages of the Pacific Islands (following dialects or places): (1) Ambrym, New Hebrides, collected by Rev. W. B. Murray, 1885.  (2) Bau dialect of Viti Levu, Fiji Islands, collected by Walter S. Carew, 1882.  (3) Gilbert Islands, collected by Hiram Bingham, undated. (4) Havannan Habour, collected by D. Macdonald, 1885.  (5) Marean dialect, collected by J. Jones, 1885.  (6) Ponape dialect, collected by E. T. Doane, undated.  (7) Rarotongan dialect, collected by Rev. W. W. Gill, 1887.  (8) Rotuman dialect, collected by Rev. W. Allen, 1886, (9) Solovia dialect of Viti Levu, collected by Walter S. Carew, 1882.

Portuguese Manuscripts.  Several hundred volumes which appear to be partly transcripts, dealing with miscellaneous subjects and dated in the 17th, 18th, and 19th centuries.

Tahitian Dialect.  Four manuscript volumes in Tahitian dialect.  Catalogued.

### D. MISCELLANY

Education.  Papers relating mainly to education and organizations of learning in France, Germany, Switzerland, China, and Japan, dated 1889–92.  57 pieces.

Italian and French Manuscripts.  "L'Arte del navigare . . ."  c. 1540.  1 vol. "Questo libro contiene cose spettante alla citta di Vegevano . . .." 1619–1707. 1 vol. "Memoires sur la province d'Alsace pour l'instruction du Duc de Bourgogne, 1697 . . . ecrits vers 1700.  1 vol.

Martini, Eve Marius Adrian (Baron).  A folio volume of visiting cards collected by Martini while a member of the diplomatic corps of the Kingdom of the Netherlands.

French Manuscripts 15th to 19th Century. Letters and documents, mainly French; many on vellum. 110 pieces.

National Society of the Daughters of the Founders and Patriots of America. Application papers. c. 36 volumes to date.

Watermark Collection. A collection of some 600 miscellaneous letters and documents dating from 1769 to 1858. In the collection is a group of about 325 papers of the one-time U. S. Consul at Rio de Janeiro, Mr. W. H. D. C. Wright.

Woman's Relief Corps. Scrapbook of material relating to the Woman's Relief Corps, dated 1905, 1920, 1921, 1930, and undated.

A reel of film reproductions of letters written by well-known persons from the time of John Hancock to Robert Todd Lincoln. Originals in The Hayes Memorial, Fremont, Ohio.

Universal Fellowship Foundation. Papers descriptive of "The Inner Church Radiant as Outlined by the Universal Fellowship Foundation." 1 ms. box. Typewritten.

Russia. Four illuminated manuscripts, 1773–85. Landgrants.

Duero River. Spain and Portugal. "Documentos y antecedentes referenters a la navegacion del Duero y caminos para sus Puertos." 1829–41. 1 vol.

Poets. American. Poems by the modern American poets, Leonie Adams, John Peale Bishop, Witter Bynner, John Gould Fletcher, Frances Frost, Archibald MacLeish, Marianne Moore, Ezra Pound, Wallace Stevens, Allen Tate, Eunice Tietjens, William Carlos Williams.

# INDEX

Compiled by C. PERCY POWELL

# GENERAL INDEX

Compiled by MARY PARKER RAGATZ

## A

Abbot, C. G., letter of submittal, v.

Abernethy, Thomas P., 13.

Abrams, Ray H., *Suppression of Minority Opinion in Times of Crisis in America*, 16.

Act of incorporation, xv.

Adams, Herbert B., xv. *See also* Herbert Baxter Adam Prize.

Adams, Randolph G., chairman, committee on Americana for college libraries, 11, 63, 79.

Adriance, Robert I., 11, 80.

Agricultural History Society, joint session of A. H. A. and, 14; luncheon conference, 23.

*Albert Gallatin Brown*, Ranck, 58.

Albert J. Beveridge Memorial Fund, xiii; members of committee on (1938), 11, 78; publication plans of committee on, 47; report of committee on, 55–56.

Alexander, Edward P., 23; chairman, Conference of Historical Societies, 89, 90.

Aldrich, Julian C., 11, 80.

Ambler, Charles H., 18.

American Academy of Political and Social Sciences, A. H. A. delegates to meeting of, 5–6.

American Council of Learned Societies, 58, 72; A. H. A. representatives on, 6, 80.

American Documentation Institute, A. H. A. delegate to, 6.

American Farm Economic Association, 72.

American Historical Association, organization and activities, xi–xiv; act of incorporation, xv; constitution, xvii–xviii; by-laws, xix; proceedings, 1–80; abstract of minutes of executive committee meetings, 3–8; question of administration of, 3, 5, 9, 24, 45, 46; question of publishing papers read at meeting of, 5; representatives of, at meeting of American Academy of Political and Social Sciences, 5–6; delegate of, to the American Documentation Institute, 6; representatives of, on the National Historical Publications Commission, 6, 7; representatives of, in allied bodies, 6, 12, 80; proposal for a journal of popular history to be identified with, 8; poll vote of executive committee, 8; minutes of council meetings, 8–12; report of the committee on appointments, 10–12; program, 13–23; minutes of business meeting, 24; treasurer's report, 24, 25–44; secretary's report, 24, 44–47; report of board of trustees, 42–44; membership problem, 46, 57–58; radio program, 47, 66; statistics of membership, 53–55; committee reports, 55–67; other reports, 67–74; question of subvention to Pacific coast branch, 73–74; officers (1938), 75–76; committees (1938), 77–80.

*American Historical Review*, xi, 4, 45, 46, 47, 71; appropriation to, 8; board of editors, 12, 78; report of managing editor of, 67–69.

*American Influence on British Federal Systems*, Whitelaw, 22.

*American Merchants and the Constitution, The*, Nettels, 17.

American Philosophical Society, joint session of A. H. A. and, 15; reception to A. H. A. and other societies, 16.

Americana for college libraries, committee on, report of, 61–64; members (1938), 79. *See also* Americana Plan.

Americana Plan, 6, 9. *See also* Americana for college libraries; McGregor Plan.

American Society of Church History, joint session of A. H. A. and, 15.

American Statistical Association, 72.

American travel. See *Bibliography of American Travel*.

American University, 72.

Anderson, E. N., chairman, George Louis Beer Prize committee, 60; chairman, program committee (1939), 78.

Anderson, Howard R., 11, 80.

Andrews, Charles M., 11, 78; council member, 75.

*Annual Report*, A. H. A., xi, xii, 4, 7; editor of, 4; report of the committee on the contents of the, 66; report of the editor, 69–70; members of the committee on publication of the (1938), 79. *See also* Ragatz, Lowell J.

*Appalachia in Transition: Indian versus White Man*, Downes, 18.

*Appeal to Reason, The*, Bainton, 17.

Appointments. *See* Council committee on appointments.

Archives, subcommittee on, International Committee of Historical Sciences, 12, 80.

## B

Bailey, Thomas A., 84.

Bainton, Roland H., *The Appeal to Reason*, 17.

Bancroft, George, xv.

Barbour, Violet, chairman, 1938 nominating committee, 55, 77.

Barck, Dorothy C., 77; sec., pro tem., Conference of Historical Societies, 89, 91; sec., Conference of Historical Societies, 79, 90.

Barker, Eugene C., 10, 77; council member, 55, 76.

Barnes, Elinor S., *Philadelphia, Convention City of 1787*, 23, 89.

Barnes, Viola F., 12, 78.

Bassett, John S., 45.

Baxter, James P., III, 3, 4; chairman, executive committee, 10, 77.

147

Beale, Howard K., 6, 10, 24.
Beard, Charles A., 11, 79 ; *Historiography and the Constitution,* 15 ; council member, 76.
Becker, Carl L., *Some Rambling Remarks about Constitutions,* 15 ; council member, 76.
Bemis, Samuel F., 12, 79, 80.
Bennett, E. E., 84 ; *Parliament and the English East African Companies, 1663–1714,* 83.
Beveridge, Albert J. *See* Albert J. Beveridge Memorial Fund.
Beyer, H. Otley, 8.
Bibliographical Society of America, joint session of A. H. A. and, 19.
*Bibliography of American Travel,* 9, 47 ; report of committee on, 59–60 ; members of committee on (1938), 79.
*Bibliography of British History,* 3, 9.
Bining, Arthur C., *History and the Changing World,* 16.
Binkley, Robert C., 12, 79 ; *The Holy Roman Empire versus the United States; Patterns for Constitution-making in Central Europe,* 22.
Birney, James G., papers of, to be published, 47, 55.
Bishop, William W., 79.
Björk, David K., 8.
Blegen, Theodore C., 12, 79.
Blinn, Harold E., *The French Labor Movement, 1880–95,* 83.
Bloomfield, Leonard. *See* Crosskey, William W.
Boak, A. E. R., 77, 78.
Board of trustees, members (1938), 77.
Bolton, Herbert E., council member, 76.
Bond, Carroll T., 11, 78.
*Book-trade Publicity Before 1800,* Hallenbeck, 20.
Bourne, H. E., 45.
Bowen, Clarence W., xv.
Bowman, Francis J., 84.
Bowman, Nelle E., 11, 80.
Boyce, Gray C., 58.
Boyd, Julian P., 11, 12, 79.
Bradley, Harold W., 84.
Bradley, Phillips, 11, 79.
Branch, E. Douglas, *Henry Louis Bouquet, Professional Soldier,* 18.
Braun, Evelyn Plummer, 8, 12, 79.
Bridenbaugh, Carl, *Cities in the Wilderness: The First Century of Urban Life in America, 1625–1742,* 61.
Briggs, Elizabeth, death, 54.
Brookings Institution, 72.
Brown, Louis F., *Ideas of Representation from Elizabeth to Charles II,* 13.
Brown, Marjorie D., 11, 79.
Bruce, Kathleen, chairman, John H. Dunning Prize committee (1938), 12, 78.
Bruun, A. Geoffrey, *The Constitutional Cult in the Early Nineteenth Century,* 22.
Buck, Solon J., treas., A. H. A., 3, 4, 7, 8, 9, 10, 12, 24, 55, 66, 75, 77, 79 ; annual report (1937), 25–44. *See also* Treasurer, A. H. A.

Buckler, Francis W., *The Establishment of the Church of England: Its Constitutional and Legal Significance,* 16.
Bucks County, Pa., plan to publish minute book of county courts of, 1684–1715, 57.
*Bulgarian Atrocity Agitation in England, 1876, The,* Harris, 83.
Burlingame, Merrill G., *The Influence of the Army in the Building of a Western State,* 83.
Burr, George L., council member, 75.
Butler, Mrs. George, *Early Books Relating to Trees of America,* 20.
Butler, Mrs. Pierce, 77.
Bylaws, xix.

### C

Canfield, Cass, 8.
Cappon, Lester J., 12, 79.
*Career of Théophile Delcassé, The,* Porter, 60.
Carnegie Corporation of New York, 73.
Carnegie Revolving Fund for Publications, xii, 7, 10 ; members of the committee on (1938), 11, 78 ; report of the committee on, 58–59.
Carroll, Eber Malcolm, 22.
Carter, Clarence E., 16.
Chaffee, Eugene, *The Clash Between North and South Idaho Over the Capitol Question,* 83.
*Chancery and the Privy Seal, 1327–36, The,* Morris, 83.
*Changing Conceptions of Property in Law,* Philbrick, 21.
Cheyney, E. P., 58, 80 ; council member, 75.
Christian, Percy W., 83.
Christy, Mary E., 11, 80.
Chronology, subcommittee on, International Committee of Historical Sciences, 12, 80.
*Cities in the Wilderness: The First Century of Urban Life in America, 1625–1742,* Bridenbaugh, 61.
Clark, Charles E., 56.
Clark, Dan E., 83 ; chairman, Pacific coast branch committee on awards, American history, 84.
Clark, R. C., 84.
*Clash Between North and South Idaho Over the Capitol Question, The,* Chaffee, 83.
Cohen, Morris R., *Constitutional and Natural Rights in 1787 and Since,* 17.
Cole, Arthur C., 11, 78.
Coleman, Christopher B., 89 ; sec., Conference of Historical Societies, 91.
Commager, Henry S., 8, 78 ; *Constitutional History and the Higher Law,* 21.
Commission on the Social Studies in the Schools, 45, 46, 47 ; report of, 70.
*Commons and the Council in Fifteenth-century England, The,* Gray, 16.
*Concepts of Democracy and Liberty in Eighteenth-century Europe, The,* Salvemini, 18.
Conference of State and Local Historical Societies, joint session of A. H. A. and, 23 ; sec. of, 79 ; minutes of, 89–91 ; financial statement, 91.